School Principal

School Principal
Managing in Public

DAN C. LORTIE

THE UNIVERSITY OF CHICAGO PRESS
CHICAGO AND LONDON

Dan C. Lortie is professor emeritus of education at the University of Chicago. A sociologist, he has specialized in the study of work and organizations. *Schoolteacher* is in its second edition with the University of Chicago Press.

The University of Chicago Press, Chicago 60637
The University of Chicago Press, Ltd., London
© 2009 by The University of Chicago
All rights reserved. Published 2009
Printed in the United States of America

18 17 16 15 14 13 12 11 10 09   1 2 3 4 5

ISBN-13: 978-0-226-49348-0   (cloth)
ISBN-13: 978-0-226-49349-7   (paper)
ISBN-10: 0-226-49348-2   (cloth)
ISBN-10: 0-226-49349-0   (paper)

Library of Congress Cataloging-in-Publication Data

Lortie, Dan C. (Dan Clement), 1926–
    School principal : managing in public / Dan C. Lortie.
        p. cm.
    Includes bibliographical references and index.
    ISBN-13: 978-0-226-49348-0   (cloth: alk. paper)
    ISBN-13: 978-0-226-49349-7   (pbk.: alk. paper)
    ISBN-10: 0-226-49348-2   (cloth: alk. paper)
    ISBN-10: 0-226-49349-0   (pbk.: alk. paper)
    1. Elementary school principals—Illinois—Chicago Metropolitan area.
2. Elementary school principals—Iowa. 3. Suburban schools—Illinois—
Chicago Metropolitan area. 4. Suburban schools—Iowa. 5. School
management and organization—Illinois—Chicago Metropolitan area.
6. School management and organization—Iowa. I. Title.
    LB2831.924.I3L67 2009
    372.12'012—dc22   2008038482

♾ The paper used in this publication meets the minimum requirements of the American National Standard for Information Sciences—Permanence of Paper for Printed Library Materials, ANSI Z39.48-1992.

{ Contents }

{ Acknowledgments }

Studies of this kind require resources—the time of many persons, money, stimulating intellectual settings, and talented assistants. I am extremely grateful to have received all of them and am delighted to express that gratitude here.

First, I want to point out the contributions made by dozens of school administrators who gave many hours of their time for interviews; principals and superintendents gave help during the pilot phases, and principals were interviewed at length in the final sample. This book could not have been written without their active assistance and generosity, generosity whose dimensions become particularly clear when we recall the constant and urgent demands on their time. That the need for anonymity prevents thanking them by name says nothing about the depth of my gratitude to those men and women—it is immense. I can only hope that the book comes as close as possible to being a full, true, and accurate account not only of what they said but what they meant.

I am most grateful for the financial support received from the Department of Education in Washington at different points in the study. Although the names of the specific granting units changed (i.e., National Institute for Education and Office of Educational Research and Improvement), the readiness of the staff in those agencies to provide sympathetic and thoughtful support did not vary—they were, in each instance, simply great. Many thanks as well to the Spencer Foundation for a timely and important grant.

The context in which one works is also significant. I was especially fortunate in that regard. At different points in the study,
colleagues at the University of Chicago provided the intellectual
liveliness so necessary to serious research. The graduate students
in the Department of Education at Chicago also invigorated the
scholarly setting. Before mentioning some persons by name, I
want to underscore my sense of indebtedness to the department as
a whole. It was a remarkable place to work.

The professors in educational administration with whom I
worked most closely in the early years of the study included Roald
Campbell, Alan Thomas, Donald Erickson and, a little later, Bob
Jewell and Kenneth Wong. Other helpful colleagues included
Charles Bidwell, Tony Bryk, John Craig, Bob Dreeben, Phil Jackson, and Fred Lighthall. I learned from each of them. Larry Hedges
helped design the sample. Kent Peterson and Marie Schilling,
graduate students at the time, were central figures during the pilot
phases and the design of the interview. Kent also played a major
part in the hiring and supervision of an excellent corps of inter-
viewers. Gary Crow and Sandy Prolman undertook the enormous
job of assisting in and supervising the development of codes, their
entry to the computer system and the conduct of various analyses.
Their contributions merited coauthorship of an earlier report to
NIE that relied heavily on their work.

Some of the data were gathered during the period when I was
privileged to work with an outstanding group of researchers from
Harvard and Vanderbilt (National Center for Educational Leadership). Led by Lee Bolman and Terry Deal, it included, among others,
Carolyn Evertson, Philip Hallinger, Susan Moore Johnson, Catherine Marshall, Jerome Murphy, Joseph Murphy, and Carol Weiss.
They were a joy to work with. Two splendid assistants—Carla
O'Connor and Daryl Ford—showed initiative and intelligence in
gathering the career information eight years after the first interviews were completed.

I was extremely fortunate to have worked for over twenty years
(primarily during the summer months) with the Bush Foundation
programs for Minnesota superintendents and principals. Headed
by that incomparable teacher and manager John Mauriel of the
University of Minnesota School of Business, it engaged all of us,

staff and participants alike, in vigorous exploration of issues in running schools and school districts. It is hard to imagine a more useful, protracted immersion in the realities of schooling than those happy months.

I recently asked several persons to review and evaluate an earlier version of the manuscript. Their responses were enormously gratifying; these very busy people took the time to read the manuscript and make many extremely useful suggestions and comments. My heartfelt thanks to Gary Crow, Robert Crowson, Ernest House, Fred Lighthall, Judith Little, and Kent Peterson. Fred Lighthall and Judith Little went far beyond the usual efforts we academics make in responding to such requests by writing detailed and enormously useful critiques and making numerous helpful suggestions. Professors Howard Bultinck and Lynn Bush of Northeastern University helped by checking for factual errors, particularly specifics that prevail in Illinois. I hasten to add the usual exoneration that must be extended to those who help writers yet do not have the final say. Attribute no flaws to these generous colleagues!

That the editorial staff has won renown for the University of Chicago Press is well established; that they combine high skill with unusual graciousness may be less widely known. Many thanks to John Tryneski, Elizabeth Branch Dyson, and Emilie Sandoz. Jean Eckentels's work on the manuscript not only improved it greatly but was done in ways that were invariably congenial. Mark Reschke supervised production with the same qualities.

Finally, to my wife Grace Budrys, my deepest gratitude not only for direct assistance with the writing but for undergoing the ways in which this project complicated our family life. I have sought to emulate her capacity to convert complex information into highly readable prose.

{ **Introduction** }

Public schools are among the major employers in the United States, providing work for millions of persons; teachers make up the largest proportion, but there are clerks and custodians, nurses and social workers, teacher aides and cooks. The total undertaking is vast and subdivided into many units; first by states, then by thousands of districts and then into an even larger number of schools. Each school building has someone in charge, a principal who is responsible for the day-to-day workings of an organization composed primarily of children and only secondarily of adults. More than half of the adults in public schools work with young children in the elementary grades, typically consisting of kindergarten and six or eight grades. This book is about the men and women who manage these familiar yet, in important respects, unusual organizations.

The perspective taken is sociological and occupational, and the emphasis is on the work of elementary principals in suburban schools. Being sociological, the focus is on career paths (seen ecologically and subjectively), the position of principal in an organizational context, core work tasks, and the sentiments that are generated by members of the occupation in the course of their daily activity. The emphasis is on modal patterns in each domain; for example, how are people recruited to the occupation and socialized into its ways? What position do principals occupy in a hierarchy of authority where they both manage and are managed by others? Are there regularities in the sentiments (positive and negative) they express about their work? What trends appear to have sufficient viability to warrant attention in future research?

The principalship is a particular kind of occupation: it is among those lines of work where one is held accountable for the performance of others who rank lower in the hierarchy, making it managerial work. Since managerial work occurs in an organizational setting, the concepts and findings from organizational studies are particularly relevant. In that light, we will pay particular attention to contextual features that are special to the principalship and examine how they contribute to the emergence of a distinct subculture. In what ways do the cultural themes we observe connect to the social and organizational contexts within which principals work?

Several types of data will be used as we seek answers to that and other questions. (The appendices deal with data sources in more detail.) The basic data consist of face-to-face interviews, 2 to 3 hours long, with a representative sample of 113 suburban elementary principals in three counties around Chicago conducted in 1980 (appendix A). A telephone follow-up took place in 1988 in order to learn the current location and position of each principal at that time. Those Chicago area data are supplemented by a larger, statewide sample of Iowa elementary principals gathered around the same period; Vittengl, the author of the latter study, developed a self-administered questionnaire based in large part on information provided by our research team (appendix B). Numerous historical studies were reviewed to form the basis for chapter 1; additional and more recent information is found in national reports prepared by the NAESP (National Association of Elementary School Principals 1978, 1988, and 1998) and other national studies.

The core suburban and Iowa materials are not recent, a fact which raises questions about their utility in understanding the current position and tasks of suburban elementary principals. The inclusion of more recent data where possible and the suggestions for research on recent changes in the final chapter are efforts to reduce the effects of that shortcoming, but they do not eliminate it. Two additional considerations, however, lessen the limitations imposed by when the data were gathered. The first is the slow rate of change we find in the structures of public schooling; I believe that many aspects of principal work have not changed significantly since our data were gathered. The second is that the empirical work done in this study, by filling gaps in the literature, provides a baseline for future research on the topics with which it deals. This study is an in-depth examination of the elementary principalship at the last point where its composition was heavily dominated by men. In addition, school districts became more subject to state and federal controls in the last two decades of the twentieth century—a trend toward centralization which deserves, in my view, close and sustained observation as it waxes or wanes in the years ahead. Persons undertaking research on schools should benefit from a baseline to determine how organizational changes have affected the management of elementary schools, particularly in suburban settings.

Why study elementary school principals? One reason grows out of research done in the 1970s and 1980s that supported the claim that elementary principals can have important effects on the quality of their schools (Brookover et al. 1979, Levine and Lezotte 1990). The significance of the principal position is widely accepted today among those who study schools and prepare school administrators; it has, at least to some extent, caught up with the previous concentration on the role of the superintendent by those who do research in educational administration. Studying the principalship has another advantage because it is a focal point in the life of schools. Principals interact constantly with the key parties involved in schooling—teachers, students, parents, and central officials. (The relationships between high school principals and teachers are less direct as they are usually mediated by an intervening layer of department chairs.) What we learn from and about principals can deepen our understanding of how American schools and school districts function; that understanding, in turn, can provide a more reliable base for efforts to improve the schools.

Why concentrate on principals who work in suburbs? There are several reasons for that choice. Our study was conceived and initiated at a time when few observers defined the performance of suburban schools as problematic; scholarly and public concern centered then, as it still does, on city schools and the schooling of minority children. Suburban schools have been and are seen as meeting standards not met elsewhere. To the extent there are general norms by which schools are judged, they come closest, it seems, to being expressed in suburban schools. I decided to study suburban schools, then, in order to learn how (comparatively) effective schools operated and what principal work was like in settings less likely to be defined as troubled.

Studying suburban school districts was attractive for two additional reasons. The organizational context of the principalship in suburban districts is less difficult to uncover and grasp than the multilayered and, at times, baroque structures found in large cities. Finally, the small size of suburban districts also makes it less costly to obtain more cases and greater variety in the district contexts where principals work, offsetting, to some degree, the part played by district differences.

THE PLAN OF THE BOOK

The sequence of chapters in the book reflects two main considerations. The first is the desire for clarity; that is, information and ideas are presented in ways which, I hope, advance awareness of the complexities found in this social system. The second reflects my theoretical dispositions. In regard to the first, I believe it makes sense to begin with the history of the position and, soon after, to present the specifics of the research setting. The same view led to the decision to split the presentation of the career data into two chapters, putting the earlier years of the career in chapter 2 and the later years, with a focus on career satisfaction, considerably later in chapter 7. I recognize the chronological bias in those decisions; I believe that presenting earlier events first, in both organizations and lives, facilitates understanding.

The order of the chapters also matches what I regard as the likely flow of causation, particularly in the public education sector. Long-established institutions precede those who staff them and although, occasionally, outstanding individuals make important and lasting changes in how they operate, the structure generally has more effect on any given person than he or she on it; the positions and attached task bundles in the organization present opportunities and constraints to which individuals respond. Furthermore, when a structure has persisted without major changes over several decades and is largely similar in most communities, common traditions are likely to emerge and affect the beliefs and values of participants (e.g., definitions of how authority should be exercised within the organization). Persistent structures, in short, shape individuals and the occupational subcultures to which they subscribe. We begin, therefore, with a brief, structurally oriented history of the position. In the same vein, two early chapters (3 and 4) deal with the authority system in which elementary principals occupy both subordinate and superordinate statuses. The focus is on how principals perceive that structure and their most frequent responses to the challenges it presents.

Chapters 5 and 6 focus on the sentiments, positive and negative, that principals express about their work. Sentiments are seen, in this context, as what we might call "cathected" beliefs and preferences; special attention is paid to such emotionally loaded sentiments as pride and pleasure, frustration and displeasure. Shared sentiments undergird the subculture that participants in a common endeavor build together over time. We look into the joys and satisfactions principals derive from their day-to-day activities in chapter 5, and in chapter 6, what we can call the "downside" of the job. Chapter 7 examines the longer-term issues around satisfaction and dissatisfaction with the career.

Chapter 8 is a summary in which the organizational context, principal tasks, and sentiments are combined into a composite "occupational subculture." As managerial work, the principalship shares features with similar positions, but this penultimate chapter concentrates on the "special" characteristics of principal work and the meanings that are attached to them.

Finally, the book ends with a chapter which is partly speculative and partly based on data on recent changes in the work of elementary principals. Its primary purpose is to stimulate further research. In addition to discussing changes that have taken place since the basic data were gathered, it projects trends which may alter, in important ways, the future work of elementary principals.

A WORD ON RHETORIC

I have chosen to use the rhetoric of management for what I believe are good reasons. Although there are organizational theories which focus on specific functions performed by those responsible for overseeing the work of others (e.g., decision making, leadership, problem solving, resource allocation, etc.), one can identify and compare members of the category "manager" without making so specific a conceptual commitment. It is also useful that the United States Census uses the category. My proclivity in doing an occupational study, much influenced by Everett Hughes, is to focus on how persons within the occupation see and define the work they do, the meanings they attach to their tasks and careers (Hughes 1958, 1971). Another critical aspect of that approach is to examine those phenomena in a comparative framework. Management rhetoric has the double advantage of being general enough to accommodate what principals say are the tasks and meanings they see as central while permitting comparisons with other occupations in which persons oversee the work of others.

Important work is being done these days on leadership as a key function of persons who head schools; the rhetoric of leadership is increasingly common in what was almost always referred to as "educational administration." I hope that this study is seen as useful to those who emphasize that perspective, for our concerns are very close. Mintzberg's treatment of leadership (1973) as a vital function among several performed by managers has, I believe, the advantage of directing our attention to other significant aspects of managerial positions. For example, the scope of leadership possible for principals becomes clearer, I believe, when we examine their position as subordinates in a hierarchical structure. The complexity of relationships with parents emerges when we realize how ambiguous the location of leadership can be in those relationships.

"I think the main thing is that this book is less about what could be than what is. In the process it tells about why what could be is so hard to bring about," commented an anonymous reviewer of this book. Let me add to that description. As I said above, I believe that knowing "what is" can help those who are eager and ready to improve our schools. Change *is* hard to bring about. It is useful to remember, however, that the constraints and obstacles that retard improvement—the inhibiting aspects of present structures—are the result of decisions we have, as a society, made in the past. We can make different decisions in the future.

The Setting

Principals do not hang up shingles announcing the opening of their new practices. The reason is obvious but important: principals always work in organizations and always have—they offer no services outside the schools that employ them. Their work is, therefore, connected to the particulars of the organized settings in which they are employed, and we will see how profoundly the nature of those settings affect them in the pages to come. How their positions were shaped over time is an important part of that story and a brief examination of that history is the major focus of this chapter. What their work looks like today reflects the development over many decades of public schools, a history, as we shall see, that has been comparatively gradual and evolutionary. Continuities that have persisted over three centuries and significant changes that have taken place over many decades shape what we encounter today. The first part of the chapter, then, centers on the historical setting.

The second part of the chapter presents background information about the suburban schools we studied—information on the specifics of the organizational setting. Some organizational variables that transcend the particular sector of public schools are included, considerations such as size, environmental turbulence, and social composition. Taking such factors into account helps us to compare the challenges facing school managers with those faced by managers elsewhere. There are also particulars of grade structure and levels of student performance. Awareness of both kinds of particulars will assist readers in assessing the findings and interpretations presented throughout the book.

A VERY BRIEF HISTORY

We live in a society where technological changes produce new lines of work almost explosively. Think, for example, of the electronics industry and the proliferation of products, services, and occupations it has produced in recent years. In contrast, the position of public school principal in the United States, having originated during the first half of the nineteenth century, looks almost ancient. Yet two other adult positions in public schools are even older; teachers and citizen overseers preceded the principalship by as much as 150 years. There were teachers employed in publicly supported schools as early as the seventeenth century; the schools where they worked were built, maintained, and supervised by local citizens selected to represent their communities. We are not studying new institutions.

Although there was considerable variation in arrangements in colonial times, schooling was nowhere sufficiently complex to require officials to coordinate activities or allocate resources within the simple schools that prevailed. Members of the citizens' governing group handled such matters. They were, in essence, trustees responsible for supervising the use of public funds obtained, eventually, through local taxation (Bailyn 1960). They hired the teacher and arranged to have the roof repaired. The teacher taught and also provided what are called "support services" today, such as maintaining stoves in cold weather, sweeping up at day's end, and bandaging whatever hurts the children sustained while running around during recess (Elsbree 1939).

That two key components (citizen boards and teachers) present at the birth of American schools persist today points to a degree of continuity in the structure of public schools; important changes made over the decades have resulted in the more complex organizations we see today. One such change is the curtailment of local board powers associated with increased controls from state and federal legislatures, the executive branches of state and federal governments, and state and federal courts; examples of such influences are racial desegregation, mandatory provisions for students with disabilities, and, more recently, increasing controls from state and federal governments based largely on how students perform on standardized tests (Campbell et al. 1990, Conley 2003).

The second major change is the development of an administrative corps, including headquarters personnel (the superintendent and central office staff) and principals for the individual schools. The existence of that corps makes it unnecessary for board members to engage in day-to-day managerial matters. Today's boards meet regularly and review recommendations submitted by the superintendent, passing or altering or rejecting them as they see fit. They continue to have the overall responsibility for the fiscal affairs of the school district and, officially, oversee school affairs in general.

The position of teachers has also undergone major changes. The teachers of an earlier era were the only adults regularly found in the one-room schoolhouse, an arrangement that persisted in some rural areas into the twentieth century.[1] Today classroom teachers work under the direct supervision of full-time administrators; they teach different grades and different subjects and work alongside various types of specialists. Their efforts, moreover, are supplemented by clerks and skilled workers performing supportive functions. In many states, teachers belong to unions that have acted to protect and advance their interests.[2] But there are also important elements of continuity. Today, as in the distant past, teaching tasks center on the face-to-face instruction of a group of children. Unlike industrial tasks that have been taken over by machines and robots; their tasks are more specialized today; the technological innovations that have persisted (there have been fads of various kinds) have been integrated into instructional programs still dominated by teachers. Most instruction, moreover, takes place in the bounded space of a separate classroom somewhat isolated from others in the building. In elementary schools, most teachers spend most of their working hours with one group of children day after day for the duration of an academic year.

Simple schools (a citizen board overseeing one teacher) prevailed over many decades; they were adapted to rural life where children were dispersed over miles of thinly populated land. But arrangements created in rural America no longer matched reality when urbanization expanded throughout the nineteenth century. Large increases in the number of students due to demographic changes (including immigration) and laws making school attendance compulsory changed that reality. As urban density increased, more and more children lived in smaller and smaller areas. It became not only possible but necessary to accommodate them in new ways; buildings with multiple rooms replaced the one-room schoolhouse. Those heading schools (ultimately titled "principal") sorted children by age levels and prior schooling, placing them in the newly created system of grades (Elsbree 1939). Teachers were assigned to classes that had become considerably more homogeneous because they no longer taught children of widely varying ages and accomplishment.

The creation of schools with multiple grades and classrooms was a major change in the organization of public education; multiple classrooms and teachers raised issues of internal authority over teachers as well as students and the question of who spoke for the school vis-à-vis the community.[3] It was widely assumed that there should be a single person "in charge" of the building. The emergence of management at the school level contrasts with the pattern that prevailed in business at the time where new positions were created by owners as part of developing technologies; for example, the organizational and productive systems built by Henry Ford and Sears Roebuck were designed and executed from the top down. At the school level, however, local management grew up and over an established and continuing teaching function and, as a result, showed greater adaptation to what previously existed than was true for structures that were developed in business corporations. The break with the past in schools was comparatively bland.

Teaching young children had always involved responsibility for their care during long periods of time; the phrase "in loco parentis" underscores the expectation that a teacher will attend to the general well-being of the child as well as the learning of students. Young children require constant supervision, particularly when in groups and outside their homes; order must be maintained and care taken to protect them from harm. The shift to a system of age-graded classes did not remove the need for close supervision; the expectation continued that teachers would stay with their students during the school day, leaving them only for brief and/or stipulated periods when another adult was assigned to supervise the children. (Concerns about legal liability eventually reinforced close supervision of the students.) Teachers became unavailable to participate in tasks that grew out of the organizational needs of the school; their contributions, where desired and sought, would have to take place primarily outside regular classroom hours. Restrictions on the availability of teachers reduced the capacity of principals to delegate school-based tasks to them; in managerial terms, principals faced and continue to face a workforce characterized by what we might call "low assignability."[4] Administrative assistants for elementary school principals, moreover, have tended to be sparse and, when present, have been vulnerable to budget cuts.

The last half of the nineteenth century was a period of transition between the largely decentralized distribution of schools and the (comparatively) tidy hierarchies that emerged in cities after the turn of the century (Cronin 1973). Arrangements varied greatly during the later years of the nineteenth century; one account (Reller 1935) is almost despairing in its efforts to generalize about the early district structures in 39 cities. But despite such variations, there appear to have been some common elements in the tasks of the head teachers (principals) during that era.

Pierce's work (1935) points up the fact that principals had much to do in this formative period. One of their central responsibilities was to place children in the emerging system of grades, children whose educational backgrounds, we presume, varied enormously. Many came from foreign countries with no preparation in English, whereas others, migrants from the countryside to the cities, had widely uneven knowledge of reading, writing, and arithmetic. It fell to the principals to deal with the parents, who were also heterogeneous and frequently had no experience with public schools or how to support their children's learning. Perhaps it is not surprising that it became less and less common for those serving as principals to continue teaching while performing their administrative duties; it became a full-time position within a few decades of its initial creation.[5]

By 1900 city school districts had, in the main, taken shape—a shape that became the prototype for other kinds of communities as well. Historical accounts and interpretations differ on the processes and motivations involved, but its formation clearly reflected changes in the society at large (Katz 1968, Tyack 1974). Centralization was fostered by technological and related developments, an observation Max Weber made in discussing the development of modern bureaucracy (Weber 1947). It became possible for those at the apex of a city system to inspect schools throughout the area (as trolleys and automobiles replaced horses) and to communicate (telephones) with officials in widely dispersed units. The expanding school population required new facilities and coordinated action in larger and larger district units; as years of schooling increased, so did the need to align the grades and curriculum from kindergarten through high school. In governance, progressive ideals challenged party patronage and encouraged appointment based on merit and professional preparation, the latter helping superintendents to wrest a degree of discretion from boards and political figures; conceptions of professionalism, buttressed by universities and state governments, aligned university programs with hierarchical ranks among school personnel. The dramatic successes of large organizations in business (from industry to retail chains) provided models of leadership, idealizing it and influencing school boards and others with power over the formation of school districts (Callahan 1962). The organizational connections within the public system of education tightened.

School superintendents played a part in shaping the emerging structure. They met and communicated across state and municipal lines to form national groups (e.g., National Education Association, etc.) working to support their claims to clear administrative powers. Callahan (1966) tells that during the 1890s they debated and worked toward a consensus that claimed administrative rights and responsibilities for superintendents, but unlike a few of their more aggressive members who pressed for legal independence, most superintendents rejected that much independence and accepted policy dominance by local school boards and their authority to hire and fire superintendents. Superintendents acknowledged their vulnerability and the need to take it into account in their behavior as school executives; at the same time, however, they supported preparation programs in universities to buttress their claims to "professional" knowledge and to bolster their prestige by acquiring advanced degrees. When journalists attacked schools and decried weaknesses among teachers, superintendents joined in and emphasized the need for "supervision" (tasks they claimed as theirs) to correct deficiencies among faculty members. Conceptions of scientific management that dominated managerial thinking during the early decades of the twentieth century built on such imagery, propounding the need to concentrate planning and specialized intellectual capacities in headquarters (central office) rather than in individual schools; that practice became routine in subsequent years and made it less likely that principals (especially in the elementary grades) would get more than a minimal number of persons to help them in managing their schools (Callahan 1962).

Tyack discusses the emergence of what educators—and the public at large—came to regard as the "one best system" (Tyack 1974). That system, initially developed in the cities, became the prototype for smaller communities including the suburbs around the cities and, in the form of regional schools, rural areas as well: it became the standard structure. Its diffusion was helped by, among other things, state regulations and certification procedures and university programs for training teachers, specialists and administrators and, as we have seen, the professional associations of school people that were dominated by school administrators (essentially male) during the formative years (Wesley 1957).[6]

Seen strictly from a structural point of view, we can depict the standard system as built by collecting smaller units (classrooms and schools) into a common organization and ranking them within a vertical hierarchy called a school district. The first aggregation combined previously physically separate classrooms headed by a teacher (the one-room school) into graded schools with multiple rooms, several teachers, and an administrative head. (The first documented case was the Quincy School in Boston in 1847, a twelve-room school modeled on schools that some leading American educators had seen in Germany (Elsbree 1939). The second aggregation pulled together, into a citywide organization, schools that were locally operated in neighborhoods and run by neighborhood leaders. The nested units continued to be headed by persons in positions associated with their previously independent standing—teachers heading classrooms and principals heading schools. The resulting hierarchy placed superintendents directly "over" principals and principals directly "over" teachers. In managerial terms, superintendents became the senior managers, principals the junior. All teachers reported directly to a principal while students, of course, were subordinated to all certified adults.

The hierarchy was not the result of an innovative entrepreneur creating an organization that produced thousands of new jobs. It was, rather, an accumulation of previously existing units. There are no equivalents to Henry Ford—whatever heroes are honored tend to be government officials (Horace Mann at the state level and William T. Harris at the federal) and the occasional superintendent (Frank Spaulding). As far as principals are concerned, one is hard pressed to find their names associated with the emergence of the modern school system.

The relationship between superintendents and boards has been the subject of a large and continuing body of study and comment; that intersection in school districts has generated considerable heat and a high degree of scholarly interest (e.g. Gross, Mason, and McEachern 1958, Cuban 1976, Blumberg 1985). Strains in the relationships between teachers and their employers have, of course, received considerable attention since teacher "militancy" developed in the latter half of the twentieth century. In comparison, the position of the principal in district structure has generated less attention. There was some conflict between superintendents and principals, as we might expect, during the period before the consolidation of schools into citywide districts, but once that phase was over, observers paid less attention to relationships between principals and their organizational superiors, a task we will undertake for suburban settings in chapter 3.

We began this section by saying that we are not studying new institutions. There is an important consequence of the long history that precedes American public schools today. Traditions, often unnoticed, have built up over the decades, which affect our thinking in ways we do not fully comprehend. One such effect is evident, I believe, in a certain "taken-for-grantedness" about schools and the positions of people who work in them. Features that have been around a long time come to seem "natural." We begin to forget that school organization is a construction built by people and, as such, could have been put together in other ways. It is useful to bear that in mind when we analyze what exists; doing so should help us to imagine possibilities for alternative futures.

THE ORGANIZATIONAL SETTING

As mentioned early in the chapter, important aspects of organizations transcend the sector in which they are located, and identifying specific ways in which they vary allows us to compare management across fields. Those included here are size, the extent of environmental turbulence, and the social composition of participants. Others are more limited in their scope, such as particulars of the district structure (i.e., the grades included) and the level of student performance. We turn now to those five aspects of the districts and schools we studied. (Some comparative data on Iowa principals in different kinds of communities—suburban, urban and rural—are found in appendix B, section II.)

Size

In terms of the number of subunits, the suburban districts (59 in all) in this study are not large organizations. They range from two to twenty-eight schools, but the tilt toward smallness is revealed by a median number of 6 schools per district. Their central offices usually have few certified positions and, modally, only two positions that outrank principals. Given limited size and relatively flat hierarchies, the superintendent, unlike that official in large cities, is not a remote figure to principals but someone with whom they interact regularly; district meetings, for example, often consist of sitting around a table together in central office. Morris and Crowson's "creative insubordination," a strategy which allows city principals to circumvent bureaucratic rigidities, is not likely to prevail under these circumstances (Morris et al. 1984). The data suggest, moreover, that many principals attended board meetings (not always enthusiastically) and got to know board members, something rare in large districts. Speaking metaphorically, these suburban districts were generally closer to being villages than cities. It is also worth noting that the small size of the districts limited opportunities for principals to move up the hierarchy, a constraint that led some principals to regret that they did not move to larger districts, as we shall see in chapter 7.

The question of *school* size is more complex, depending on how one counts participants in school affairs. Adults reporting directly to the principal averaged 24 full-time employed persons, a mean that includes teachers and other staff members. By some standards, the schools were not that large: 82% had fewer than 500 students with a median of 375. If we use the span of control concept of traditional management theory, 24 persons reporting to the principal is high, but not outrageously so. But given the disciplinary and placement responsibilities of principals, should students be ignored in the span of control question? If at least some are included, how do these schools compare with firms and other organizations staffed entirely by adults? When we add the physical dispersion of teachers and students into separate places, the difficulties involved in maintaining close surveillance over subordinates become even more apparent.

There is, moreover, another complication. If we consider interactive complexity rather than span of control, the scope of the principals' responsibilities expands; that is, the schools they head are, in terms of interaction, considerably "larger." Some have numerous volunteers coming in on a regular basis; one school, for example, had one hundred such persons per week. All schools have interested parents whose satisfaction, as we have already intimated, is considered of great importance. Some parents are regularly involved as PTO members and volunteers, but others vary in the frequency and intensity of their engagement in the school. And, as March has pointed out, some organizations (he calls them "organized anarchies") have variable boundaries among their characteristics (March and Olsen 1976). In schools, many, even hundreds, of persons who are normally uninvolved can, if aroused, become highly and emotionally engaged. One aim shared by principals is, in fact, to prevent explosions of parental alarm about school events. Seen interactionally, then, schools are somewhat larger organizations than they appear initially and, if serious trouble arises, can expand to intimidating proportions.

Environmental Turbulence

The suburbs around Chicago (like many others) were undergoing demographic changes and the organizational turbulence those changes produced during the 1970s and 1980s brought with them insecurity of employment for those working in the schools. The children of the "baby boom" years were moving out of the elementary grades; drops in enrolment caused "reductions in force." The abbreviation RIF resulted in "riffing," a synonym for dismissal among teachers and, when schools were closed, losses of position by principals. (Principals in our sample usually accepted teaching positions in the same districts.) Position loss shows up in our data; asked whether they knew of any principals who had been let go within the previous four or five years, 59% of the respondents answered yes (Q. 47D, appendix A).[7]

Most respondents (88%) identified recent changes that had taken place in their schools and/or communities (Q. 14). Some (39%) of the mentions were benign, such as the introduction of a new academic program. The majority of mentions (61%), however, referred to threatening events such as enrolment drops, school mergers, school closings or rumors of such, teacher firings, financial problems, and the like. There was, in short, considerable turbulence in the working environment of many of these principals; the threat and actuality of school closings were recurrent themes in the interviews. And fear of losing one's job, as they say, has a way of concentrating the mind.

Where closings were taking place or rumors flourished that they would, the relative power of the board and superintendent vis-à-vis principals increased. It appears that the principals, in the main, perceived themselves in a buyers' rather than sellers' labor market during the study period. It is generally the case, as we shall see, that stability in district location far exceeded movement across district lines, a fact that probably reflects, at least to some degree, a tight job market. (There are indications that things are different today;

newspapers are likely to refer to "shortages" of qualified persons to fill principal positions, particularly in large cities.)

Social Composition

The term "suburban" may, for some readers, carry connotations of uniformly high socioeconomic standing. In the Chicago suburbs of 1980, however, socioeconomic homogeneity was not the rule; it is true, of course, that white families so far outnumbered African-Americans that to describe the suburbs as racially segregated, albeit de facto, was clearly justified. But apart from the severe constraints imposed by race, we find considerable variation in economic status and educational levels at both the district and school levels.

Families headed by hourly workers (skilled, semiskilled, and unskilled) composed a third (31%) of the families while a little over a fifth (22%) stood at the more prosperous end of the scale with heads who were executives, managers, proprietors, and professionals. The preponderance of families—the large middle (47%)—consisted of white collar persons, that is, small business owners, salespeople, and clerical workers (based on census data). The occupational distribution was remarkably similar by schools when principals were asked to describe the occupations of their students' fathers; hourly workers amounted to 35%, high-status occupations 21%, and owners of small businesses, clerks, and sales personnel, 44%.

The principals were also asked to estimate the educational level of their students' parents; the sample means were 44% high school graduates, 22% some college, 25% college graduates, and 3% additional professional training. (A bare 6% referred to partial high school or less.) As college graduates, the principals' formal schooling exceeded 73% of the parents and, including their graduate study, 97%, an impressive number. Such advantages in formal schooling provided a prestige resource that was, in all likelihood, useful in the principals' relationships with parents.

African-Americans, as noted above, were uncommon. In 75% of the schools, they numbered 5% or less of the student body; in 62%, 2% or less. The segregated pattern is clear at the other end of the spectrum, where African-Americans constituted 97% or more in 6 schools. A modicum of integration is visible in 15% of the schools where African-Americans ranged from 10% to 60%.

District Grade Structure

Most schools in Illinois (Chicago being an important exception) are divided into two layers consisting of high school districts (grades 9–12) and elementary districts (K through 8). The districts at each level have their own school boards as well as professional and supporting staffs, making them essentially distinct and separate from each other. That feature is not the national norm where most school districts (called "unit districts") include kindergarten through grade twelve. (Nationwide, the U.S. Census reports that 6.3% of all students are found in strictly elementary districts.) In the suburbs we studied, issues of curricular integration are handled by committees composed of secondary and elementary representatives. All elementary school districts are aligned with particular high school districts, an arrangement that allows for closer integration than would otherwise be the case.

The consequences of this dual organization for elementary principals will be occasionally mentioned in subsequent chapters. Readers will be able to get a sense of its relative importance when we present comparative data from studies (e.g., Iowa, NAESP studies) where unit K-12 districts are either the rule or dominate the data. In the main, there seem to be few differences attributable to the grade structures involved in the school districts.

Student Performance

A substantial majority (71%) of the principals reported that their students performed above average on national achievement tests, 22% said average, and a mere 7% below average (Q. 10G). Thus it was possible for these principals, comparing their students with national figures that included rural and city students, to boast about the relative standing of their students; for most of them, the generally high outcomes probably reduced the salience of achievement test results. They tended to describe their students (Q. 10F) favorably in other respects; when their comments were coded as positive, negative, or neutral, positive comments outnumbered negative comments by a ratio of 3 to 1. Students were praised for obedience, strong effort, and social skills; negatives included poor social adjustment, families showing little interest in education, and children who were "spoiled" by overindulgent parents. In general, however, there were few occasions (as we shall see) when our respondents portrayed their students as problematic.

In conclusion, it appears that when compared with the explosive decades immediately prior to our study, times during the 1980s were relatively harder for principals in the suburban grade schools. Insecurities around employment had replaced the often exhilarating opportunities of previous years when more schools were opened than closed. It is wise to bear these changes in mind when we consider the internal power relationships and career contingencies that faced the respondents in this study. We begin our examination of the latter—early career processes—in the next chapter.

The Early Career

School administration was created during the nineteenth century with the birth of two major positions—the superintendent of schools and the school principalship. It was not long before each position was incorporated into state systems of career regulation formed to certify teachers. The principal position, the first step after teaching, required a specific minimum of time working as a class-room teacher and completion of a university program of study overseen by the state. The result was that entry to the position was restricted to persons who had first served in another position: it became a two-stage career. That one must first train and be certi-fied in one position (teaching) before one can enter another (the principalship) is an unusual feature of the kind of management we are studying; the fact that management in schools is subject to state licensing sets it apart from the vast majority of managerial occupa-tions where no such arrangements prevail.

That entry to the principalship is staged provokes particular questions about how persons are recruited to, and socialized into, the occupation. To what extent do principals reflect the social com-position of the teaching force? Are they the same kinds of people? Second, what career steps are involved in becoming a suburban elementary principal and how are they selected for the position? Finally, what does the newcomer, already experienced in the work of schools, need to learn in order to perform the new role? These questions provide the focus for the three sections of this chapter.

SOCIOECONOMIC ORIGINS

Since only teachers can become principals, we might expect the social composition of the occupation to reflect that of the teaching staff, but this was markedly not the case in the 1980 sample we drew. While most elementary teachers were (and still are) women, only 15.2% of the sample members were female, 84.9% male; for the country at large in 1985, the NEA survey reported that men constituted 13.8% of elementary teachers and women 86.2% (National Education Association 1987). School district choices were just beginning to reflect the moves toward equality for women that were changing the economy and, ultimately, the principalship in suburban Chicago. In regard to race, the sample of principals was 9% African American, close to the 10.4% "non-white" teachers reported in the NEA survey. As we shall see later, the distribution of men and women and whites and African Americans varied by the socioeconomic level of persons living in the school districts. Gender, however, was the largest and most dramatic difference between the principals and those who occupied teaching ranks.

If the principals were anything but representative in regard to gender, how did they compare with teachers in other respects? For example, how do their socioeconomic origins compare? Entry arrangements in teaching have facilitated recruitment and, as a consequence, have provided a route for upward mobility into the middle class; is the same true for entry to the principal position?

The socioeconomic origins of the sample principals, as far as we can tell, resemble those of teachers in general. For example, the percentages of fathers who occupied white and blue collar jobs look similar to those in the 1985 NEA survey of teachers in elementary teaching. Table 2.1 lists the occupational groupings of teachers in our suburban sample and compares them with those in the NEA study.[1] Testing for upward mobility in our data made it clear that a considerable number of the men and women in the group moved up from families where the fathers occupied lower income occupations and had lower educational levels. When we compare occupational prestige the mean is 60 for the principalship versus 43.9 for the fathers' occupations. (See Hauser and Featherman 1977 for information on the National Opinion Research Center's prestige scale

Table 2.1. Occupation of Fathers: Elementary Teachers and
Suburban Principals

	Teachers (All)	Principals (Suburbs)
1. White collar workers	51.2%[a]	51.8[b]
2. Blue collar workers	36.1%[c]	42.7[d]
3. Farmers	12.6%	5.5
	99.9	100.0

a. Includes clerical and sales, managerial workers and self-employed, professional and semiprofessional worker
b. Includes clerical and kindred workers, sales workers, managers and administrators, professional, technical and kindred
c. Includes unskilled workers, skilled or semiskilled workers
d. Includes craftsman and kindred workers, operatives, laborers except farm, service workers
Source: NEA study, Status of the American School Teachers 1985–86, National Education Association, Research Division, 1987.

used here.) Ninety-one percent of sample members had acquired more years of schooling than their fathers. (In Iowa, the comparable number is 94.7%). The principalship, like teaching, has provided the opportunity for a substantial number of persons to move up the socioeconomic ladder. We note here that the costs for teachers to qualify for an administrative certificate are not very high because certificate study is often available on convenient schedules that permit working and studying simultaneously and school districts usually subsidize graduate study in their salary schedules or, in some cases, help with direct tuition support.

In discussing their choice of teaching, the responses given by the principals look very similar to those for teachers in general. Some decided early (one-third before finishing high school) while the rest decided during college (46%) or after working or serving in the armed forces for a short period of time (21%). The list of attractions they gave is also familiar—working with children, affection for a particular subject, influence from teachers in or outside the family, opportunities for service; familiar constraints (limited funds and/or limited awareness of alternatives) also appeared. The aspirations mentioned as alternatives (the high status professions, business management) reflected the American dream of "moving up."

To what extent did the respondents enter teaching with the thought in mind that they would eventually leave it for administration or other kinds of work (Q. 5C)? Sixty-two percent expected to stay, 38% to leave. Asked whether the expectation of leaving played a part in the decision to teach, around one half (56%) said yes, it did (we can call them "sojourners"). Those who saw their teaching years as preparation for administrative or college work constituted 19% of the total; most respondents developed the ambition to become principals while already working in schools. The mean number of years spent teaching before becoming a principal was 7.2 (S.D. 4.3) years, suggesting that there was ample time for most to become socialized into the world of teachers and to develop sensitivity to how they defined their relationships with administrators. (The Iowa data show the suburban principals there moving up faster than others—7.6 years versus 9.5 for city principals and 8.1 for those in rural areas. Appendix B discusses the Iowa data in greater detail.)

Becoming a principal, respondents expected, would bring them increases in extrinsic rewards (Q. 6, money 60% of mentions, greater influence 41%, and prestige 17%). An interesting aspect of the responses, however, was the denial by 25% of a premise in the wording of the question, that is, the principal position would be "better" than what they were doing at the time, namely, teaching. I suspect that those who expressed discomfort with the phrasing thought it implied more separation from teaching than they liked, that they preferred to stress their common interests with teachers and to reduce rather than emphasize the social distance between them. The suggestion that the relationship to teachers might be special will receive considerable reinforcement as we proceed.

GETTING IN: TWO PERSPECTIVES

The issue of promotion to principal in the suburbs can be seen from two perspectives—an ecological, spatial one involving geographic moves and an organizational one focusing on selection processes. We begin with the first.

A small proportion (15%) of the sample grew up in suburban Chicago (table 2.2). The numbers of those who originated in other

Table 2.2. Location of Birthplace

	Men		Women		Totals	
Place	White	AA[a]	White	AA	N	%
1. Chicago suburbs	15	0	1	0	16	15
2. Downstate Illinois	30	0	1	0	31	28
3. City of Chicago	24	1	7	1	33	30
4. Other U.S.	17	4	4	3	28	25
5. Other nations	2	0	0	0	2	2
Totals	88	5	13	4	110	100

a. African Americans

places are similar to each other—Chicago (30%), downstate Illinois (28%), and other points in the United States (25%).[2] We move next to the routes followed by our principals to two destinations; the first deals with the geographical moves to the suburbs around Chicago, the second to their first full principalship, the point selected to signify entrance to the occupation "principal." In regard to the first destination, the population of the suburbs and their schools exploded during the nineteen fifties, sixties, and early seventies. Along with many of the families they served, the vast majority of the principals were migrants to suburban life.

Since the certification of teachers is a state function, districts recruited primarily from colleges and universities within state boundaries. (Arrangements that exist for cross-state certification have not eliminated localism in teacher and principal careers [Kaye 2006].) Seventy-three percent of the principals were born and raised in Illinois and 66% of the respondents attended college there.

It is interesting that although most of the principals grew up in other places, 65% of them took their first teaching position in the suburban ring around Chicago (table 2.3). That high percentage points to the importance of early choices in these careers; it underscores the point that when one began in the suburbs made a difference. It demonstrates as well the significant part played by colleges in the relocation of young graduates, easing the transition from their original communities to work in suburban settings. For example, those attending downstate colleges were drawn primarily from downstate communities (data not shown) but rarely returned

Table 2.3. Location of First Teaching Position by Location
of College Attended

	Location of College			Totals	
	Metro Chicago	Downstate	Other U.S.	N	%
1. Chicago suburbs	34	24	13	71	65
2. Downstate Illinois	2	2	2	6	6
3. City of Chicago	10	0	2	12	11
4. Other U.S.	0	0	20	20	18
Totals					
N	46	26	37	109	100
%	42	24	34	100	

to them; 24 of 26 went directly from college to teaching in the
Chicago suburbs.

What routes to the Chicago suburban ring were followed by
the remaining 35% who arrived later after working in schools elsewhere? Half came from other states, half from Chicago or other
places in Illinois. Some moved in short hops, others in longer. Most
of these later arrivals (68%) began teaching in suburbia after working in a nearby town or city for a year or two; they took short hops.
Those who moved farther were primarily women (4 of 5 cases); at
the time of the study, women generally worked longer as teachers
before becoming principals.

The remaining dozen moves, usually from a greater distance,
were made by men who began their employment as rural superintendents. The remaining six began their careers as principals by
moving to a suburban district, but four of those had previous administrative experience such as assistant principals. Only two men
moved directly from classroom teaching elsewhere to suburban
principalships.

One's chance of becoming a Chicago suburban principal, then,
rested heavily on having taught in a local suburban school; 89%
of the respondents had done so (10 of 12 who did not had at least
some administrative experience). That the dominant criterion was
the demonstrated ability to teach (one presumes effectively) in a
suburban school indicates that suburban employers did not hold

Table 2.4. How First Principal Position Attained by Gender (Q. 7)

	Men		Women		Totals	
	N	%[a]	N	%[a]	N	%[a]
1. Promoted within district	61	66	14	82	75	68
2. Appointed from other district	32	34	3	18	35	32
Totals						
N	93	100	17	100	110	100
%		84.5		15.5		100

a. Column percentages

"outside" teaching experience in high regard. In fact, there was a limited tendency to hire outsiders even when they had adminis- trative experience. Given the preponderance of local selections, it is highly likely that experienced outsiders were regularly rejected in favor of local persons without such experience. There was a marked preference for persons with suburban credentials.

Turning now to routes into the first principalship (wherever it occurred), we find that access could take place in two ways. Per- sons could be promoted from inside a district or appointed from outside, usually, in the latter case, from a nearby district. Table 2.4 presents the data by gender. The data are presented in terms of the first position as a "full principal," excluding semiadministrative po- sitions (usually part time) and the few who held positions as rural superintendents.

Once more the preference is for insiders; 68% of the principals first attained the position inside the districts in which they were working as teachers or low-ranking administrators. The proportion for women was higher at 82% versus 66% for men, suggesting that women probably faced more difficulties in crossing district lines. Superintendents and their boards chose, two out of three times, persons with whom they had direct and sustained contact during their service as district employees. Both parties displayed caution, the employer by selecting familiar persons with demonstrated local records and employees by accepting a known employer and district setting. Modally, neither party chose the riskier alternative.[3]

Job markets can be placed on a continuum from open to re- stricted; the open end presupposes few credentials for entry, the closed end numerous requirements that rule out many potential candidates. Becoming a suburban elementary principal required educational credentials at both stages of the career and experience working in schools; those formal credentials apparently exercised a localizing influence, favoring those who were born and grew up in the state of Illinois. We have also identified powerful informal requirements in the situation we studied—a preference for men over women and local, suburban experience over employment in other locations. We turn now to another important aspect of access to the position—specifically, mechanisms of promotion from teacher to principal. What patterns prevailed there?

Respondents were asked whether anyone "gave them a hand" when they moved into their first principalship (Q. 7B). Responses were examined in light of whether the person was promoted internally or appointed from outside the district. The reason for paying attention to that distinction was that when internally promoted persons were helped by senior administrators (central officials and senior principals), the helpers would usually continue to hold influential positions within the district and be available to assist such beginners as they coped with their new responsibilities; the sponsors, moreover, had a reputational stake (how good is his or her judgment?) in the success of the newly appointed person they had recommended for the position. Those who helped local teachers to move to a principal position elsewhere could not, obviously, provide the same degree of continuing assistance; they could, however, be willing to provide advice not available to those who did not receive such help.[4]

Sponsorship was the modal pattern (73%) among principals who were promoted internally; close to 3 out of every 4 said they had help from superordinates. Superintendents and assistant superintendents were mentioned most often as sponsors. In some cases, principals-to-be were asked to apply for the opening, in others, they talked about being groomed for promotion. ("They brought me along.") The career of the protégé was, at times, helped when a friend moved up the hierarchy (e.g., from principal to superintendent) and appointed him (this was strictly a male pattern at that time) to the vacated position, a kind of link between two careers. Some instances involved a principal championing a member of his or her staff. Whatever the particulars, active support from district influentials provided the protégé with a competitive edge; all in all, sponsorship contributed to the bias toward promoting insiders and to the pattern of "homosocial" advancement in which persons favored others like themselves. (e.g., male superintendents favoring males for promotion.)

Most of the principals who moved into principal positions in districts other than their own received help in making the move; 69% reported such assistance across district lines. They probably received help when no vacancies were available in their home districts; they had bosses who were willing to wax enthusiastic about their abilities, some phoning officials in other districts on their behalf. Some candidates were provided, for example, with "inside" information about impending vacancies that were not widely advertised.

The importance of assistance from sitting administrators in the first instance of principal appointment—internally or externally— points to an important limitation in access to these positions. Most new principals had the active support of persons in influential positions, a fact indicating that a considerable degree of self-perpetuation in administrative ranks prevailed at the time; those inside the ranks of educational administration obviously had much to say about who would join their ranks. Relatively few individuals who were unable to win such support made it into the principalship; active support from a senior educational administrator can be added to the list of informal qualifications that were usually required to obtain the position.

We have seen that the careers of these men and women displayed considerable stability through time; most, having attained the position of principal, stayed put. Such stability underlines the significance of early decisions in the career as we have already noted—what happened early very often shaped a lifetime of work in this field. That stability, coupled with employer preference for insiders (a preference reinforced by the personal intervention of senior administrators) raises questions about the values underlying this system of recruitment to the principalship. Two themes seem particularly relevant—a widespread pattern of caution on the part of both employers and employees and a bias in favor of organizational continuity rather than change. We will have occasion later

Table 2.5. Principals' District SES by Gender and Race

District SES	Men N	%[a]	Women N	%	Totals N	%
1. High status						
White	30	31.6	2	11.8	32	28.6
African American	0	0	0	0	0	0
2. Middle status						
White	37	39.0	7	41.2	44	39.3
African American	1	1.1	1	5.9	2	1.8
3. Low status						
White	21	22.1	4	23.5	25	22.3
African American	6	6.3	3	17.6	9	8.0
Totals						
White	88	92.7	13	76.5	101	90.2
African American	7	7.4	4	23.5	11	9.8
Grand Total	95	100.1[b]	17	100.0	112	100.0

a. All percentages column based
b. Abbreviation for rounding error

to consider the ways in which this kind of career system supports similar and other features of the occupation and its culture.

The districts in question, as we mentioned earlier, were not all alike in their socioeconomic standing; they were classified into three levels—high, medium, and low.[5] Table 2.5 presents data on the distribution of respondents by gender and race.

The advantages that white males enjoyed over others is evident in table 2.5, a state of affairs that prevailed widely in 1980. In addition to the overall numerical domination of men in the position, we see that white males were considerably more likely to work in higher status and higher income districts; 70.6% were in high and middle status districts compared with 53% of the white women and a mere 18% of African Americans in the sample. The white women were, modally, located in the mid-status districts; nine (9) of eleven (11) African Americans worked in low-status districts. No African American was employed in a district that did not have a majority or substantial number of African American students. Their careers were almost entirely segregated in both racial and social class terms.

There were notable differences in the prior work experience of men and women. Women were more likely to have taught in the early grades; 76% of them compared with 10% of the men had some teaching experience in the primary grades of kindergarten through third grade. The men taught principally in the intermediate grades of four through six (45%), grades seven through eight (33%), and a handful in high school (3%). Ten percent of the males specialized in teaching music, special education, and physical education, usually working across the elementary grades.

LEARNING THE INS AND OUTS

A two-phase career means that the principalship is not an entry job; those who become principals have already undergone substantial work socialization. They have held regular positions for several years and done so in a presumably acceptable fashion in (usually) suburban school districts. They were not newcomers to the demands of regular work and very few were "greenhorns" in suburban settings.

The principalship is, of course, a different job. We can uncover some of the changes beginning principals confronted by comparing their demands with those they faced as teachers. Whereas teachers spend most of their working hours with children rather than adults, the opposite is true for principals. In the earlier grades, teachers work with 20–30 students throughout the academic year while those who worked in junior high schools or departmentalized upper grades worked with perhaps 120–160 students; principals in our sample had general responsibility for 200–600 youngsters. Teachers' psychic rewards center on their relationships with students; they have no responsibility for the conduct of adults. Principals, on the other hand, head organizations composed of adults as well as children and are invested in the performance of those adults as well as the students. Every fall represents a new start for classroom teachers who begin with a fresh group of students, putting problems from previous groups behind them. For the principal, the opening of school is not so pristine an experience; most of the students, families, and staff members are the same as the previous year, bringing their characteristics and outlooks with them. In contrast to teachers, principal relationships with particular students and their families tend to be long-lasting.

For most of our principals, the transition from teaching to principal was abrupt. Although around half had some prior administrative experience, only 13% felt that it constituted significant preparation for the new position; of those, only two did not talk about things they had to learn. In their first day on the job, the rest of these men and women began work without a clear idea of what they are were expected to do; they knew practically nothing, for example, about the many routines they were expected to carry out; they were forced to rely heavily on the building secretary, if they were lucky enough to have an experienced one, during those initial months (Casanova 1991). They were, suddenly, "in charge" of the building and the custodians who maintained it; they were expected to cope with calls about late busses or snarls in the lunch program. Their school served hundreds of students, some in programs with which they may have had no previous contact (e.g., special programs for the handicapped); those who taught in the junior high grades faced very young students for the first time and oversaw curricula in reading and arithmetic that were new to them. Parents arrived with complaints they expected the neophyte to correct. And perhaps most starkly, they had to learn to relate to teachers no longer as peers but to muster the authority of the boss and to use it proficiently. It is obviously a good thing for these men and women, as we shall see later, that they usually had considerable support during this early period.

Table 2.6 presents responses (multiple responses were sought) to the following question (Q. 8): "Principals have told us that they had to learn a good deal on the job during the first year or two. What were the most important things you had to learn?" The readiness of respondents to identify what they had to learn is evident in the mean number of mentions—2.6 per principal. We will examine responses to this question in some detail.

Interactive Issues

The first two categories in table 2.6 deal with interactive issues that confronted beginning principals; taken together, they constitute

Table 2.6. What They Learned (Q. 8A)

	M[a]	% M
1. Specific Relationships		
Teachers	50	18
Parents	35	13
Students	15	5
Central officials	5	2
Subtotal	105	38
2. "People Skills"	33	12
3. Adapting the Self		
Change behavior	29	10
Accept new realities	22	8
Reframe (cognitive)	8	3
Miscellaneous	7	3
Subtotal	66	24
4. New Knowledge		
Administrative specifics	34	12
Instructional programs	26	9
Subtotal	60	21 (r.e.)
5. Time Management	10	4
6. Miscellaneous	4	1
Total mentions	278	100%
N = 107	Mean number of mentions per respondent = 2.6	

a. M refers to mentions in all tables.

50% of the mentions. The movement from teacher to principal clearly required acquiring new interpersonal abilities, both general "people skills" and building relationships to teachers, the parents of students, students, and central officials. The third category, "Adapting the self" demonstrates that it is no small thing to move up the hierarchy in elementary schools; it requires change in habits and behavior, acceptance of new realities and modification in how one thinks about schools. We are seeing a new "round" of socialization as these men and women acquire dispositions distinct from those they acquired while teaching. Categories 4 and 5 refer to acquiring new administrative and instructional knowledge and learning how to manage time.

The newcomers to the position had to develop their general abilities to relate to others, to increase what they frequently referred to as their "people skills" (table 2.6). Some were surprised to discover how important such skills proved to be; some criticized their preparation programs for not making them more aware of their importance. They found that working with adults and exercising authority over them differed from teaching children.

> Dealing with adults is quite different than dealing with the children in the classroom. In the classroom, you are God. Not so with adults. (19C, Male, 41)[6]
>   You step into it like a lamb. (104B, Male, 53)
>   Human interaction is the ballgame in being a principal. (79A, Male, 46)

One gets additional detail on the transition from teacher to principal from the more specific responses tallied in category 1. The material on teachers is especially important, for it is the largest single category (18% of mentions, 47% of N) and deals with what we will see, time after time, is a critical relationship for principals. Although there is no single dominating response, most of the comments revolve around learning how to relate to teachers from a new position of official leadership. Specifics varied, showing that different persons did not necessarily encounter the same problems in making the transition.

Some respondents began their new work with mistaken perceptions of teachers that they had to correct. Those who had taught exclusively in junior high grades, for example, were surprised to discover that teachers in the earlier grades were in some ways unlike their former colleagues in the upper grades; other new principals were surprised to see that teachers could, despite their certification, perform badly. Teachers, they discovered, included some who acted in ways their new principals had not, such as failing to meet deadlines instituted by administration; on the other hand, some new principals were taken aback when they encountered teachers who would treat a casually expressed comment as an order to be obeyed; they were astonished at the readiness of some teachers to accord them unquestioning authority.

Concern was expressed about "getting along" with faculty members, with figuring out ways to establish rapport with them. Explicit references to authority issues pointed up differences in the challenges they presented; while some said they had to screw up their courage to be assertive, others talked about learning to curb the urge to make "solo" decisions in favor of fostering more teacher participation in decision-making. Several discussed their change in status and the social distance from teachers that it brought in its wake. In a couple of instances, there is sadness as they talk about losing the closeness they had with former teacher friends. Promotion, it is clear, is not always free of loss.

One set of tasks vis-à-vis teachers received particular attention—the evaluation of teacher performance. (This is not the last time we will encounter such concerns; see chap. 6.) Some complained that they were not prepared for this task; it seems that university programs in administration offered limited guidance in this area. New principals, having worked alone, had few opportunities to observe their colleagues; they were now expected to act as experts, sometimes in subjects they had never taught (e.g., early reading and mathematics) or with children who were younger or older than those with whom they had dealt. Over time, classroom observations would help them to build a base for comparing teacher styles and to see effective practices to pass on, particularly to inexperienced teachers; at the beginning of their careers, however, their practical knowledge about instruction was limited largely to their personal experience.

One third (33%) of the respondents mentioned learning, in a phrase they often used, "how to deal with parents." Unlike teachers, parents have not been socialized to the explicit (and tacit) norms shared by school workers; as persons outside the organization and its controls, they are less predictable. Furthermore, the relationship to parents differs from what they experienced as classroom teachers. First, as mentioned above, there is the matter of scale—a principal needs to connect to dozens and dozens, and in some cases, hundreds of parents; it helps, of course, if they develop the ability to relate to them easily and are able to communicate a readiness to be accessible. They learn how to use web sites, newsletters, and the like to inform parents. Second, principals are expected to respond—effectively when parents are dissatisfied (often with a teacher) and press the principal to rectify the situation. As we shall see in greater detail later, the "irate parent" not only complicates the principal's day with difficult-to-handle emotions but if she (usually the mother) continues to be dissatisfied, may appeal to central office, endangering one's standing with the bosses. Finally, the principal is seen by others, unlike a teacher, as the spokesperson for the entire school. That designation carries responsibility for enhancing its reputation and increasing the goodwill of the community-at-large; they come to see the parent-teacher organization, for example, as an instrument to advance the public's image of, and increased support for, the school.

> You try to resolve cases so you can send everyone away happy. To justify a staff member's actions to the community can be hard. My staff must keep me informed so I can justify their actions. (29C, Male, 52)
>
> I discovered the importance of image in the community. You can offer good service and still not be thought of [as] a good school because of a bad image. People make a judgment on the basis of a 15 minute conference with the principal. What do I mean by image? That means how one looks, acts, dresses and relates to parents. (8C, Male, 37)

The transition to principal may involve new challenges vis-à-vis students. Some principals, as we have seen, had not previously dealt with small children if they had taught only in the upper grades. Others talked about the differences between disciplining students as a teacher and standing at the peak of the control system as principal—the range of interactions with students becomes narrower and disciplinary actions can carry more serious consequences.

> I had to become familiar with elementary children. You talk to them differently, and they have different needs. (48A, Male, 34)
>
> I had to learn how to deal with children as the chief authority figure in the school. (61C, Male, 45)

There are, of course, many interactions between school staff and students directed toward maintaining order. Most such actions do not involve a wider social network; they go unnoticed outside the immediate classroom or gym or playground. When students are referred to the principal for his or her disposition, however, the decisions become potentially significant for a wider audience; teachers have expectations of support that the principal must take into account while parents, on the other hand, may be drawn in if they consider the principal's decision inappropriate. One of the things new principals must learn is how to balance support for faculty members and respect for parental feelings about what disciplinary steps are or are not appropriate. (Some principals involve parents and teachers in developing statements about disciplinary procedures in order to develop practices and policies rooted in consensus.)

Adapting the Self

Sociologists have observed that occupational roles and activities can shape how people tend to behave and how they tend to see the world—in short, to affect "personality" (Becker et al. 1968). Furthermore, persons can be aware that changes are happening or have happened; principals identified three kinds of changes they had observed in themselves, changes that added up to 24% of all the mentions.

The largest single proportion talked about how they had to adapt their behavior to succeed as principals. They had to exercise greater self-control, to watch what they said and did, to deliberate when making decisions, and to stay with their decisions once they were made.

> I learned to bite my tongue, to think before I acted. (9C, Male, 38)
> Not to make snap decisions and to keep calm. (12C, Female, 3)
> I had to learn how to make a decision and stick to it. That was hard, tough. I also had to learn to make decisions amidst pressures from all sides and I learned that most decisions are about 50% right—until you go into administration you don't really realize that. (114B, Male, 47)

One is reminded of terms used by others to describe proper behavior for those in a position of authority, for example, the French

"sangfroid" and the British "stiff upper lip." They connote a similar need for self-control and steadying calm, the importance of
avoiding premature decisions, the wish to appear as someone who
is in and under control. One must, despite doubts, stand by one's
decisions. Listening to others before acting (particularly subordinates) may not be a regular feature in that traditional, somewhat
military image of leadership; it probably emerges among principals because, when dealing with adults (particularly when those
adults see themselves as professionals), they feel a greater need to
listen more carefully than they thought necessary when teaching
children.

Some of the responses say, essentially, that one must learn to
accept and live with the less desirable features of the new position.
Among them is the sense of being alone, of having lost the easy fel-
lowship with fellow teachers. And that pressures and stress are part
of the new position. Another realization is that when one becomes
a principal, the code of "live and let live" one subscribed to as a
teacher no longer applies; one must accept being held responsible
for what other adults do. Another managerial truth strikes some
as well: it is not possible to please everyone all the time. Universal
popularity isn't in the cards.

> You have to adjust to being alone—when you walk out of the build-
> ing, you feel you have it all on your shoulders. Everyone will want
> to share their problems with you but you can't always share with
> others. You are really alone. (65B, Male, 37)
>
> For example, supervising the playground. As a teacher you think
> of just your own class. I had to be responsible for the whole school.
> Teachers just can't leave for a cup of coffee—the playground has
> to be covered. I became much more aware of the legalities. (35B,
> Male, 41)
>
> The pressure—it comes from all sides. You don't see it as a
> teacher because the principal is the buffer. (44B, Male, 32)
>
> The reality of having to deal with problems created by other
> people, having to react to, not control situations, having to deal
> with problems made by someone else, not by me. (5C, Male, 31)
>
> I learned that I couldn't please everyone all the time. I had to
> take a stand and displease some people. (86B, Male, 32)

Finally, respondents talked about needing to make cognitive changes, for example, to "read" people to decide whom to trust. One's frame of reference had to broaden to think about the school as a whole—"to think like a principal."

> To think in terms of the whole school rather than in terms of the 25 to 30 students in your own classroom. And leading a group of teachers and providing leadership to them. You didn't have that before. (120C, Male, 56)

The transition from teacher to principal, in short, required changes in how these principals managed their emotions and their dispositions. They sought a "cool" and controlled way of responding to problems; they learned to take time and care in what they said and did. They came to accept unfavorable aspects of the job—the responsibility for the mistakes of others, the sense of aloneness, the need at times to displease others, and to cope with the stresses built into the job. Their thinking had to adapt to the demands of leading a larger and more complex group of personalities and the need to coordinate diverse interests. Becoming a principal may have built on their prior experience as teachers, but for many, it meant that they had to make serious changes in themselves, to shape a self that helped them contend with—and, if fortunate, master—the demands of their new positions.

New Knowledge

Occupying the principal's office carried the need to handle responsibilities that were brand new to most entrants. There are many details involved in the day-to-day operation of the school, details for which the principal is ultimately responsible. "Administrative specifics" referred to in table 2.6 include, in order of frequency of mentions, budgeting funds and related duties, "paperwork," maintenance of the school building, scheduling classes and personnel, bussing, and a substantial number of tasks that were mentioned only once.

The rhetoric used when principals talked about administrative duties did not glorify those duties; there were several references to "administrivia." It is not that they considered them expendable.

(With one exception—they often regard the reports they are required to complete for state and federal agencies as a waste of time.) It is, rather, that they did not seem to take pride in performing administrative tasks or talk about them as serious and important matters—they are portrayed in the language of necessity, not choice. Here are some examples:

> The mechanics of it. After the first year I had a new secretary so we learned together—the mechanics of budgeting, scheduling, paperwork,—garbage. (103A, Female, 58)
>
> How to take care of administrivia, such as filling out reports, locking doors, replacing paper towels. I had to tell people little things to do. I didn't expect that. (82C, Female, 52)
>
> I had to learn details, like making sure the paper is flowing, that the corners of the building are clean, is the number of kids on the bus right? (32C, Male, 46)

Learning about the instructional program is accorded more importance by those respondents who mentioned it as something they had to learn about in their beginning years. Those responses, moreover, did not occur often among those who had experience in the earliest grades; they were most heavily concentrated among those (usually men) who had specialized in music, special education, or physical education; for them, elementary curriculum and regular instruction were new. Given that few women mentioned this topic and that their backgrounds were modally in the primary grades, it seems that learning about early reading and mathematics instruction was particularly problematic, at least for some men, during their early years as principal.

> I found out how little I knew about the primary grades. I spent the first year going through a reading program with a teacher. I would learn by watching teachers teach. (24C, Male, 61)
>
> Getting acquainted with the elementary curriculum—that was the most challenging. (68A, Male, 54)

Close to one-fifth of these principals (18%) admit to beginning their careers with a serious disadvantage in their ability to evaluate, supervise, and assist the teachers in their instructional work; they were unfamiliar with the specifics to be taught (e.g., the advantages and disadvantages of particular pedagogical approaches) and had no experience teaching in the early grades. One wonders about how this gap in their technical knowledge affected their acceptance by teachers and the readiness of faculty members to regard them as suitable judges of their work. In these instances, it is clear that reaching a position of "educational leadership" would, at the very least, take some time to occur. (The final entry in table 2.6—time management—will be discussed at some length in later pages.)

Not Really Alone

It would be easy to misconstrue the meaning of talk about being "alone." The statements focused, of course, on learning to work alongside persons with whom one could no longer be as open and frank, of experiencing a degree of reserve in interactions with subordinates who were, not long before, peers. The reality is, however, that almost all the new principals had someone who would give them help in establishing themselves in their new positions. When asked about help during that period (Q. 8B), 99% of the respondents named someone as helpful to them (table 2.7). Administrators—central office persons and principals—account for 61% of the mentions; when we examine individual cases, it turns out that 88% of the respondents had either someone from central office or an experienced principal helping him or her. These beginners were welcomed as new members of administrative ranks; at the same time, they were coached on the appropriate behavior, and in all likelihood, the beliefs and norms of the group (e.g., "Make sure you're in charge.") New principals were helped whether they were promoted internally or appointed from outside. Their resocialization as administrators combined advice and support from experienced practitioners alongside the inevitable experiences of trial and error they underwent as brand new principals.

What may be somewhat more surprising is the substantial number of mentions (18%) of help from teachers. Sometimes the teachers they turned to were the more experienced ones; the new principals probably felt more comfortable accepting help and advice

Table 2.7. Sources of Help during Early Period (Q. 8B)

	M	%M
1. Central office		
Superintendent	36	
Other Central Official	31	
Subtotal	67	33%
2. Principals		
1 mentioned	27	
2+ mentioned	31	
Subtotal	58	28%
3. Teachers		
General	17	
Some	19	
Subtotal	36	18%
4. Secretary	13	6%
5. Other		
Family member	14	
Friend	5	
Miscellaneous	12	
Subtotal	31	15%
Grand Total	205	100%
N = 111	Mean number of mentions per case = 1.8	

from them. The rhetoric usually centered on the readiness of faculty members to be "supportive" or "receptive" or "helpful," with references to "they taught me" or even "watched over me." In such instances, we could see this initial period not only as a "honeymoon" (a common term among educational administrators) but as a kind of de facto apprenticeship where faculty members, and quite possibly superordinates as well, extend a kind of exemption from normal expectations of performance in order to let the beginning principal learn the trade.[7]

Families and friends could also play a part in the induction of these new principals. Sometimes a spouse or friend worked in schools, and teacher spouses helped their mates anticipate possible reactions of staff members to particular decisions. One principal told of having a network of friends built up over the years to which she could turn on a large variety of issues.

We turn next to the context in which principals played out the things they learned on the job. We begin with the "up end" of the authority system—the principal as subordinate to persons in the central office. That too was a largely new experience—most teachers have relatively little contact with central office officials.

Looking Up

Principals are employees of a school district who work under the authority of the senior administrator, the superintendent. At the same time, they are "in charge" of their own schools. They occupy the classic "middle management" position referred to in organizational writing: they stand under the boss and over others who report to them. Yet they do so with a twist; they do not operate, as many middle managers do, alongside those of higher rank in the same physical setting but as heads of discrete, dispersed, and bounded units, schools with names and distinct identities. As heads of such visible units, they have greater public presence than middle managers whose terrain is less distinct and visible to the community-at-large.

The focus of this chapter is on the principal as a subordinate official in a vertical system of authority. Relationships "up" are examined in five chapter sections. After a brief review of the public context of principals' work and the formal structure within which it is carried out, we will examine the extensive system of controls exercised over principals by those above them; we will pay particular attention to those areas where principals have a degree of discretion, to "apertures" in the district control system. The third and fourth sections present the perspectives principals take toward the exercise of authority over them. In the third, we discuss the expectations they attribute to their bosses; what do the principals think is wanted of them? The fourth part looks into the ways in which respondents frame their relationship with those above them and how they believe central officials should exercise their authority. The next chapter will deal with authority exercised by principals on their teachers and staff.

A VERY PUBLIC SETTING

Managerial work is similar, in some ways, in a broad array of situations. For example, the need to elicit suitable effort from subordinates, a central theme in the study of organizations since the classics of Barnard (1950) and March and Simon (1958), preoccupies all who occupy managerial positions; the extent of the manager's stated authority and capacity to exercise it can vary significantly depending on the organizational context. That and other aspects of the work can differ sharply; compare for example, the settings of Roman Catholic bishops, sales managers in car dealerships, department chairs in universities, Silicon Valley high tech managers, and ironworker crew chiefs toiling hundreds of feet above ground. Since different managerial settings make different demands, we will expect responses to differ as well. I wish to concentrate here on one of the most significant special characteristics of the work of elementary school principals—the very public nature of the conditions surrounding those to whom they report and the very public context of their own daily efforts.

The funding of public schools underscores the assumption that the services they provide are a public good. Adult taxpayers, quite apart from whether members of their families do or do not make use of them, are legally bound to provide the financial support they need to operate. Local taxation, although supplemented by state funds, incorporates the expectation that schools will be responsive to local citizens who can register satisfaction or dissatisfaction with their performance by voting for or against requests for increases in operating and/or capital expenditures (Wong 1999). Those who hold responsible positions in public education consequently have a strong and continuing interest in local public opinion; their ability to meet educational goals, and, of course, their economic resources, depend largely on its favor.

Taxes for local schools loom large in the awareness of citizens. They are higher than those required for other municipal services—

schools serve more people on a regular and protracted basis, for example, than police or fire departments. The form they take, moreover, is the highly visible, annual, and rarely popular property tax. An aging population, moreover, means that families not using schools exceed those who do. Given the American tendency to be wary of public expenditures and the strong interest shown by local media and citizen taxpayer groups in school budgets, a "culture of thrift" prevails in many school districts. Those who manage them have learned that allegations of waste and inefficiency can crop up with relatively little provocation. In the lingo of organizational theorists, the presence of "slack" is not a regular event.

Superintendents and principals, particularly in compact suburban districts, are highly visible and highly accessible figures. Accountability runs from the top to the bottom of the governance and managerial structure; board members who govern schools live in the community and, as elected officials, are sensitive to the concerns of their neighbors. Like others elected to public office, they prefer that if they do not continue to serve, it be the result of personal and not voter choice. The decisions they make are not only reported by local newspapers, television channels, and radio stations but are regulated by state laws requiring transparency. Superintendents, their careers at stake, are expected to have acceptable justifications for what they recommend to the board and for the administrative decisions they make.

Scholarly work in education and practitioner culture routinely treat the superintendent's position as highly vulnerable. That vulnerability is consequential not only for superintendents but for those reporting to them, a condition which is particularly true for principals. Many, if not most, of the events that create public alarm occur in and around schools, putting principals in line for superintendent displeasure. At the same time, principals work in a local context where persons can and do approach them to express a variety of concerns; accountability runs "sideways" as well as upwards.

Brief mention should be made of another aspect of principal work that flows from its public nature. Officials in the public sector are expected to operate in terms of what sociologists call "universalistic" standards: all persons should be treated fairly, with "fairly" often defined as "in the same way." Schools are organized as bureaucracies where there are explicit rules and procedures laid out for officials to respect. Caring for individual children, however, particularly in times and places where such individual attention is emphasized, creates strains between attention to personal needs and commitment to observing standard rules and procedures (Bidwell 1965).

Sociologists since Waller have pointed to conflicts that arise at the school level, particularly between the parents of students and those who teach them, and we shall see evidence of such tensions as we proceed. The sources of conflict include the unusually powerful demands that schools make of families, the presence of coercive elements in the relationship, the lack of choice by families in who will teach their children, and the lack of choice by school personnel in regard to whom they will teach. Although tensions arise in both private and public schools, there are some which are exacerbated when schools are located in the public sector.

SCHOOL DISTRICT STRUCTURE

The structure of urban districts, as we saw in the first chapter, became the standard format for American school systems, including those that were developed in the suburbs. The boards of local school districts today, though less autonomous than they once were, continue to possess broad legal powers *within* the districts they govern. As corporate entities, they are in charge of school property and, in formal terms, can be held responsible for just about everything that happens in the schools. (Unlike some universities where the formal structure features a separation of powers between trustees, president, and faculty, school districts' formally stated powers are concentrated at the board level.) The board states policy for the district and makes decisions on its fiscal affairs; it is the official employer of all who work in the district. The extensive formal powers accorded boards means that decisions that might be construed as essentially managerial or professional in other bodies are more likely to require board approval before they attain official standing.

On the other hand, the realities of school affairs require considerable "delegation"; school districts can hardly be managed on a daily basis by part-time, elected board members. The gap between the formal definitions of structure and what must prevail for thousands of children to be organized into a going concern day after day requires potent "informal" elements in a continuing structure—a structure which has many traditional features. The board exercises its powers primarily through decisions made at regular meetings where members vote on agenda items prepared, usually, by the board chair and the superintendent. Boards appoint the superintendent, as specified by state law, to be their primary agent, chief advisor and overall manager of district affairs on a day-to-day basis.

Superintendents stand at the top of a pyramid of line authority that includes everyone employed by the district—assistant superintendents and principals, teachers and librarians, office workers and bus drivers, custodians and nurses and, ultimately, students. The superintendent is authorized to speak for the school district under the presumption that what is voiced, if not always a direct specification of school board views, is at least consistent with them. Despite their readiness to delegate the daily operation of the school district to the superintendent and others, however, boards retain the right to disagree with the superintendent's recommendations and to question his or her actions. Boards can be highly accommodating, but even the most docile, like aircraft carriers or troops held in reserve during wartime, compose "a force in being" respected by wise school executives. The superintendent is expected to propose, but ultimately it is for the board to dispose.

Despite decades of experience with this structure, the exact boundaries between the respective domains of boards and superintendents are not always sharp and consensual. In fact, discussions of the appropriate boundaries between boards and superintendents are common at education meetings and in professional journals. The focus of this study, however, is not on the subtleties and at times bewildering variations in how school boards and superintendents relate to each other but on the position of the elementary school principal, a position shaped by two general patterns. The first is that decisions made at the apex of the decision-making structure (boards and superintendent acting together) are authoritative for any particular school and any particular principal. The second is that superintendents are hired and dismissed by boards, making them subject to the evaluations by members of the board; there is, moreover, widespread agreement within the field, as we have said, that persons holding the position of superintendent are vulnerable to dismissal.

The first pattern, the concentration of power at the apex, means that individual schools are entirely dependent units; no school has the financial resources or legitimation to operate without district authorization and support. District authorities decide when and where to open schools and when and where to close them, they determine what persons will head them and they set the salary levels of those employed in them. In the course of daily operations, principals are expected to call on central office to clarify policies and procedures; they are also expected to discuss changes they intend to make with central office. In sum, there is no ambiguity about the subordinate position of the school and the principal who heads it: both clearly belong to a larger entity holding legitimate authority over them. The policy that matters most to principals is "district policy," which expresses decisions made by board members and superintendents and reflects their decisions on how to respond to state and federal government initiatives.

Although superintendents get a degree of employment security from the multiple-year contracts they (usually) sign with boards, it is only a slight exaggeration to say that they serve at the pleasure of their boards. Conventional knowledge among superintendents (an observation based on years of personal contact with them) is that it is best to move along, if one can, when the relationship with the board sours, as, for example, when board members overrule increasing numbers of one's recommendations. Job "survival" is a common theme in the talk of superintendents—they are acutely aware of colleagues' resignations that are less than completely voluntary. Waller (1967) identified such occupational hazards years ago (his father was a superintendent) and subsequent scholars have paid close attention to the vulnerability of superintendents (e.g., Blumberg 1985, Callahan 1962, Cuban 1976, Getzels, Lipham, and Campbell 1968, and Gross, Mason, and McEachern 1958). One of the ironies in public education is that while many superintendents appear to be assertive and confident executives, we find the simultaneous presence of widely shared job anxiety within their ranks; such concerns, it appears, shape their behavior, including how they oversee principals. The specific connections between superintendent concern with public opinion and the principals' perceptions of how they are evaluated will become clearer later in this chapter.

We turn now to the feature of school district structure alluded to in the opening paragraph—the "distinctness" of its internal units. Scholarship in the field of education, following Weick (1976), has often described internal relationships as "loosely coupled." That looseness is affected by, among other things, the "thick" boundaries around subunits within school districts and the rich internal lives that are not immediately apparent to those who do not belong to them. Schools are distinct units but, perhaps less obviously, so are individual classrooms.[1] The boundaries around each, physical and sociological, affect the ways in which insiders and outsiders perceive and interact across them.

Our common experience of elementary schools underscores their reality as distinct social units. They are readily identifiable with architectural forms that set them apart from their (usually) residential settings. The visibility of physical boundaries is matched by generally understood norms on who may enter them and under what circumstances; anyone who is not granted permission to do so regularly is expected, in most places, to report first to the principal's office. They display strong internal relationships around shared extracurricular activities, which can and do vary from school to school. Affiliation and identification of students (and of some school employees) are more likely to focus on schools rather than school districts. There are symbols (e.g., names such "terriers" or "wolves") played up in publications, internet sites, and the like, which set them apart one from the other, intended to create the "school spirit" Waller discussed decades ago (Waller 1967). Competition in athletics and student exhibitions (e.g., science fairs, art shows) reinforce school identity. Where school location has been stable for some time, a school may come to be identified with a particular neighborhood, acquiring attachments and strong sentiments on that score.

A more subtle source of internal differentiation is evident in classrooms organized under a teacher who works with the same group of students for a full academic year. Most teachers and most students, in fact, spend the vast proportion of their work and study time in that setting. (The exceptions include gym teachers and other specialists who work with children of different ages.) That kind of differentiation in district structures will receive closer attention in the next chapter.

This review of public school social structures (a brief summary of a complex subject) aims to introduce the organizational context within which principals work. They work in a bureaucracy in which formal powers are concentrated at the board level but, given the part-time engagement of such citizens and decades of state rules and regulations, one finds large-scale delegation of management to the highest official, the superintendent. Delegation to the superintendent and, in turn, by that official to principals has, over the years, produced understandings, many of them tacit and not always stated in precise ways, on the need for "managerial prerogatives." Given that informal organization looms so large in this social world, the actualities of school organization are not revealed fully in official documents and statements. Other kinds of empirical study are necessary to supplement documentary information and to work out the ways in which districts and schools are in fact managed.

Internally, districts are marked by distinct layers of authority and managerial responsibility; one set of officials handles overall district affairs at the central office, principals are in charge of schools, and within schools classroom teachers work with a specific group of students for a full academic year. Seen that way, school districts reveal a threefold structure with a superficial resemblance to the Russian dolls in which smaller dolls are nested in larger ones; it is superficial because, unlike the dolls, the boundaries between the units are constantly penetrated. Formal separation of powers may be lacking, but, given the distinctness of the components, one would expect such a social system to be marked by "adjustments" and "negotiation." Principals stand at the intersection of district and school realities, straddling and coping with both worlds. We turn now to some of the complexities they confront as they interact with those higher in the system.[2]

CONTROLS AND APERTURES

As implied in previous chapters, it is relatively easy for citizens to get in touch with members of the board and employed officials in suburban school districts. For although the formal structures found in suburban districts mimic large city school systems, their smaller and relatively more villagelike settings result in considerably more interaction across school and community boundaries. Newspapers and other local media serving such communities, less focused on national and international matters, allocate relatively more space and time to local schools. Accountability, therefore, means more than responding to intermittent elections and advocating increased tax resources when needed; officials need to respond to events and issues as they occur and cope with citizen requests and complaints as they come up. Such close and steady attention tends to make school operations more consistent with districtwide policies and practices. "Deviations" in any particular schools are denounced by central officials when they become controversial. As in other organizations, those in charge expect compliance; board members expect superintendents—and superintendents expect principals—to comply with their decrees. Boards are mandated to heed and implement state laws and policies and, in some domains, federal rules and regulations as well. Failure to comply may result in the loss of funds from government agencies and, today, mandatory changes in schools within the district. In order to strengthen compliance, school district authorities employ a wide array of specific controls over the schools. But as Chester Barnard warned in his classic work, it is a mistake to assume that subordinates will comply automatically with the wishes expressed by management (Barnard 1950).

Kent Peterson developed a framework to study such controls using the same initial data base reported in this study (Peterson 1983). The types of control processes he identified include those found in many organizations, for example, supervision, input controls, behavior control, and output control. They involve specifics such as supervisory visits, controls over money and personnel, reports, job descriptions, rules and the like and, finally, the evaluation of performance. Such hierarchical controls are common. Two other types of control—selection/socialization and environmental controls—are not as common in other kinds of organizations. Selection/socialization includes professional programs in universities and the work experience required by the state for the certification of school administrators; the reliance on state certification is rare among managers in other sectors. "Environmental controls" arise in the interaction with persons who matter but are outside the organization; in the case of principals, this means that community (primarily parental) responses and sentiments are built into the control over, and evaluation of, principals. Peterson concluded that controls over elementary principals—taken as a whole—were "multiple and pervasive."

Persons who govern complex organizations, however, face another challenge in addition to obtaining compliance with their policies and practices. They must provide enough flexibility in the authority system to allow managers at lower levels to make timely and appropriate decisions in their domains. We have already noted that school systems have internal subsystems—schools and classrooms—which make comprehensive and rigid centralization neither feasible nor desirable; principals and teachers need sufficient "space" to cope with the daily exigencies they face and to find solutions to unexpected as well as foreseeable problems. Bureaucratic functioning requires a workable combination, then, of central control and subunit autonomy. We turn now to an examination of district controls with those requirements in mind. To what extent do these controls differ in the extent to which they constrain principal action? What mechanisms exist to provide flexibility for principals in their work?

Controls over Three Domains

In addition to the question of what kinds of controls are exerted, then, there is the substantive question of what aspects of school decision-making are controlled and what differences, if any, prevail among those distinct domains. This study paid special attention to three such domains—control over money, curricular control, and personnel decisions. The first two present a picture of considerable centralization, the third less so.

(1) The ways in which funds were distributed to the schools varied in their details, but two general observations can be made. First, principals were allowed, at most, sharply limited funds to disperse as they saw fit; any substantial amount of money required approval by the central office and school board. Recall that by far

the largest amount of money spent in schools is for salaries, which are usually administered by central office as a result of collective bargaining (87% of the suburban districts were unionized) and for individual teachers were based on criteria such as years of schooling and seniority. There were occasions when suburban principals influenced the money received by a staff member (e.g., hiring for after-school programs, summer school work), but such occasions were relatively infrequent and the amount of money limited.

The modal approach used by district officials to decide how much money a school received was based on student population—a per capita allotment (Q. 34 A, B). A simple per capita procedure prevailed; it was used in 57% of cases with an additional 12% combining it with principal requests; in 29% of the cases principals emphasized the part played by their requests. In most cases, then, more-or-less equal division prevailed; in instances where principal requests in budget preparation took place, it did not permit significant variations in the amount of money allowed various schools. (It did, however, give principals more voice in how money was used within their schools.) Since board members reside in various sections of a school district, it is unlikely that efforts to favor a particular school will go unnoticed or unquestioned; the norm of universalistic distribution of public goods does not lack guardians in these public schools.

(2) Curricular standardization (formal, written curriculum) is modal in these suburban school districts. Written objectives for each subject in each grade were very common (they averaged out in the main subjects at around 75%); and districts adopted a single textbook at a similar rate. Most principals reported that efforts were made to align objectives and texts to either standardized or criterion-referenced tests. Overall, curriculum emerges as a domain where, modally, major efforts were made to standardize across the several schools. Although principals may have had opportunities to contribute to that content (for example, they could run trials for later adoption by the district-at-large and/or serve on district curriculum committees), individual schools were expected to adhere to, and principals to implement, a common districtwide curriculum (Q. 38 A–C).[3]

(3) The domain of personnel decisions presents a mixed picture, but principals had more discretion in this area than in financial and

curricular matters. The principals said they were able to hire the particular teacher they wanted (82% so reported; Q 35A). Central office may have participated in the process by providing names to the principal and, perhaps, doing some initial screening before the principal became involved, but comments about that kind of assistance were normally favorable. Principals cherished the opportunity to select teachers for their schools; it allowed them to take an active part in shaping the faculty with which they had to work so closely. (Principals in nearby Chicago did not have the same hiring powers at the time of this study.)[4]

There were, however, restrictions in regard to personnel matters. Principals reported they had limited influence on processes of collective bargaining; 66% said they did not have enough influence. At the same time, however, the consequences do not appear to be that serious because 78% said that they had enough freedom to deal with teacher matters within the terms of the prevailing contract (Q. 36 A, B). Eighty-four percent reported that they had to use a standardized district approach in evaluating their teachers; we will encounter some of their complaints about such requirements later (Q. 37). A final constraint was that district officials retained the right to transfer teachers into their schools; 79% said they were expected to accept transferred teachers regardless of their preferences in the matter (Q. 35B).

Flexibilities in Control

What we have seen so far indicates that controls exercised over principals by their superordinates were substantial. We stated earlier, however, that we expected to encounter flexibility in the system to permit submanagers to make many of the decisions they faced on a daily basis. The School Act of Illinois states, "The principal is in charge of the school." Suburban superintendents interviewed in pilot interviews prior to this study made it clear that they expected the principal to run the school, in essence "to be in charge." Such expectations carry the implied presence of working authority for the principal, authority which presumably carries the right to make independent decisions as well as to carry out district policies and practices. A full examination of this issue would, of course, require extensive and intensive observation of district operations; what we do have, however, indicates that significant apertures existed within the control system, openings that allowed principals to exercise a degree of discretion within their schools.

(1) The first opening in the system of control has already been mentioned—that is, differential control by domain. We saw that principals were generally allowed considerable freedom in faculty hiring. The particular orientations of principals could, as a result, shape their faculties and, presumably, the actual implementation of curriculum. In some instances, the limited interest of superintendents allowed principals to make decisions in other areas related to instruction (e.g., the superintendent of one principal showed no interest in curricular matters, allowing her wide discretion [12, Female, 32]). Discretion in instructional matters also showed up when principals were asked whether central office expected them to implement a particular form of classroom organization; 76% replied no, central office did not while the 62% who said they personally tried to influence classroom organization did so primarily on the basis of their own preferences (Q. 40A, B). This means, I believe, that principals were granted significant leeway in implementing pedagogical approaches in their schools, that the how was less firmly specified than the what. (Teachers are also likely to say that they are freer in regard to how they teach rather than what they teach.)

How closely do teachers adhere to the prescribed curriculum? We asked principals (Q. 39 A, B) to describe district expectations in regard to teachers staying within the prescribed curriculum versus using their own judgment on a scale of 1 (stick to) to 6 (use own judgment)—the mean was 2.5, with heavy concentration (67%) at 2 and 3. Principals' responses to the question of what teachers actually do was slightly closer to "using their own judgment" with a mean of 2.9 and a concentration of 55% at 3 and 4. Clearly, there is some "play" in the system. This connects, I believe, to the boundaries within schools and a degree of readiness by administrators to respect the teacher's hegemony in her domain.

(2) Writing years ago, Blau and Scott discussed the distinction between close supervision that emphasized compliance with particular procedures and supervision that emphasized results (Blau

and Scott 1962). Principals were asked to describe how the central office wielded its authority (Q. 45A). When principals were asked about the degree to which central office relied on the use of rules and directions concerning their work, the modal response was low use with 62%; 34% said medium use and 5% high use. The picture is different when we compare how they responded to a similar question about central office reliance on results; in that case, 33% said high use, 41% medium use, and 26% low use. (The kinds of results expected by central office will be discussed below.) This is another way, then, in which flexibility figures in the overall control of school principals; most were supervised in ways that allowed the wider range of options present in an emphasis on results rather than more constraining compliance to particular practices and procedures. As we shall see, these responses allowed for considerable attention to questions of community satisfaction.

(3) It is useful to recall that we are examining relatively small suburban districts, not the tall vertical hierarchies found in large districts such as New York or Chicago. District size affects interaction between principals and superintendents in several ways. In large districts, there may be close to no personal connection between the two; in most of our districts, as we saw in the previous chapter, the principals were well known to the superintendent who appointed them and were often sponsored by them. In very large districts, principals and general superintendents meet primarily on ceremonial occasions or in subgroups. By contrast, the principals in this study had opportunities for one-on-one interactions and met regularly with the superintendent to discuss district affairs.

In short, interaction between principals and their bosses was usually more frequent and mutually engaged than those found in large districts in cities or, for that matter, the extensive county districts so common in the South.[5] The more frequent and informal interactions in these suburban districts make it more likely that the views and sentiments of the principals were known to the superintendent, and, as a consequence, had greater influence on superintendent decisions. To the extent that was true, principals were asked to adhere to fewer unfamiliar and uninfluenced edicts than their colleagues in very large districts. As a consequence, the meaning of the controls exercised over them differed. It is one thing for a submanager to be expected to obey a directive whose basis is un-known, quite another to respond to policies and procedures that have become familiar in advance and which might, in at least some cases, include one's preferences. On this phenomenological level, centralized control in our relatively small suburban districts is in all probability experienced as less constraining than it would be in larger organizations.

(4) Another mechanism that differentiates control from central office is "selective supervision." Perhaps the reader recalls being in a classroom where the teacher seated a child in front "so I can keep an eye on you." It seems there is a somewhat similar process among the adults in school systems; around half (48%) of the principals reported that different degrees of supervision were exercised by central office over principals within their districts (Q. 43). Asked why they thought that took place, they provided various answers; the most frequent were the superintendent's evaluation of the principal, whether the principal was having problems, and the number of parental complaints that central office received. It seems clear that at least in those districts, the degree of discretion in decision-making that was allowed a principal varied with the level of trust and rapport that prevailed between superintendent and principal.

The data at our disposal, then, comment on the two sides of district management with which we began. The controls were varied and potent—boards and superintendents could and did assert their formal authority over principals and individual schools. Yet there are signs of openness in the system of district controls, of a system which falls short of complete centralization. The districts are structured, it appears, so that superintendents can exercise discretion in a variety of ways. It also appears that in general, principals are permitted more discretion in putting their staffs together and supervising instruction than is true, for example, in how money is spent. Teachers, it seems, are also granted some leeway in cur-ricular matters; the authority system shows some deference to the identity and requirements of the Russian dolls inside the district. As far as principals are concerned, evidence that they are supervised less than their peers in the district is likely to be seen as an indica-tion of confidence in their ability and consequently experienced as rewarding. In that respect, the ways in which superintendents exercise authority can function as part of the incentives they have at their disposal.

WHAT PRINCIPALS THINK IS WANTED

The system of hierarchical authority, and the controls that derive from it, are intended to direct the decisions and behavior of principals in the district; in a sense, they constitute the operationalization of district objectives. They are authoritative messages but, like any messages, their effects depend essentially on how their content is perceived. We looked for those perceptions by asking principals two broad questions—one asked about the results their organizational superiors expected from their efforts and the other asked how central office evaluated their performance (Q. 45B, Q.47A).

The first data come from a follow-up on the question asking about the part played by rules and directives versus results in district controls. As we have just seen, respondents reported that results received greater emphasis. All respondents were asked to identify the most important kinds of results expected of them.

The leading response (table 3.1) centers on the central functions of a school—the results of the instructional program (26% of mentions, 66% of respondents) and, adding to the category, the 3% and 9% additional mentions and respondents regarding a positive evaluation of their school's instructional program. Student learning, as we might expect, leads the list of results emphasized by central office with 29% of the mentions. What may be less expected, however, are the numerous responses that mention the public reaction to the school and the principal, answers that are almost as frequent as student learning (25% of mentions, 63% of respondents). Central office, these principals said, had a strong interest in how the public reacted to the school and the principal; public satisfaction is one of the two leading results that matter to the bosses. There is a duality here in which student learning and community approval dominate the list.

What accounts for the importance of public satisfaction? As I see it, it results from a combination of organizational and personal interests. Officials, elected and employed, want to ensure financial support, and support in general, for their schools. On the personal

Table 3.1. Most Important Results Watched by Central Office (Q. 45B)

Result	M	%M	%N
1. Instruction			
Student performance and progress	75	26	66
Quality of instructional program	10	3	9
Subtotal	85	29	—
2. Public reaction: positive or negative	72	25	63
3. Teacher performance, reactions	47	16	42
4. No trouble for central office			
Compliance: rules and procedures	23	8	20
No waves, all smooth	20	7	18
Subtotal	43	15	—
5. Student behavior and relations			
with students	11	4	10
6. School atmosphere, climate	9	3	8
7. Miscellaneous	25	9	22
Total	292	101 (r.e.)	—

N = 112

level, board members prefer to have the option of running again—successfully if they choose to do so. Superintendents have vital career interests at stake.

There are two other kinds of response that are substantial although they occur less frequently. The first refers to teachers and how their behavior reflects on the principal (M = 47%, N = 16%). The content of those responses is mixed: they include judgments about the principal's influence on teacher performance and how enthusiastically teachers support the principal. Teachers are portrayed in twofold terms; they are described both as objects of the principal's leadership and constituents whose approval is sought. One way to summarize these findings is that principals believe they should be seen as "leading" their faculties but not in ways that might offend. A duality appears not unlike that we just discussed: goal achievement is qualified by the desire to win support and avoid disapproval.

There is another category (trouble for central office) where avoiding offense stands at the heart of the matter. First, the principal should avoid deviating from the rules and procedures laid down by central office; these responses (not strictly logical in terms of a question about results) indicate that some principals believe that central office is paying close attention to their compliance with its rules (e.g., getting reports in on time) and its policies (e.g., how extracurricular activities are to be scheduled).

Central office can also be displeased by a principal who "makes waves," who roils the calm of district waters by too much questioning of its policies and procedures or by making decisions that upset constituents (internal or external), which may embroil central officials in conflict situations. Theorists who uphold the value of conflict in organizational life would find few supporters among these principals and, if their depictions of central officials are accurate, their bosses. Controversy is defined as bad, calm as good.

As seen by these principals, then, what results matter most to central office? Students should learn. At the same time, however, the public must be favorably impressed by the principal and the school. Teachers should be perceived as following the principal's leadership; at the same time, they should also be seen as approving how that leadership is exercised; their views toward the principal should be positive. The principal should strive to avoid whatever creates trouble for those of higher rank; he or she should adhere to district rules and procedures and run the school smoothly and quietly with a minimum of conflict. These specifications illuminate why several principals in our pilot study selected the word "diplomat" as the best word to depict their work.

One more observation on responses to this question. Although there is clustering around the main themes, principals mention a variety of results that their superordinates pay attention to in evaluating their work. The miscellaneous category, for example, contains a largish number of unique responses. There is no single "bottom line" that dominates the responses to the exclusion of others; as a group, principals portray themselves as accountable for a diverse set of outcomes with a diverse set of persons.

The themes in table 3.2—responses to the evaluative criteria used by the superintendent—are similar to those we have seen in table 3.1. The order of the themes, however, differed—respondents focused less on student learning and more on ensuring that superintendents were pleased with the calm and good order surround-

Table 3.2. Evaluation Criteria (Q. 47A)

Criterion	M	%M	%N
1. No trouble for central office			
Compliance: rules and procedures	44	12	39
No waves, all smooth	37	10	37
	81	22	—
2. Public reaction: positive or negative	72	20	64
3. Instruction			
Student performance and program	31	9	28
Quality of instructional program	29	8	26
	60	17	—
4. Teachers' performance and reactions	54	15	48
5. School atmosphere, climate	21	6	19
6. Student behavior and relations with students	14	4	13
7. Relations with central office	7	2	6
8. Miscellaneous 1	25	7	22
2	26	7	23
	51	14	
Grand Total	360	100	
(N = 112)			

ing the school and the principal's adherence to district policies and practices. Again, it was important that the public be satisfied. Instructional outcomes, however, received a substantial number of mentions. Teachers continued to play an important part in how principals thought central office viewed their performance; what they said and how they behaved (presumably in terms of concerns to central office) mattered. The proportion of infrequent answers (miscellaneous 1 refers to low frequency answers and miscellaneous 2 to single answers) was even higher than in table 3.1.

How should we interpret the decline in mentions of instruction when the focus is directly on evaluation of the principal? If we examine indications of student performance and progress we find that it ranks third in this array rather than first as in table 3.1; emphasis on the quality of instructional programs, in contrast to student outcomes, also increased in table 3.2. I suspect that this may point to a shared belief among principals and their bosses that given high uncertainty in how administrative decisions and actions affect student learning, it is easier (and perhaps fairer) to focus on the quality of a principal's relationships with key groups and efforts to improve the instructional program than it is to make judgments about his or her direct impact on student learning. (More research with data designed to test that possibility is obviously needed in today's climate marked by heavy state and federal government reliance on standardized tests.)

When we put together the responses to the two questions, the themes are clear. Students should learn and the instructional program manifest high quality. The public should be satisfied. Teachers should reflect favorably on the principal's leadership. Principals should avoid irritating central officials by disregarding their rules and directives or failing to contain conflicts that may otherwise come to the attention of central office. Once again we find the absence of a clear and dominant "bottom line" that is deemed to be overwhelmingly important. What stands out, however, is that educational goals (at times competing goals) must be achieved in a harmonious atmosphere both inside and around the school.

The particular duality has important implications for how principals go about their work. For now, let us consider one such implication; to the extent that steps designed to improve instruction might offend the public (or an active part of it), the principal may well hesitate to take them. The possibility of trading off instructional potential for public approval will not be missed by principals. The need to get both instructional results and public approval draws attention to the benefits of compromises—when they are indicated—that will satisfy both objectives. Instructional gains are clearly desirable; it is best, however, if they can be realized in ways which, at the very least, do not offend parents and other members of the school community. Caution is, all considered, probably best.

The superintendents (and associates who assisted them) assessed the performance of the principal based on information they received. What sources, as seen by principals, did they rely on? How do those perceptions compare with the processes principals have identified in the earlier questions?

Table 3.3 has much in common with the two tables we have just reviewed. The primacy of community members as a leading

Table 3.3. Perceived Sources of Evaluation Information Used by
Superintendent (Q. 47B)

Source	M	%M	%N
1. Parents and community	56	24	50
2. Superintendent's observations	42	18	38
3. Teachers	32	14	29
4. Superintendent's staff	29	12	26
5. The principal (self)	27	11	24
6. Board members	17	7	15
7. Reports, other written materials	16	7	14
8. Test scores	5	2	5
9. Don't know	4	2	4
10. Miscellaneous	8	3	7
	236	100	

N = 111

source of superintendent information is reinforced in these data. Teachers also figured, ranking third.[6] Table 3.3 differs in the addition of observations the superintendent does for him or herself; principals also see themselves as playing a part in the evaluation, mentioning face-to-face interaction and the reports and other written materials they send to central office. Board members appear for the first time in this data series. They have the opportunity to form judgments on their own. They are privy to achievement tests at various schools, observe principals at meetings, hear comments from neighbors and, in some instances, are parents of children in the principal's school.

An interesting feature of table 3.3 is the low proportion of principals mentioning test results as important in the superintendent's evaluation. Only 5% of respondents did so despite the fact that most of the districts (well over 60%) administered some type of standardized tests. It seems likely that if they were important to the superintendent, principals would hear about them, at least during their annual reviews. We should not conclude, however, that this means learning outcomes were ignored; the contributions of teachers and parents undoubtedly include judgments about academic outcomes. What may be taking place here is that principals are saying that given uncertainties in assessing student outcomes, they expect that superintendents would rely more on collective judgments than on any single measure—a tendency Thompson (1967) links to situations marked by uncertainty. (One expects that there would be more emphasis today on test scores. They have not only increased in number and frequency but are widely publicized by the press and Internet and, where results are really bad, can lead to interventions from state officials under the No Child Left Behind Law.) This lack of emphasis on test scores at the time of our study may support the inference we have just mentioned, that participants in school administration (principals and central office personnel alike) did not place high value on this kind of information. It is also likely that principals were not sure, given their limited control over the teaching staff and gaps in the relevant knowledge base, exactly how to direct their own efforts to raise those scores.

WHAT PRINCIPALS WANT

We conclude this chapter with an examination of how these principals see the relationship with central office and what they prefer—and what they dislike—in that regard. We look as well at responses to a specific question asking respondents to identify the one area in which they would like to have greater discretion. The responses also provide information on how the principals perceived the authority system in which they worked.

On Help and Hindrance

One of the advantages of open-ended questions is that they can be used to uncover the concepts that respondents use in their thinking about a particular topic; their terms expose the frames they use to perceive and evaluate a particular object or, as in this case, a particular relationship. This can be seen in the responses obtained to three questions about the relationship between principals and central office, specifically a question with two parts that asked first how central office actually helps them to get their work done and then what central office might do to be more helpful. A separate question asked principals to identify ways in which central office

Table 3.4. Principals' Views on Central Office Assistance or Hindrance

	(1) Q. 50A How helps			(2) Q. 50B How help more			(3) Q. 51 How make harder		
	M	%	Rank	M	%	Rank	M	%	Rank
1. Support (All types)	72	32	1	15	11	4	19	9	5
2. Resources (All types)	60	27	2	33	25	1	30	15	3
3. Provide ideas	34	15	3	12	9	5	—		
4. Time claims	25	11	4	16	12	3	41	20	1
5. Autonomy	19	9	5	7	5	7	31	15	2
6. Communication	7	3	6	10	8	6	18	9	6
7. Know school	—	—	—	23	17	2	15	7	7
8. Include principals	—	—	—	5	4	8	13	6	8
9. Management (Poor)	—	—	—	—	—	—	26	13	4
10. Miscellaneous	5	2	—	12	9	—	11	8	—
Total	222	99		133	100		204	102 (r.e.)	

could make their work harder (Q. 50A, B, Q. 51). Code categories were developed to identify the ways in which central office actions were seen as either helpful or obstructive. We will consider each question separately and then attempt a summary; responses are presented in composite table 3.4.

In responses to Q. 50A, we find that two aspects of the relationship dominate: central office helps, as these principals see it, when it gives them support (32% of mentions) and when it provides them with resources (27% of mentions). Since, as we have seen, district authority and control over money are concentrated in central office, principals are dependent on those officials for authorization of their actions and the receipt of needed resources. In one sense, the distribution of such support and resources is built into the organizational system; public schools could not operate without them. Yet these principals seem to appreciate it when they are forthcoming, suggesting that resources and support are perceived, at least to some degree, as involving elements of choice and discretion; they are not entirely cut and dried, preset, and routine.

Central office is seen as helpful when it provides the principal with support (e.g., political cover, emotional reassurance) and resources (e.g., funds for a special project) that go beyond the minimum they might expect. They also mention, less frequently, other forms of help such as providing useful ideas, efforts by central officials to limit their time demands on the principal, respect they show for the principal's decision-making autonomy and the clarity of their communications.

Although responses were somewhat different in the second question (responses to Q. 50B deal with how central office could help more), the differences are relatively modest. Providing resources became the most frequent response and giving support received less emphasis; support and protecting the principal's time, however, remained among the top four responses. A new wish is mentioned and attains second rank—principals want central officials to know the principal's school better, presumably believing that they would act differently if they had a better grasp of the realities faced by the principals. Five principals wanted more opportunity for participation in district decision-making.

The data provided by the third question (Q. 51—what would make things harder?) are, of course, more negative in tone and content. The unwillingness of central officials to exercise restraint in making time demands on principals becomes the most frequent response and is followed closely by what principals saw as invasion of their autonomy by central officials; 35% of the answers refer to what principals consider to be overbearing behavior by central officials. The managerial practices of central officials receive more attention in these responses—poor administration (13% of mentions), poor communication (9%), not knowing the respondent's school (7%), or failing to include principals in district decision-making (6%). Insufficient resources remain a potential hindrance, but support declines and providing ideas disappears. Fewer resources are clearly seen as hindrance while less support and fewer ideas are less frequently defined in that way.

We would expect that providing resources and support would rank high on the positive end of these responses (i.e., Q. 50A). The more critical responses to Q. 51 point to the potential difficulties between principals and officials in central office. One is the stress of central office demands, which can eat away at the principal's control over his or her schedule; principals, as we will see, have particular problems in defending their time against incursions from other people. Another difficulty occurs when too little respect is shown for the managerial prerogatives principals believe they need. As head of a unit nested within a larger whole, the principal faces an administrative superordinate—the superintendent—who possesses markedly greater powers; the fiscal, policy, and other dependencies of the units principals head make it difficult to protect the boundaries between the school and the district. These principals, in short, want those who rank above them to show what we might call a kind of noblesse oblige, to exercise restraint in the use of their superior authority and to acknowledge that principals need an area for independent decision-making.

Negative effects are also associated with other aspects of the managerial style of the superintendent and administrative staff. Problems identified by principals included procrastination and vacillation in decision-making behavior, poor communication, inadequate knowledge of the principal's school, and failing to include principals in district deliberations. These principals, probably like middle-rank managers everywhere, appreciate steadiness and predictability, clarity in communication, decisions that take their particular situations into account, and respect for, and interest in, their views on how the organization-at-large should function.

How, then, can we summarize the way these principals frame their relationship with superordinate authority? What criteria do they apply to the behavior of those above them in the authority system? Three themes seem to catch the perspectives we have just reviewed.

(1) The superintendent and central staff are framed as providers. Do they supply the resources the principals believe they need to do the job? Do central officials provide support such as backing the principal in other vital relationships (i.e., teachers, parents)?

(2) The relationship is defined in terms of boundaries between the district and the school. Are the (appropriate) boundaries respected? Do central officials show self-restraint in their demands, such as avoiding heavy incursions on the principal's time in their requirements for paperwork, attendance at district meetings, and

the like? Do they permit principals enough latitude to make the decisions that principals consider theirs to make?

(3) Managerial standards are invoked, performance standards that principals probably share with managers in other sectors. Are directives clear? Does the boss avoid vacillation? The principals want superordinates to take account of the specific circumstances in his or her unit and, in some instances closely related to that wish, include them in district deliberations.

When we review the standards the principals applied when talking about relationships up the hierarchy, other points emerge. There is no questioning of the basic authority structure in school districts; there is no indication that these principals believed relationships should differ in any fundamental way. We do not find them challenging the right of their organizational superiors to hold them accountable for the outcomes described earlier in the chapter. They do not reject the premise that they should exhibit the substantial social skills and other capacities required to satisfy those complex criteria. One way to summarize their view is that these principals want bosses who realize—and take into account—that they too are bosses. They want the resources, support, authority, and orderly surroundings they consider necessary to discharge their managerial responsibilities.[7]

On Autonomy and Discretion

It is clear that there are some tensions built into this vertical managerial structure, that the balancing of central and local school interests is not necessarily assured. Although principals did not challenge the basic structure within which they work, some did emphasize the need for central office to allow them sufficient "space" in which to make school-related decisions. How serious is that concern with autonomy and discretion? We turn to a question which provides information on this issue (Q. 41A, table 3.5).

Respondents were asked "In your situation, in which area of your work would you most like greater freedom?" In a somewhat unusual response in these interviews, 33 respondents (31%) rejected the premise of the question, saying there was no such area, that they had all the freedom they needed and wanted.[8] An additional 13

Table 3.5. Where Principals Would Like More Freedom (Q. 41A)

	N	% N (107)
Complete denial	33	31
Partial denial, area indicated	13	12
	46	43%
Those citing an area (N107–33 = 74)	74	69%
1. Teachers and curriculum	M	%M
Curriculum and instruction	26	27
Hiring & firing teachers	14	14
Evaluation of teachers	11	11
Incentives for teachers	5	5
Other teacher supervision	7	7
Teacher contract	2	2
	65	66%
2. Other		
Money & budget	10	10
Control over principal time	10	10
More support less control	2	2
Miscellaneous	11	11
	33	33% (r.e.)
Total mentions	98	99% (r.e.)

responded with a partial denial, saying that although they generally
had enough freedom, they nonetheless cited some aspect of their
work. Thus a sizable proportion of the respondents (43%) indicated
that a lack of freedom was not an important issue for them in their
work. This overall response suggests that one should exercise caution in asserting that principals are, on the whole, eager to have more
autonomy in their work and the increased responsibility that would
presumably result from that increase. Thompson expressed skepticism about the wish for clear discretion and accountability within
administrative ranks; it seems that many principals are quite content
to share whatever accountability they may face with their colleagues
in higher-rank positions (Thompson 1967). (The advantages of not
being fully accountable for events that take place under one's juris-
diction play a part in the discussion of loose coupling in chap. 9.)

It is interesting, however, to examine the matters cited by those principals who did express the wish for more freedom in their work. The specific responses piled up in one general category— instructional matters and relationships with teachers; those responses compose 66% of the total. The specifics included areas where the principals were relatively constrained—the content of the curriculum, evaluation procedures, incentives for teachers, and collective bargaining processes. Although most have considerable say in hiring teachers, there are some who do not and wish they did.[9] The less frequent responses deal with wanting fewer financial constraints and more freedom in the use of their time.

The discussion of principal socialization in chapter 2 made it clear that relating to teachers, a major focus of what they said they had to learn, suggested the importance of that relationship. The data in this chapter reinforce that theme, telling us that more freedom and discretion in their relationships with teachers play a prominent part in what they want from central office. Why should these principals show such concern with their relationships with teachers? We will seek an answer to that question—along with others—as we examine data on those relationships in the next chapter.

On Being in Charge

Having examined the authority exerted over the principal, we turn now to the authority the principal exercises over others. The focus is primarily on the principal vis-à-vis teachers; the latter, we shall argue, comes closest to being the core relationship among those persons with whom the principal interacts regularly. The word "core" is used to identify that relationship, both collectively and individually, which is simultaneously the most important and the most difficult for the principal to establish and sustain. That combination of importance and intricacy gives it great salience. The first part of the chapter discusses why I consider it both important and intricate and the second part explores how principals think and act in response to the challenges that emerge in the relationship. The chapter concludes with a discussion of authority resources and how principals use them in relating to teachers.

CONSTRAINTS ON INFLUENCE

One need not study schools for years to realize that teachers are especially important to the work of principals. Teachers, after all, perform the central tasks expected of schools; day in and day out, they work with students and carry the major responsibility for their learning the prescribed curriculum. For the school-at-large to achieve its goals, then, requires that objectives be met in the physically dispersed and bounded classrooms where faculty members preside.

Principals acknowledge the special significance of their relationship to teachers; that is evident in our data, which underscore the significance and complexity of the relationship. We have just discussed in a previous chapter how principals emphasized it in learning the job and, more recently, the dominant part teachers play in where principals want more freedom vis-à-vis central office. In addition, principals rank faculty members highest when asked to identify the resources they need to get the job done (Q. 21). In talking about how they spend their time, activities involving teachers were mentioned most frequently (Q. 16A). We asked principals about their reputation with others, specifically, whose mattered most to them (Q. 53B). The largest number of responses went to teachers. (More on that item below.) As we shall see, primarily in chapter 5, there are multiple ways in which teachers affect the rewards principals experience in their work. In short, principals care very deeply about their relations with teachers.

What Are the Complexities in Overseeing the Work of Teachers?

Asked to discuss what tasks were the hardest to do well, the largest proportion of the suburban respondents (57%) emphasized supervising and evaluating teachers; as data in chapter 6 will indicate (table 6.1) exercising influence over teachers leads the challenges principals face in their work. Although specific responses to that question will be discussed later, we turn now to considerations that constrain the ability of principals to supervise those who work under their authority.

We begin with the public schools' contractual arrangements, which are rare outside the public sector and, even in that setting, seldom so consequential. One might wonder how principals deal with these crucial subordinates who have assured occupancy of their positions (tenure) and are financially compensated not on the basis of merit ascribed to them by their managers but in terms of seniority of service and the number of college credits they have accumulated. Furthermore, as we shall see, there are other considerations that make it difficult for those who are expected to manage teachers. The principal's situation vis-à-vis teachers is, we can say, marked by low levels of "pliability."

Contractual Arrangements

Teachers who obtain tenure (a process that took two or three years in Illinois at the time of the study but today requires four consecutive years in most places) have assured employment for the duration of the time they choose to work in a district, a right which can last until retirement. Although there are circumstances under which tenured teachers can be dismissed, instances not based on decreases in school population are relatively rare (Bridges 1990). The threat of dismissal is used sparingly by administrators; it is conventional, in fact, to avoid talking much about it at all. Overall, serious negative sanctions for teachers play a small part in school management.

In regard to positive incentives, the payment of money is so circumscribed as to be, in most cases, of only minor import. Salary schedules are based on experience and schooling and are set at the district level, in our suburbs, primarily through the process of collective bargaining. (Centralized salary setting exists as well in districts that are not unionized; it goes back to the formation of the standard district structure.) An individual principal may help a teacher to augment salary income by assigning additional work beyond regular working hours, such as before or after work, on weekends, or during the summer. Historically, most elementary women teachers have shown little interest in promotion to administrative positions, a fact that limited the use of career assistance as an incentive. (We speculate in chap. 9 that this is probably changing today as more women aspire to and move up the hierarchy.) The contrast to how managers in business organizations relate to their employees is marked; they can and do use a variety of negative sanctions and positive material incentives, such as fear of being fired, individual increases in pay, and the prospect of promotion. In many firms, the existence of more complex internal organization (e.g., separate departments with their own hierarchies) means a larger number of potential promotions. School managers have comparatively few such incentives to offer their teaching staffs.

The large part played by intrinsic rewards in teaching has received repeated affirmation in research on teaching. Some of those rewards (the proportion is difficult to establish) will be affected by the actions of the principal, but, given the critical part played by student responses to the teacher, it is unlikely that it plays a major part. As we shall see later in this chapter, however, principals are not without some ways in which they can reward staff members they consider deserving.

Special Features of Teacher Work

Teaching possesses a variety of additional characteristics that limit the extent to which principals can influence what they do. We will discuss five here. Most of the constraints are what we can term "taken-for-granteds" to persons who work within the system; to varying extents, they are uncommon in other fields. Points 2, 3 and 4 below appear to me to be the most likely to be special to schools. Efforts to professionalize (1) are, of course, widespread and the tendency for labor unions to build seniority into various benefits suggests strongly that the press for equality by limiting managerial authority (5) is not restricted to school teachers.

(1) Parameters due to professional socialization

Decades of university and state engagement in preparing elementary teachers, coupled with the many ways in which practices have been diffused throughout the nation, have produced considerable "conventionalization" in the work of teachers—there are widespread similarities associated with particular grades, subjects, teaching styles and task responsibilities (Goodlad 1984). Although American schooling has never been nationally centralized, other mechanisms have produced widespread similarities (including curriculum) across the country.

This educational "taken-for-granted" standardization has a somewhat invisible nature; as in culture generally, people are often unaware of the many ways in which it affects what they think and do. For example, it will not occur to principals to question the importance of reading in the first grade, to refuse to accept disciplinary referrals from teachers, or to tell a faculty member that she must stay after school to help with the paper backlog in the office. Persons appointed as teachers have absorbed ideas about what pedagogical practices are desirable and what work is suitable for them initially as students and later in the course of their college and university preparation.

Although programs in teacher preparation, supplemented by the "apprenticeship of observation" I discuss in *Schoolteacher* (1975), reduce the burden of teaching newcomers about the job, they also reduce the scope of what teachers will consider acceptable administrative intervention. There are local choices and preferences, of course, and school administrators can insist they be taken into account. The point is not, however, that teacher socialization removes the relevance of administrative decisions, but that standardization sets parameters around what will be accepted as their decision-making terrain (Hanson 1981). Grade schools do not operate like free-wheeling new firms on the frontiers of technology or small enterprises where an owner hires and fires at will and changes employee assignments as fast and as frequently as she or he wishes. In addition, most principals work in schools that were established before their arrival—in some cases, long before; the local practices of individual schools can take on the force of tradition. If places where people work are put on a continuum of conventional behavior and standard practice at one end and free-wheeling, start-from-scratch places at the other, schools are closer to the conventional and routine end of the array. In the language of March and Simon (1958), much of what happens in classrooms and schools is "preprogrammed."

(2) Subalterns and supervision

The vertical line of authority in school hierarchies does not end at the point where principals oversee teachers—challenges to authority occur more often among students than among adults employed in schools. Teachers are expected to deal with "classroom management" or, in old-fashioned lingo, maintain discipline over students. Getting and keeping control can test even the most experienced teachers and, at times, the principals who are expected to back them up. Many years ago Waller depicted the school as a social order whose equilibrium could never be taken for granted (1967).

George Homans, in discussing leadership, pointed out that it is necessary for the top official to support subalterns, a proposition that applies to principals (Homans 1950). They usually avoid undermining the authority of teachers by not correcting or reprimanding them in the presence of students, believing that such restraint is needed to uphold the teacher's authority over students and that they share a common stake with teachers in maintaining that order. Occasions when principals observe teachers at work are generally limited; the claims of other duties, the dispersion of classrooms, and the span of control facing principals reduce the frequency and/ or duration of classroom visits. The restraint exercised to support the teacher's authority means that when principals observe something they would like to see changed in the teacher's behavior, they must often put off their suggested corrections until later. This is one of the constraints, then, that reduces the potency of the principal's direct supervision of the teaching staff—it is mostly after the fact.

(3) The inner life of classrooms and formal evaluation

Firsthand, intensive accounts of life in elementary classrooms by Philip Jackson (1968) and others (Bossert 1979, Smith and Geoffrey 1968, Kidder 1989) reveal that individual elementary classes, despite many overt similarities, are characterized by distinctive inner lives. Despite the numerous and important similarities found in large sample studies such as Goodlad's (1984) intensive, "microscopic" studies reveal subtle and significant differences that can complicate supervision; for example, teachers develop rules and routines special to their groups and foster relationships among students that press them toward particular patterns and interpersonal dynamics. The particular personalities of the teacher, coupled with the makeup and nature of particular classes, make no class exactly like any other. Interactive patterns may change in unexpected ways over the academic year, making earlier observations obsolete. It requires protracted and sensitive viewing by a perceptive observer to discern the complexities of that inner life and to grasp the basis for teacher decisions, which are deeply immersed in her perception of the class and which possess intuitive elements the teacher may find it hard or even impossible to articulate. The inner life of a classroom is not all that easily discerned.[1]

It follows, then, that anyone charged with overseeing and evaluating the performance of teachers in these distinct, complicated small worlds faces a difficult task. Principals, having themselves taught and quite possibly recalling that complexity, may believe that the teacher's intimate knowledge of the situation grants her expertise that they do not possess. That is not to say, of course, that principals do not believe that their observations, based on what may be considerably longer contact with particular students and families than the teacher's, and, often, more years of experience in schools, are without merit. What is does mean, however, is that thoughtful principals recognize the limits they face when evaluating the performance of teachers. We have already noted that principals find supervision and evaluation of teachers among the most demanding of their tasks, an issue which will receive more attention later (chap. 6).

(4) "Two realities" of school life

What has been said has already implied a view of schools that takes account of two levels—or realities—that are found within them. Schools can be seen as consisting of two kinds of organizations. We can focus on the school-as-a-whole, as an integrated organization, or, on the other hand, we can view the school as a collection of separate classrooms or "studios," within which teachers work most of the time with a set group of students. Seeing the oversight duties of the principal from those alternative viewpoints helps us to identify aspects of the principal's position vis-à-vis teachers we might otherwise miss. The discussion of the "inner life of classrooms" above proposes that individual classes manifest significant differences from each other, a quality that complicates comparisons for principals and makes evaluation based on standardized forms and terminology difficult to carry out.

In what other ways might the duality represented by the school-as-a-whole and the school-as-separate-studios affect the exercise of authority by the principal? It appears likely that the existence of those two orders of reality require particular strategies and tactics on the part of principals. The principal heads an identifiable unit—the school—which has its own identity and position among the schools in the district. It is subject to district policies and procedures to which the principal is expected to adhere; at the same time, the principal must organize a wide range of activities based on specific realities in a particular school. Some students of organizations urge the principal, as the head of a unit, to work toward a common sense of mission, to develop a "vision" that unites the efforts of those in the school; some argue that in order to be potent, the mission must translate into specific norms and values—a subculture—that prevails throughout the school (Deal and Peterson 1999).

At the same time the principal must relate effectively to teachers who are themselves managers of groups of persons and who expect those managerial responsibilities, and their distinctiveness, to be recognized, acknowledged, and, ideally, commended. They differ as well in their readiness to view the principal as a professional overseer; they range from extremes of eager compliance to cool disinterest. There is potential for conflict between the requirements of these two aspects of a school, that is, school as a unity and school as composed of distinct subgroups. Heavy emphasis on common elements and shared norms, for example, can overwhelm attention to the uniqueness of teachers, their classes, and their needs as well as their particular perspectives on authority. Balance requires finding ways to integrate common themes in the mission with specific, identifiable contributions from dispersed and (to varying degrees) diverse subunits. So stated, it seems that organizing and sustaining an elementary school requires high awareness of internal operations coupled with sensitive manipulation of significant symbols; given the subtle nature of these issues, the interpersonal demands on the principal's leadership are anything but trivial. Complexity is standard.

(5) The preference for equality

Finally, there is a strain in teacher culture that focuses on a strong preference for equal treatment from those in authority. Today it gets expressed in collective bargaining and contracts that emphasize "objective" characteristics such as seniority and schooling as the basis for salaries and, when student enrolments drop and teachers are "riffed," insistence on seniority as the ruling criterion for retention. The preference for equality appeared well before the rise of unionism; it showed up in teacher resistance to merit pay decades ago. It seems to get expressed more frequently in teachers pressing for mechanisms that reduce administrative authority rather than in making strong demands for full participation in policy decisions (Lortie 1975).

Recognition of this press for equality may be evident in the anxiety principals express about evaluating teachers (chap. 6). When principals complain that they have to make judgments without "objective" evidence, they may be indicating that, at least to some extent, they share the concerns with equality expressed by teachers. Do such views persist from their earlier experience with and socialization into teaching?

SOFT MANAGEMENT

We turn now to a set of questions intended to identify the beliefs and preferences that our suburban principals express in regard to dealing with teachers. We will look for reiterated themes in a set of somewhat different but closely related questions. To what extent, and in what ways, do their views reflect the particular complexities we have mentioned above?

We begin with what we can call a "mirror" question that asked respondents to describe the images they hoped various other persons would have of them: it read "In a word or two, what kind of reputation would you like to have in the eyes of teachers" (Q. 53). Table 4.1 summarizes the 244 responses (mentions), which were coded into 10 categories. Those 10 categories were then combined into 4 clusters of similar responses.

There are four distinct themes in table 4.1. What we can call the "close" and/or "warm" responses lead the list—these occur when principals wish to be seen as caring persons who are easily approachable by their faculty members. When we add the second leading theme—the moral virtues of fairness and trustworthiness—61% of the responses add up to what is consistent with an image of the principal as someone with whom it is safe to be open and frank; the closest word I can think of, although far from perfect, is "confidante." They also want teachers to perceive them as knowledgeable, serious professionals and as persons who have the ability to take action; those more conventional and

Table 4.1. The Reputation Sought with Teachers (Q. 53)

	M	%M
Cluster A "Warm and open"		
1. Caring, understanding, supportive	51	21%
2. Friendly, approachable	31	13%
Subtotal	82	34%
Cluster B "Trustworthy"		
1. Fair	49	20%
2. Trusted, shows integrity	17	7%
Subtotal	66	27%
Cluster C "Expert"		
1. Competent, professional	30	12%
2. Positive role model	2	1%
Subtotal	32	13%
Cluster D "Doer"		
1. Firm, gets the job done	14	6%
2. Provides professional leadership	12	5%
3. Decision maker	5	2%
Subtotal	31	13%
Miscellaneous (1 response each) and not codeable	33	14%
Total	244	101 (r.e.)

vigorous managerial abilities, however, do not occur as often as themes of warmth and trust. The softer, gentler sides of authority outweigh those of knowledge and strong action; these are not managers who want to be feared—as leaders, they want willing followers who trust them enough to communicate openly and freely with them.

The next question asked principals to choose among various ways in which they could improve instruction in their schools, surely an important issue (Q. 23). This was a card question with seven alternatives (for the full list see table 4.2). Each principal was asked to select a first and second choice in terms of its effectiveness in improving instruction; the question sought to identify principal beliefs about the value of alternative strategies and, not shown in the table, to explain their choices.

Table 4.2. On Improving Instruction (Q. 23 not original order)

Strategy	first		second		%all
	N	%	N	%	M
1. Conferring with teachers about ways to work with students or about instructional matters of any kind	63	56	22	20	38%
2. Providing teachers with resources, services and support	29	26	43	39	32%
3. Improving faculty quality through hiring and replacement	10	9	14	13	11%
4. Planning instructional programs which are tied to assessing student performance	6	5	13	12	9%
5. In-service training provided by the teachers themselves	4	4	8	7	5%
6. Evaluating teachers formally and supervising them closely	0	0	9	8	4%
7. In-service training conducted by outside experts	0	0	2	2	1%
	112	100	111	101 (r.e.)	100

The concentration on two alternatives is striking—the first two in the table, "conferring with" and "providing for teachers"— account for 70% of all first or second choice answers. These principals saw themselves as working to improve instruction alongside and in concert with teachers, in a sense as partners. They believed that what happened in their interaction with teachers—transactions of mutual discussion and provision of support—were more potent than the five other strategies they might select, all of which had a handful of supporters. They link the potential for improving instruction directly to their interpersonal transactions with members of their faculties. Principal influence is seen as effective provided it takes place under a particular set of circumstances. Directness is held hostage to maintaining a trusting and cooperative relationship. You do not simply "tell them."

Respondents were asked to say more about their choices and why they saw them as effective. Close to equal percentages produced four reasons. Conferring with teachers, they stated, allows the teacher to choose the problem for discussion: they assumed that working from the teacher's agenda was desirable. Mutual discussion allowed both parties to work together in an equal and collegial way. Solutions arrived at jointly, they believed, were more likely to elicit teacher commitment to carrying them out. Finally, conferring together provided an opportunity for both the principal and the teacher to learn. This set of reasons comes, in the writer's view, very close to what was termed the "confidante" or trust relationship sought by principals in their responses to the reputation question. The emphasis is on openness, sharing, equality, and clear communication; the assertion of authority per se is played down. It is, in addition, one-on-one interaction with teachers rather than an approach to the faculty as a whole; it connects with an image of the school as a set of studios in which the principal acts as an unpretentious mentor and reliable confidante connecting to teachers individually, teachers who are free to express their particular concerns. Beneficial influence is a product of those one-on-one exchanges. It implies, it appears, an additive process in which principals build their influence over instruction teacher by teacher, individual by individual.

Asked to develop their second most frequently chosen response— the principal as provider—the principals stressed two ideas. More resources and support provide better results as they are needed to get the job done and/or teachers will work harder when they have them. It is important to note that resources include not only physical resources (space, equipment, etc.) but psychological reassurance when self-doubt threatens one's confidence and political "cover" if parents attack; the principals sees buffering, such as in dealing with hostile parents, as an integral part of the productive processes of the school.

Providing for teachers can be directed to the faculty-at-large as well as to the individual. For example, a few principals mentioned, in citing points of pride, that they were able to prevent the school from being closed—school closings threaten the job security of all involved. They took pleasure in citing instances when the school—principal and faculty—attained success (admittedly not often) in challenging central office and winning out in a controversy (Q. 49; Crow 1985). Providing for faculty members, individually and collectively, presents opportunities for the principal to create obligations and to demonstrate the kind of initiative that produces respect from staff members.

A word or two on the infrequent choices. At the time the interviews were conducted, teachers were being laid off rather than hired; it was not a period when many principals had the opportunity to rebuild their faculties, making the hiring and firing alternatives weak options at best. It did, however, lead the lesser choices in mentions. In-service training became more widespread in the 1980s and 1990s and might, today, get more support than it did with this group. Neither linking programs to testing nor close supervision linked to evaluation received any significant support; few principals were favorably impressed by the more aggressive managerial approaches they entail. (The principals in this study would hardly have responded enthusiastically to state and federal initiatives placing heavy emphasis on standardized testing; that issue is discussed in the final chapter of this book.)

In our exploration of principal beliefs, another question presented respondents with five situations labeled "dilemmas" that could arise in the supervision of teachers (Q. 22). They were asked to choose answers posed as either/or options. We will focus on two of the responses that were highly modal; they point to widely shared beliefs on the part of the principals in the sample. Two of the response patterns, numbers 1 and 5, show low consensus as the principals split on both (table 4.3).[2]

A strikingly large 92% of the respondents rejected the chance to support close and detailed supervision of their teachers in favor of looser arrangements for supervision (number 4); they preferred latitude that permitted teachers to exercise a degree of personal discretion in their teaching. Responses here are similar to what they said above in their choices for improving instruction: those choices did not require close supervision. The image of what constitutes good supervision, as was also evident in their responses to

Table 4.3. Five Dilemmas (Q. 22)

	N	%
1. Take action versus hold off for morale		
Take action	66	59
Hold off	45	41
	111	100
2. Evaluation important versus increases social distance		
Important	98	87
Distance	15	13
	113	100
3. Include teachers versus emphasize efficiency		
Include	87	78
Efficiency	24	22
	111	100
4. Detailed guidance versus latitude		
Detailed guidance	9	8
Latitude for judgment	104	92
	113	100
5. Clear written rules versus case-by-case		
Rules	54	49
Case-by-case	56	51
	110	100

the reputation question, comes closer to colleagues sharing their views than the principal imposing his or her preferences. This is not to say that principals were never engaged in influencing their faculties; for example, we observed that many were ready to press for forms of classroom organization they preferred. These principals sought to avoid what might be construed as giving orders on instructional matters, preferring greater reliance on persuasion and other indirect approaches. They chose managerial behavior that allowed teachers some opportunity to use their best judgment, a stance that respects the boundary between the principal's office and the classroom and reflects the constraints we discussed early in the chapter. As will become evident when we discuss the authority resources available to principals, however, it did not rule out the readiness to use them to enhance their influence.

The second modal response showed a preference (78%) for sharing decisions with faculties and foregoing whatever efficiency gains might be thought to result from moving ahead without them (number 3). Obtaining consensus for such decisions reduces the likelihood that teachers will be displeased; these principals, as evident in the advantages they cited in selecting "conferring with teachers," believed that participation increases commitment to action on decisions. Yet it is useful to recall that teacher participation in schoolwide decision making cannot always be arranged. It may be constrained by district officials or, as can also happen, lack of teacher interest in schoolwide affairs.[3]

Let us recapitulate the beliefs and preferences these principals expressed about supervising teachers. We found them (mostly) wanting to be seen as warm, caring persons who were worthy of trust and the open communication that accompanied it. In terms of improving instruction, they placed their relationship to individual teachers at the heart of that effort, expecting that improvement would result from conferring with teachers and providing the resources they needed, a strategy that combined close, more-or-less equal interaction and the provision of support. They preferred loose rather than close supervision of teachers and leaned toward inclusion of staff members in schoolwide decisions. The image projected is of high value placed on bonds to individual teachers and to the goodwill and follow-through they associate with including the faculty in schoolwide decisions. The choices reflect the two perspectives—the school-as-a-whole and the school-as-separate studios.

Two more questions asked the principal to report on what she or he did in relating to faculty. The first was somewhat general; after their responses to the five dilemmas question, they were asked "what are some other characteristic ways in which you relate to your faculty?" The second question was more specific, asking them to talk about how they rewarded staff members.

Eighty-three principals (79%) answered the question which followed the five dilemmas (Q. 22). Their responses, presented in table 4.4, show some refinement of, and in some instances, redundancy with, the data we have already reviewed. The wish to be seen as warm and accessible is developed in category A, where principals

Table 4.4. Ways in Which Principals Relate to Faculty (Q. 22 [6])

Ways to relate	M	%M
A. Getting and being close to		
1. Informal, sociable relations	11	8%
2. Much time spent with teachers	15	11%
3. Open door, accessible	19	14%
4. Listens, helps personal problems	18	13%
	63	46%
B. Help and support		
1. Help with work problems	15	11%
2. Back teachers, facilitate	10	7%
	25	18%
C. Seek out participation	15	11%
D. Reward and rebuke		
1. Reward	5	4%
2. Reward and rebuke	2	1%
	7	5%
E. Work closely with subset	3	2%
F. Students come first, teachers second	2	1%
G. Miscellaneous single responses	23	17%
	138	100%

N = 83, 79% of base of 107 who responded to follow-up question.

talked about making various efforts to get close to faculty members; they emphasized informality and sociability, spending time with teachers, making themselves freely accessible, and, in some cases, showing concern about the personal problems of teachers. Other indications of trying to build closer ties include being helpful and supportive and seeking out teacher participation in making decisions. Infrequent responses in this context included using rewards and rebukes, working with a subset of teachers and emphasizing the primacy of student over teacher interests.

If we regard the first three categories (A–C) as directed toward building goodwill with teachers, 75% of the actions they mentioned fell into that classification. These modal responses include interactions with the faculty as a whole and close contact with individuals. The emphasis is clearly on building relationships with teachers that will allow them to have influence over their work; goodwill is assumed to be the bedrock for such influence.

To the extent that principals defer to teacher preferences, it can be best understood, I believe, as directed toward establishing and maintaining goodwill—the central resource, as they see it, in their ability to shape the behavior of and generate favorable attitudes in the faculty. Recall as well that many perceive central officials not only as wanting satisfied teachers but also as relying on them to provide evaluative information on principal performance (chap. 3). Teacher preferences constitute an important part of the social context within which principals make decisions and exert their authority.

ON DISPENSATIONS, RECOGNITION, AND PRIVATE PRAISE

Managers are normally able to use various types of incentives in order to mobilize the best efforts of those who work for them. We have seen that elementary school principals, viewed comparatively, have few such incentives. They are not, however, without some. Table 4.5 presents the responses to a question asking principals how they reward their teachers (Q. 24B). It read "Since you can't give teachers more pay, in what ways can you reward desirable teacher actions?" We note that there were few references to rewards in the general question we have just discussed: were respondents, perhaps, a little uneasy talking about using their authority in potentially divisive ways? Giving out differential rewards, after all, entails the risk of contravening teacher views on fairness and equality of treatment. Asked directly, however, they were quite ready to identify a set of rewards they found useful. The mean number (2.6) shows that they had no trouble in naming a variety of them.

Forty percent of the mentions made by sample members are classified as dispensations, as favors that principals can choose to allocate. They control, as heads of schools, various kinds of scarce resources which they can distribute as rewards. For example, they can choose teachers for popular workshops or other special events that carry exemption from regular duties. They can arrange to cover classes for a teacher who needs time away from work (sometimes doing it themselves). In dealing with class assignments, they

Table 4.5. How Principals Reward Teachers (Q. 24B)

	M	%
1. Dispensations		
Resource allocation	38	14
Rule-bending	23	8
Prestige appointments	21	8
Positive evaluation	17	6
Promotion potential, money	12	4
	111	40
2. Praise/recognition	83	30
3. Praise, private	54	20
4. Misc. & other	28	10
	276	100

may favor someone by not assigning particularly difficult students to them. They can "bend the rules" (the strategic leniency identified by Gouldner years ago) to permit, for example, early departure from work (Gouldner 1954). They can appoint teachers to prestigious committees in the school or district; a few were ready to say that they used teacher evaluation as a reward. In some instances, they may be able to distribute extra duties that are remunerated or work to increase chances for promotion to administrative ranks for those who desire it. It is worth noting that dispensations are normally visible to others who do not receive them; being obvious, they have the capacity to produce negative feelings such as envy and charges of "playing favorites."

Thirty percent of the responses consist of instances of praise for a teacher in which the positive statements were recorded in some way; as more than the ephemeral stuff of a spontaneous interchange, they constituted more lasting recognition. They might occur in a note to the teacher with a copy in the teacher's personnel file or broader attention in a newspaper or school publication. The extent of the recognition varied, depending, of course, on how widely it was publicized.

The third category—private praise—contributed 20% of the mentions. Receiving praise is, quite possibly, more rewarding for teachers than for persons in many of other kinds of work. I paid considerable attention in earlier research to the extent to which teachers feel uncertain about the outcomes of their work—there are many occasions on which teachers feel doubt about and disappointment in the results they see (Lortie 1975). Such feelings of uncertainty can make compliments from authority figures particularly reassuring. In comparison to the first two categories of rewards we have discussed, moreover, it can be private and less likely to offend others on the staff.

Given its high value to teachers and its apparently "low cost" nature, one might ask why praise does not dominate the responses. One possibility is that generous praise—even if private—is likely to be remembered and may be used to counter negative comments the principal might find it necessary to make in the formal evaluation of the teacher; if so, principals may feel that reassurance must be rationed lest it complicate later actions on their part. That formal evaluation can force the rationing of recognition is probably another reason why principals express so much ambivalence about it.

The principals in this study knew they were expected to be "in charge" of their buildings, to establish and maintain authority over the adults as well as the children. To the degree that they believed they needed to assert control by using potentially unpopular dispensations and granting recognition to some persons, they were ready to do so. As they learned in becoming principals, there was no way to avoid at least some social distance between themselves and faculty members, no matter how hard they hoped for the closeness they preferred. Although the incentives available to them are modest when compared with many other authority systems, using them helps principals to manage their faculties and provides opportunities to reinforce the behavior they wish to see in their teachers.

Teacher sensitivities obviously play an important part in the modal responses we have reviewed. We should not overlook, however, that teachers have an investment in the presence of principal power. They have a stake in its existence: they rely on that authority to help them deal with fractious students, overbearing parents, and even, at times, obnoxious behavior from colleagues. They have little interest in undermining the authority of the principal; they are more likely to look for ways in which that authority can be shaped to serve their interests.

Teachers are not alone, of course, in seeking to influence principal decisions; the superintendent and central office staff, parents, and others in the local community also let principals know what they want and expect. Principals, moreover, are men and women with their own views on what is best for the children charged to their care. The significance and complexity of their work becomes more evident as we realize that it falls to them to establish and sustain the balance among the various viewpoints and interests that play on them as they manage their schools.

{ **5** }

The Rewards

All work produces comfort and discomfort, good times and bad. We turn first to the positive side of principals' work, to the rewards they experience in their daily round. Learning about the gratifications people obtain in an occupation is to learn much about its nature; the drive to make the most of available pleasures affects much of what people do at work. At the same time, the less pleasant aspects, that is, the tough problems that are hard to solve, also play a part in shaping their behavior on the job and their sentiments about it. This chapter focuses on the positives, the next on the problematics of school management.

We can conceptualize some of the rewards earned by principals as stretched over time. There are longer range satisfactions that come from work which is defined as socially and morally valuable; recent research reveals that people who have chosen vocations to serve others report the highest levels of work satisfaction. A recent report from the NORC General Social Survey (Smith 2007) illustrates that connection; it found, more specifically, that educational administrators were among those persons who were most content; they were among those occupations in which more than 60% of the members said they were satisfied with their jobs. Performing well in work that serves others is doubly rewarded; one can enjoy a sense of competence from affirming one's craft while, at the same time, achieving worthwhile purposes. In service occupations, doing well generally coincides with doing good.

There are, on the other hand, shorter range pleasures that spark one's day, such as feeling proud about a particular accomplishment, receiving recognition, or having especially congenial contacts with co-workers. Such rewards are less than fully predictable, varying from time to time; there are occasions when good feelings give way to exasperation and disappointment. That principals' work is so highly interpersonal makes the flow of rewards, particularly those which are short-range, somewhat erratic; much hinges on the actions and responses of others. Uncertainties about principal rewards will begin to emerge when, in the final pages of the chapter, we explore how principals assess their own performance and the difficulties that occur when they try to do so.

PERSPECTIVES ON REWARDS

There are different ways to approach the rewards experienced by elementary principals. One is to begin with their position and the official expectations held for it; to what extent do principals attach feelings of satisfaction to meeting those expectations? Our earlier data and analyses pointed to a dual set of expectations held by those who govern school districts, namely, the advance of student learning and the achievement of harmonious relationships with parents and co-workers (chap. 3). To what extent do positive sentiments expressed by principals coincide with those imperatives? The extent of that coincidence tells us something about integration in school districts and its relationship to career processes. If principal sentiments are aligned with official purposes, we can infer that, at least to some extent, the ways in which persons are recruited, selected, and socialized into the job have the effects intended by those charged with governing school affairs. Without rendering an overall judgment about the efficacy of the system we are studying, we can observe whether it works in internally consistent ways or is subject to significant strains and stresses.

Another perspective we can take is to look for the ways in which the rewards the principals talk about connect to those around them, that is, the kinds of affect, and emotional intensity, they attach to different relationships. What relationships within their role set do they find most rewarding? Learning about those relationships tells us which aspects of their work generate strong sentiments and are therefore more likely to shape their performance and the subculture they share with others in the occupation. This chapter will deal with issues of interpersonal connection along with how principals respond to the dual imperatives of student learning and the maintenance of harmonious relationships.

Main Satisfactions

We asked sample members to talk about the main satisfactions they derived from their work—that is, the aspects of their work they found most rewarding. Their answers are presented in Table 5.1. Two responses dominate: indications that the students are learning and statements that the school is well-run. Since those two responses together account for 59% of the mentions, we will examine them in some detail, starting with those that refer to student learning.

The rhetoric used by respondents in a substantial proportion of those responses (around half) is particularly interesting. They used the word "seeing" in referring to learning outcomes, using the verb

Table 5.1. Main Satisfactions from Work (Q. 54)

	M	%M
1. Students learn	75	31
2. My school is well run ("Managerial")	68	28
3. Teachers learn, improve	28	12
4. Recognition, appreciation	24	10
5. Worthwhile work	12	5
6. My good performance	11	5
7. Less frequent responses	18	8
People work (4), parent contact (4), job variety (3), income (3), schedule control compared with teaching (2), good associates (2)		
8. Miscellany (1 mention each)	4	2
Totals	240	101 (r.e.)
N = 113	Mean number of responses − 2.1	

in ways that suggests reliance on personal, direct observation of students. (The language is similar to that used by physicians when they talk about their clinical observations.) More indirect indicators such as teacher reports and district achievement tests are rarely mentioned; in fact, scores on achievement tests were referred to only twice in the 75 responses to student learning.

One subgroup of principals in this category (19%) left no doubt that their main satisfactions involved direct contact with students:

> To really get superinvolved with the kids and let them feel good about themselves and that school should be a happy place. I look for ways to make this a pleasing place while good learning is going on. (98B, Female, 45)
>
> Working with the kids, seeing them develop, seeing them learning. If that's happening, I'm doing everything else right. (19C, Male, 41)

Although these principal responses sound much like those we might expect from classroom teachers, there is one respect in which learning outcomes are more apparent to principals. Unlike classroom teachers whose contact with students is usually limited to one year, principals can have contact with students over the entire span of their elementary school period.

> Seeing students progress, seeing them read, and so forth. I have the opportunity to see kids improve over time. Little kids become sixth graders, that's great to see. (28B, Male, 51)

Another subtheme in principal talk is also found among classroom teachers—later contact with students. There is special joy attached to students returning to express appreciation or meeting former students who are doing well.

> Seeing them go to high school and achieve, then you know you've achieved. When kids come back and remember what you've done then you know what you did was long lasting. (37A, Female, 45)
>
> I like meeting those kids 8, 10 years later and finding out that they've turned out to be decent citizens and that you've had a hand in it. (13C, Male, 50)

Finally, one respondent points to an advantage linked to longer service in a position.

> When you've been in one school as long as I have, to see some of the kids you've had succeed. Especially the ones who have had problems, the ones that you've worried about. When they come back years later and share some important memory they have of their years here. (97B, Male, 49)

This strong similarity of principal and teacher sentiments—satisfaction attached to indications of student learning and appreciation—points to a degree of affective continuity among those who leave the classroom for the principal's office. There is a similar emphasis on psychic rewards connected to seeing students learn; there are, at the very least, traces of their prior socialization as teachers. Unlike teachers, however, there is another axis—the operation of the entire school—which looms large in the subjective world of these elementary school principals.

The category "my school is well run" in table 5.1 (this will be abbreviated to "managerial" in the text) is a somewhat heterogeneous category organized around a single idea—the "school works well and I take satisfaction in that fact." There are various ways in which the effective operation of the school is indicated; the following quotations illustrate that variety.

> Having the building run smoothly in all aspects—classrooms, students, parents. (118A, Male, 44)
>
> The ability to organize and find the plan is working smoothly. Something that I've had a lot of planning and input on and that goes smoothly. To come out of running a good meeting—the meeting moves along, decisions are made and people leave feeling good. You go home and feel good. (27C, Male, 50)
>
> Operating my school successfully. Positive climate, learning effectiveness, responsibility, using money well, making it the most pleasant place to be as I possibly can. (47B, Male, 41)
>
> Knowing the staff and the children feel free to talk about any problems. And they all know what is expected of them. (40B, Female, 50)

The main satisfaction is planning and implementing programs
or action throughout the year. I do enjoy planning. In general, a
feeling that the school is really working well and that the kids and
teachers are pretty happy. (70B, Male, 42)

One of the striking features of these managerial responses is
the marked emphasis on smooth operation and the satisfaction of
those involved in and around the school. These mentions reflect
one side of the responses given by the principals when they were
asked about the grounds used by central officials in evaluating
them. It appears that, in the main, these principals see no contradiction between what they believe their employers look for and
they themselves take pleasure in achieving.

School administrators often separate out their responsibilities
for the professional, technical leadership of faculty members from
their general administrative duties. With that usage in mind, references to improving the capacity of teachers are presented separately in table 5.1. (If answers dealing with teacher improvement
were included in the general managerial category, that category
would have the largest number of mentions.)

Principals take satisfaction in helping teachers with their work
and find it particularly gratifying when they feel they have contributed to the faculty's improvement by doing so:

Seeing teachers improve, showing more sensitivity, becoming more
child-centered and less self-centered. (49A, Male, 56)

Working with kids and influencing teachers to do a better job
with the children. (114B, Male, 47)

It's great to see teachers in class smiling and not hollering.
(108A, Male, 33)

Others talked about instilling confidence in their faculty members and "inducting beginning teachers into the profession." One
could conceptualize an emphasis on improving teachers as an investment in the capital of the school, as adding to its corporate
potential. While student learning may have few obvious effects on
the school's potential over time, the multiplier effect that can result
from teacher improvement can have long-range significance.

It is not surprising that recognition and appreciation from others should produce satisfaction for those who are fortunate enough to receive them.

> Having everyone—parents, teachers, and students—provide me with positive feedback. It was a completely successful year, and it feels good. (5C, Male, 31)
>   Doing a job well, having myself feel that and others feel that and meaning it. That's a good feeling. (22A, Male, 32)

The definition of education as a public service has its advantages, as the following shows.

> It's good knowing you are doing something worthwhile. Knowing that you can affect achievement and the self-respect of students by what you do. You can make a difference. (50C, Male, 48)

The rhetoric of change did not feature prominently in responses to this question, but there were a few (6) who framed their efforts in those terms.

> Bringing about, providing for positive change. Not just in program but in people—students, teachers, parents, and self. (111B, Male, 47)

A word about the infrequent responses. Few are surprising, save, perhaps, one—the low frequency of material rewards; income receives only three mentions. The rewards that are mentioned by these principals are largely subjective and psychic in nature. The dominant view respondents express about money is dissatisfaction, a point we will discuss later in the book.

Referring to the first question we asked at the beginning of this section, we see that the satisfactions these principals report are consistent with what they believe is expected of them by their organizational superiors. There is a strong emphasis on student learning, and talk about running the school well includes clear references to harmony (e.g., "smoothness") and the satisfaction of those engaged in and around the school. (For similar findings in Iowa, see appendix B, Q. 36. There, too, we find that student

learning and managerial prowess dominate the responses.) There
is no sign of tension between the principals' sense of satisfaction
and the mandate they believe they have been handed. The recruitment and socialization processes we described earlier appear to
have produced people who link their own satisfactions to—and
are therefore motivated to achieve—the twin goals of student
learning and harmony sought by superintendents and, one presumes, their boards.

Sources of Pride

The next question we consider asked respondents to cite a specific
and recent (within last year or so) work achievement that was their
greatest source of pride (Q. 55). The responses deal with actual oc-
currences. They are also tilted toward events which principals see
as showing their ability to meet significant challenges; one does not
feel pride in performing simple tasks. Talk about what we can call
craft pride, therefore, tells us what aspects of their work they find
challenging and important; it helps us to understand what principals define as good and reveals, at least to some extent, the "working goals" that animate their day-to-day efforts.

One of the more striking aspects of Table 5.2 is the concentration of responses on what takes place in the school unit. If we de-
lete the 12 district successes and 2 other district references classified
as miscellaneous, we find that 90% of the comments are located at
the school level. Strong feelings about achievement—those which
occasion pride—center on the immediate domain of the principal
and events that take place there. The school is the cathected site;
that is, what happens there matters most.

The largest set of responses focus on projects and innovations
initiated by the principal and accepted by the teaching staff (33%).
They consist of three kinds—concentrated effort and changes in a
particular subject, other instructional changes, and changes that are
(usually) organizational in nature. Reading (8 mentions) dominates
the subject matter category, which also includes mathematics, science, and writing. Principals get involved in subject matter in various ways; examples of the activities they mentioned were working
alongside classroom teachers to demonstrate new approaches,

Table 5.2. Sources of Pride (Q. 55A)

		M	%M
1. Projects and innovations			
a. Subject matter		13	
b. Other instructional		16	
c. Other changes		12	
	Subtotal	41	33%
2. My school runs well and/or is improving			
a. Runs well		12	
b. Has improved		13	
	Subtotal	25	20%
3. I solved particular problems			
a. United the school		7	
b. Other problems		9	
	Subtotal	16	13%
4. Success in district matters			
a. Curriculum		6	
b. Other		6	
	Subtotal	12	10%
5. My work relationships are good			
a. Teachers		6	
b. Parents		2	
c. Students		1	
	Subtotal	9	7%
6. Career events		5	4%
7. Special recognition		3	2%
8. Miscellaneous (1 mention each)		12	10%
Grand Totals (N = 111)		123	99% (r.e.)

commenting on student work in math papers, and arranging for a specialist to help teachers improve their teaching of reading.

The "other instructional changes" are essentially of two types—developing programs for particular students (e.g., gifted, hearing impaired) or fostering new ways to deliver instruction, such as team teaching, learning centers, videotapes, and the like. (Computer-assisted instruction was just beginning at the time.) The third category consists of activities that support instruction but do so less directly; examples are increasing the number of parent volunteers, programs of staff development, and work on discipline policies and procedures.

Why are changes so prominent in this list of things to be proud about? Several reasons come to mind. First, changes initiated or fostered by principals resolve the authorship issue, making it easier for the principal to claim and present them as his or her achievement. The undertakings in question, even where others might have been involved in their initiation and implementation, could not have succeeded without the active engagement of the principal; carrying out changes in the school-at-large falls squarely within his or her domain. Second, innovation can be seen as more creative and/or intellectually challenging than maintaining existing programs. Instructional changes, to be effective, require the accurate diagnosis of student needs and designing fresh ways to meet them effectively. Third, change involves predicting the responses of staff members, countering what might prompt them to resist the change and discerning whatever adjustments are needed to make the plan work. When it does so, it validates the principal as a "leader," as someone who can persuade others to change their professional behavior in ways they may not have done without his or her intervention. Furthermore, most of the occasions for pride were instructional changes or steps taken to improve it, actions that support the image of the principal as an "educational" leader, an image that figures prominently and favorably in the rhetoric that prevails in administrative circles. Finally, it may be a frequent response here because achieving change is defined as difficult; its accomplishment, therefore, merits the special badge of pride.

In the second major category ("my school runs well and/or is improving"), the principals tie themselves to their schools and therefore connect their sense of the school's condition with feelings of pride. The criteria that underlie their evaluations replicate themes that are increasingly evident in the data, which, taken together, add up to the principals' image of what makes a good school. What goes into that image?

One quality is smoothness, a calm and orderly school without crises or, at most, crises quickly resolved by an alert principal. Another is the happiness of teachers and students. A good school, presumably, provides satisfactions for those who study and work in it. The school's programs are strong and effective; achievement test results get better; students perform well when they move on to higher grades. Teachers cooperate with each other and the principal; they treat students well, presumably reducing the frequency of parental anger. The school is marked by cohesion, especially among the adults, and, of course, the children behave themselves. These components make up what these elementary principals consider idyllic; their attainment produces pride.

Principals also feel pride when they have solved problems, particularly if the effort involved high interpersonal skill. The most common occasion for such pleasurable feelings is success in unifying a school where there were potential bases for schism and discord.

> I developed two separate staffs from two separate buildings into one solid staff. It happened when they closed one school and brought them all over here. (4B, Male, 49).
>
> I think the work we did in integrating our new (Hispanic) students into this particular building. We had a theme—"It's a small world." I tried to point out things that all people have in common no matter what their origin. It helped us demonstrate to other schools in our district that were experiencing closing how to integrate two school communities. (113C, Male, 42)

Some problem solving might be a matter of staff management.

> I had a positive influence on the school; it hadn't been a good situation. A clique of teachers, inbred, were living off each other. I worked with that and got four transferred. It made me proud. I broke it up. I withstood the clique. (32C, Male, 46)

Another principal took pride in helping those in the school cope with its impending demise.

> To have kept our parents, teachers, and youngsters at ease with our school closing. To have kept morale very high even under a tenuous circumstance. (115B, Male, 48)

Pride associated with districtwide activity, more often than not, resulted from work on instructional matters; over half of the mentions referred to leadership in district decisions about reading, mathematics, or other academic topics. Other points of pride included creating a district newsletter, heading a study of absenteeism, and negotiating a new bus contract. One principal, having previously served as assistant superintendent for several years, felt good about his part in keeping the administration together during a serious crisis. The remaining categories contain few surprises as principals talked about strong relationships with teachers and others, successful career events (e.g., surviving a first year as principal in a tempestuous situation) and receiving honors from their peers.

Members of particular occupations normally share sentiments about the tasks they are expected to perform; we particularly expect that to occur in fields where structural and technological changes occur slowly and there is time for common definitions to emerge and spread. Work in schools is among those fields, making the concept of occupational culture particularly useful in that setting (Hughes 1958, Van Mannen and Barley 1984).

We have already begun to see the emergence of shared themes characteristic of such a culture among our sample members. As we examine more data on principal likes and dislikes, we will find repetitions in the content of those themes. From the analytic point of view, such redundancy is advantageous. Reiteration of specific ideas in responses to different questions increases our confidence that we have identified relevant and significant themes. Such repetition, however, can prove irksome for the reader; I hope that we can navigate successfully through the rocks of repetition and the hard place of inadequate discussion of the themes found in the data. Major themes are used as the basis for chapter 8.

Favorite Tasks

We turn now to the task preferences of the principals. One (perhaps obvious) point should be registered at the outset. Tasks and interactions, and sentiments about them, are not always aligned in the same way. There are some tasks, of course, which are never popular; as we mentioned earlier, one does not expect to encounter principals reveling in preparing reports for state and federal agencies. Interactions with persons, however, can be sources of either pleasure or discomfort, depending on the circumstances. Meeting with parents at a PTO gathering can be positively enjoyable, especially when parents show appreciation for their child's schooling and/or offer useful assistance. Yet few occasions are more dreaded than the angry call from a mother denouncing her child's treatment by a teacher. We find similar ambivalence when principals talk about students, teachers, and central officials.

Table 5.3 presents the responses given to a question asking about the tasks they most "like to emphasize" (Q. 16B). The two categories that dominate—instructional engagement and relational tasks—connect to the familiar themes of student learning and fostering favorable relationships. Together they account

Table 5.3. Tasks They Like to Emphasize (Q. 16B)

	M	%M
1. Instructional engagement		
A. Classroom location	42	26
B. "Broader" engagement	39	24
Subtotal	81	51
2. Focus on relationships		
A. Students	20	13
B. Parents	12	8
C. Teachers (no mention of location)	12	8
D. Combinations of parties above	8	5
Subtotal	52	34 (r.e.)
3. Other		
A. Student discipline	8	5
B. Administrative noninstructional	6	4
C. Placement of individual students	3	2
D. Solving problems	2	1
Subtotal	19	12
4. Miscellaneous: Single mentions	7	4
Grand Totals	159	101 (r.e.)
N = 112	Mean number of mentions per respondent – 1.4	

for 84% of the mentions, and the two themes are vigorously af-
firmed when principals talk about what tasks they most like to do.
In fact, if we add mentions under the third category, which support instruction (i.e., discipline 5% and student placement 2%) to
those classified as instructional engagement, the total for the two
themes exceeds 90%.

The instructional tasks principals like to emphasize can take
place either in classrooms (26%) or elsewhere; a quarter of the
references to instructional activities did not specify the location,
referring to the full range of engagements such as supervising curriculum and working on new programs. Classroom engagements
might entail direct work with students such as teaching a class or
tutoring students or simply observing the teacher at work. Working with students can have a supervisory function (e.g., doing informal evaluation of the teacher's teaching, setting an example)
but need not do so; principals often talked about enjoying interaction with the students as intrinsically gratifying.

The responses under the second category in Table 5.3 focus directly on pleasures derived in relating to students, teachers, and parents. Given that many of those contacts take place when teachers
and students are engaged in teaching and learning, they frequently
center on instruction. But there are occasions when the principals
can enjoy the children in a more "sociable" sense. For example,
some arrange to have students visit the office on their birthday
where they present them with a small gift while others mention the
special pleasures associated with making awards to students; some
male principals talk about spending and enjoying time playing baseball or basketball with the boys. (Asked about "fun" in their work
[Q. 20B], principals emphasized contacts with children [68%] and,
to a lesser extent, interactions with teachers [19%]; 2% mentioned
parents, but none central officials.)

There are opportunities for sociability and enjoyable collegial
engagements with faculty members. Although many interactions
with parents revolve around the academic problems of students,
they need not and even those that are can be free of conflict; such
contacts can present principals with opportunities for pleasant
feedback. Some principals enjoy their public relations efforts with

parents; a few seem to be particularly drawn to parents and make repeated statements throughout the interview about the pleasures they get from such relationships.

To recapitulate, then, these principals prefer to emphasize instructional tasks and relationships with those "in close" to their schools. Although those interactions usually center on instructional matters, they also offer opportunities for pleasurable interactions of an expressive rather than purely instrumental nature. They do not mention purely administrative functions either in the school or the district at large. In fact, it is almost as if the district does not exist when they talk about what they like to emphasize; mentions of interactions with central office do not appear in their answers to this question on preferred activities. These responses reaffirm the localization of positive sentiments to the school that we saw in responses to the pride question.

The Good Day

Responses to the question asking them to describe a "good day" (table 5.4) reiterate the wish for smooth running days marked by rewarding relationships ("positive feedback") and student learning ("see good things in classrooms"). If one can get something done and interact with teachers and students, one's time is well spent. The responses also point up the tensions introduced by time pressures, discipline, and other working conditions we shall discuss later in the next chapter. The following quotations depict both the delights the day can yield and the absence of impediments that prevent productive work.

> When things go smoothly with a minimal number of students sent up for discipline, the faculty is happy and content with what they are doing, or, in a meeting, you get a compliment from the superintendent. On a good day, I could get time to do what I need to do. Time is a precious commodity. (16C, Male, 40)
>
> I have some of those . . . A good day is when I can step back and watch the school function smoothly. Everything clicks. I am amazed at how much is going on. When I can get out there to the

Table 5.4. Components of a Good Day (Q. 18)

	M	%M
1. Day is "smooth"	59	21
2. Able to get something done	55	19
3. Receive positive feedback	38	13
4. See good things happen in classroom	35	12
5. Interact with students and teachers	34	12
6. People are happy and smiling	27	10
7. Less frequent mentions:		
Interact with parents—10		
No paperwork to do—5		
Busy day—5		
Sociable contacts—2		
Run special program—2		
Miscellaneous single mention—12		
Total less frequent	36	13
Grand Totals	284	100%

classrooms and see it. When teachers feel successful about their lessons and tell me about it and I can see it in a classroom. When a parent comes in and says how do you know my kid so well. (25C, Male, 41)

The literature tells you to prioritize, but that's a lot of hogwash. When a child bashes his head in or a parent screams you can't say sorry, my priorities today don't include time for that. (55B, Male, 38)

A good solid visitation in class. I like to see growth in kids. To see pupils on task and enjoying school. I would see teachers happy with what they are doing. It reflects that maybe what I'm doing is rubbing off on the staff. (70B, Male, 42)

The ability to get into a classroom and see something exciting that is happening there. To perhaps have only a few discipline problems sent to the office. And there's a lot of trivial stuff—busses here on time, no fights in the lunchroom, no angry parents. (89C, Male, 54)

The good day is smooth and calm and the flow of preferred activities is not obstructed. There is no flood of discipline cases. The teachers show up, ruling out the need to hunt down substitutes.

There are few (or no) upsetting events such as accidents, complaints, late busses, angry parents, and quarrels within the staff. Such benign circumstances allow the completion or near completion of the principal's agenda: he or she is able to concentrate on a sensitive conference with a teacher or organize the first meeting of an important committee. Challenging activities (e.g., a special education staffing) go well. The emphasis is on achievement. As one says, "I solved a problem and everybody was happy about the solution" (15, Male, 38).

The accomplishments that make for a good day, however, need not be the principal's. Twelve percent of the mentions went to the pleasure they felt when they saw good things happening in the classroom, such as a well taught class or indications that students were enthusiastic and, from all appearances, learning. Seeing such effectiveness reassures the principal that central purposes are being realized on his or her watch. (There were hints that visits to such successful classes were sometimes made to provide the principal with that reassurance.)

Ten Additional Hours

The final question on principal definitions of the positive introduces a touch of fantasy. It is hypothetical and stimulates ideal responses by asking: how would you choose to spend ten additional hours at work provided that, magically, those hours did not take time away from your private life? The responses are tabulated in table 5.5.

The preferences expressed are largely similar to those we have seen elsewhere. Most center on greater engagement in instruction and devoting more attention to relationships with students, teachers, and parents. But two don't fit that depiction. One is relatively minor; the distaste for paperwork is sometimes linked to procrastination and uncompleted tasks, which weigh on the mind. Some enjoy the relief that comes from a clean desk. A larger number of mentions (22%), however, refer to augmenting one's professional knowledge by reading and visiting other educational locations. These principals believe that more study would make them better equipped to lead instruction; the emphasis is on curricular and related issues.

Table 5.5. Ten More Hours (Q. 19A)

	M	%M
1. More time with students	27	22
2. Read, study, learn	27	22
3. Work on teacher improvement	19	16
4. Be in the classrooms	16	13
5. Curriculum and program	11	9
6. Catch up on paperwork	8	7
7. Work with parent community	6	5
8. Longer range planning	3	2
9. Miscellaneous single responses	5	4
Grand Totals	122	100

I do not spend the time I should on the valuable things I could read
and study in order to become an educational leader, not a manager.
I'd read about how we could help our gifted children and more on
pre-adolescent youngsters. (37A, Female, 45)

Reading. My *Kappan* magazine. School law. Whatever is available to help us understand why we are not doing well in math and
reading. (39B, Male, 59)

Probably curriculum. Learning about curriculum areas and elementary school programs. That's as much a function of my special
education background as anything else. I was hired for my special
education background and have to learn the rest. (62B, Male, 33)

Finally, answers to this question on using additional time point
up some earlier observations in this chapter, particularly that relationships with students can be intrinsically pleasurable. The leading
response ("more time with students") is composed largely of comments about doing more direct instructional work with students,
either individually or with groups. Much is talk about what is normally teacher work and not, in any usual sense, management—a
deviation, if you will, from the logic of hierarchy that symbolically
defines the principal's time as too valuable to be spent on tasks performed by subordinates. What this suggests (once again) is that
the transition from teacher to principal involves limited change in
identity and work preferences; the principals in question continue to

yearn for and seek out the satisfactions attached to teaching. In some respects, principals—not under the same pressure a teacher feels to maintain class discipline and the appropriately measured stance— are freer to engage in playful interactions with individual students. Whatever the rewards of running a school may be, they do not, it seems, negate the pleasures of working directly with children.

Summary

What have we learned by examining the positive sentiments of these principals? Do they reflect the emphasis we found earlier on the importance of the dual imperatives of student learning and harmonious relationships? What relationships seem to be most significant when principals talk about the good things in their work?

The sentiments, as I read these data, are closely linked to the mandates of achieving student learning and doing so in ways that produce positive feelings on the part of those who are involved. Instructional outcomes and engagements are prominent in responses to the questions. They are closely connected to feelings of satisfaction, craft pride, and the principals' task preferences. We find that to a large extent, principal talk about student outcomes are similar to those we hear from classroom teachers, and the differences, not major, are the result of differences in position and perspective. The principals take special pride when their actions produce instructional improvements; the tasks they like best are directly connected to instructional activities. Good days are free from the distractions that rival engagement in instructional matters, when principals are able to act on their preferences, to immerse themselves in curricular and classroom matters, to visit classrooms, and to watch students learn. Given ten more hours, most would like to spend more time with students and teachers and tasks connected directly to instruction.

To a somewhat surprising degree, our respondents seem to fuse the fostering of good relationships with effectiveness in their managerial responsibilities. Their talk moves back and forth between describing comfortable relationships with teachers and students and improvement in the performance of their schools. We hear little talk about shrewd allocations of resources or powerful strategic decisions; when they talk about specific achievements, as in the pride item, leadership is linked to persuading faculty members to improve or healing schisms based on school closings or ethnic divisions. There is a strong emphasis on the personal actions and interactions of the principal with students and teachers, a reiteration of the belief we noted in the last chapter that the best way to improve a school is to relate closely to teachers, to persuade them to do things in a better way, and to support their efforts to do so. In a sense, they seem to frame their leadership responsibilities primarily in terms of how they—as persons—connect to teachers and students.

Although it is clear that principals enjoy being actively involved in helping students to learn, it is also clear that they enjoy interacting with children as activity in and of itself—kids seem to provide them with their happiest moments. Given the ratio of children to adults in elementary schools, that appears to be a good thing for those who have chosen this line of work.

EVALUATING ONE'S PERFORMANCE

Psychic rewards, subjective in nature, require individuals to make judgments, among other things, about how well they are performing in their work. Occupations differ, however, in what help is available to members to make those judgments. When businessmen say they "keep score" by comparing their money income with others', the issue of psychic rewards is resolved by subordinating it to the strictly material. Major league baseball players make few moves that are not, one way or another, turned into statistics, which assign "scores" (batting averages, earned run averages, etc.) to individuals as well as teams. Television performers cannot, in evaluating themselves, escape the omnipresent and powerful ratings assigned to their shows.

Philip Jackson has pointed out that evaluating teachers is not difficult—at the extremes, that is, of high ability and incompetence; the difficulties lie in the broad middle (personal communication). The situation is somewhat similar when principals evaluate themselves but, if anything, more difficult; the effects they have on students (the ultimate test of competence in schooling) is, given its indirect nature, more difficult to measure. There are outstanding principals who, in the eyes of those observing them, make a visible difference, and chances are good that they are aware of their strong performance. By definition, however, most principals are not outstanding, and so they face the task of assuring themselves that they are doing well without the specific criteria and quantitative symbols found in business, baseball, or television. How, then, do they answer the question "How am I doing?"

The suburban principals were asked two questions on how they evaluated their performance. The first asked them to say what they watched in order to tell how well they were doing. The second question asked about the difficulties they encountered evaluating their performance.

The responses to the first question (table 5.6) are striking: feedback from other persons dominates strongly. Direct and specific

Table 5.6. What Principals Watch (Q. 17A)

	M	% Subtotal	%Total M
1. Feedback from other persons			
Teachers	107	46	32
Parents	71	31	22
Central office	32	14	10
Students (grouped in series)	14	6	4
School secretary	4	2	1
Board members	3	1	1
Subtotal	231	100%	70%
2. Performance of others			
Students	42	69	13
Teachers	13	21	4
Classroom observation	6	10	2
Subtotal	61	100%	19%
3. State of the school			
Works well	12	60	4
Climate good	8	40	2
Subtotal	20	100%	6%
4. Personal feelings	10	—	3%
5. Miscellaneous (1 mention each)	8	—	2%
Grand Total	330	—	100%

references to achieving school goals are not common, although they are probably implied. Principals guide their performance less by any direct evidence of such achievement than by messages they receive from others, particularly teachers, parents, and central officials. Those messages constitute 70% of the mentions. What are we to make of this marked emphasis on feedback from others?

Several features in school management are likely candidates for an explanation of this heavy reliance on what other persons say about one's performance. One lies in the emphasis we have seen on achieving harmony in relationships in and around the school. The approval of others tends to fuse with evaluating one's performance since their approval is itself evidence that one is fostering goodwill and winning public acceptance.

Another factor lies in basic uncertainties that bedevil those who work in public education. There are the multiple goals and standards that can be and are applied to school affairs by different individuals and organized groups. (As once expressed by Robert Wood, "education is a continuing constitutional convention"; speech in Boston, 1960.) Although some persons and some governments act as if improved achievement tests are the sole end of schooling, it hardly exhausts the specifics that parents and others bring in their evaluation of school activities. One need only recall Bloom's taxonomy of cognitive, affective and conative goals to see the oversimplification involved in reliance on a single quantitative measure of schooling outcomes (Bloom et al. 1956).

Americans, moreover, have a long history of ascribing broad purposes to their schools, such as assimilating immigrants, developing responsible citizens, inculcating behavior appropriate to employment, providing public entertainment through sports, and so on. There are conflicts about how to teach reading and evolutionary theory that arouse citizens at local, state, and federal levels of government. School schedules are adjusted to changes in the employment patterns of parents. Arguments can rage over how the budget should allocate funds for extracurricular activities; chess and drama enthusiasts vie for the same dollars eyed by parents who want an orchestra for the school. Multiple functions and multiple interests, in short, produce multiple constituencies; school managers face serious difficulties when, and if, they seek uniform criteria to guide their choices. Recall as well the differences in values among educators signaled by the uncertainties the principals express when discussing teacher evaluation.

There are technical uncertainties as well. Scholars in the field of educational administration have long lamented what they call "the weak knowledge base" in their field (most recently, Elmore 2007). Cause and effect relations are notoriously problematic in work that is basically "people work," and it is hard to find work more basically "people work" than elementary schooling. Thompson identifies three sources of constraint on what he calls "cause / effect premises" that make for uncertainty in the knowledge of managers (Thompson 1967). All are present in the work of school principals—incomplete knowledge, the dynamism of the objects worked on, and the amount of competition from others in the same area. Students provide the dynamism and to name only two, television and families, the competition.

To quote Thompson again, we get help in understanding principal reliance on others from his comments on ambiguity and its effects. Although his propositions were stated in terms of the behavior of organizations rather than individual managers, the emphasis on ambiguity seems appropriate here. He contrasts situations where beliefs about the knowledge of cause and effect are complete and incomplete and the outcomes sought feature either crystallized or ambiguous standards of desirability. When such standards are crystallized, one can use the test of efficiency when knowledge is complete and the instrumental test when it is incomplete. Ambiguity in regard to both cause and effect beliefs and standards of desirability, however, makes it difficult to use those tests. To quote him directly, he says "Now what we want to suggest is that when standards of desirability are ambiguous or when cause / effect knowledge is *believed* incomplete, organizations turn to (social) reference groups" (p. 87). I believe that the central idea he advanced, essentially that when standards are fuzzy and solid know-how is lacking, managers (my substitution) define effectiveness largely in terms of the judgments of other people.

There are two additional sources of uncertainty that we can mention here. One was the uncertainty of employment during the study period, which was marked by school retrenchment. Nor is knowledge of where one stands in a bureaucracy all that certain; superintendents, like other employers, may be less than fully candid with their employees in regard to their prospects for the future.

We should also note that principals turn to several different parties for information on how well they are doing. The interests of those different parties are not necessarily aligned; teachers and students and parents and bosses do not perceive events from the same vantage point nor press for the same responses from principals. Those differences add to the uncertainties principals face, pressing them to satisfy as many parties as possible. Wolcott remarks on a tendency of principals to think that everything is important, to avoid assigning priorities to their activities (Wolcott 1973). Such a tendency seems consistent with a strong bent toward not only hoping for consensus but perhaps relying on a degree of vagueness in specifying one's priorities.

The problem of ascertaining how one is doing is exacerbated when principals, perhaps unavoidably, rely on feedback as their primary indicators of performance. That difficulty is clear when we review the responses to the second question asking principals to discuss any difficulties they had in evaluating their performance (table 5.7). Most (86%) of the principals accepted the premise that they experienced such difficulties, but some (14%) denied it.

Table 5.7. Difficulties in Self-Evaluation (Q. 17B)

	M	% M (difficult)
1. Problems are internal (self)	39	35%
2. Information is unreliable	37	33%
3. Some areas hard to evaluate	11	10%
4. Lack of clear criteria	11	10%
5. Insufficient time	2	2%
6. Effects not clear	2	2%
7. Miscellaneous (1 mention each)	9	8%
Grand Total	111	100%

(Usable cases—N = 107
Principals who find it difficult—N = 92, % all N = 86%
Principals who deny it is difficult—N = 15, % all N = 14%)

The two major problems that these principals faced as they sought to monitor their performance emerged, in large part, from their heavy reliance on feedback from others. Thirty-three percent of the answers dealt with the unreliability of the information others provided them. Teachers, the major source of feedback, obviously had reasons to give their bosses reassuring information and positive messages on both the principal's and their own performance. A long-established proposition of organizational study is that good news travels up the hierarchy much more readily than bad, a tendency that apparently has not escaped the notice of principals who expressed skepticism about what they were told. Parents may also be motivated to flatter the principal in the hope that it will gain advantages for their children, and, as we have just noted, superintendents may find it advantageous to downplay any negative views as well.

The other major difficulty cited by the principals (35%) is a personal tendency to interpret events in ways that reassure them on the quality of their own performances—that is, to be less than fully objective in reading the signs and signals on which they rely. It is interesting that so many realize and express that concern, an awareness that matches the ambiguities that surround them. There are additional difficulties built into the process of evaluation itself, such as the lack of clear standards in general and/or in particular aspects of their responsibilities.

These difficulties in monitoring their performance and evaluating how well they were doing reduced the assurance principals felt about their efficacy. It is one of the major costs, it seems, of managing under circumstances of high uncertainty. Sensitivity to the reactions of a wide range of individuals means more occasions when one will feel, and take seriously, the sting of criticism. Chances are that one learns, under such circumstances, to avoid, or to take, those actions which reduce the likelihood of offending others. We might expect these difficulties to produce greater emphasis on cautionary and prudent rather than bold and risk-taking management. As we noted in chapter 2, there are interesting parallels to such tendencies in career decisions and processes of socialization.

Complications and Complexities

What is hard about being an elementary principal? What is the downside? Those are the questions we turn to in this chapter. We will look at conditions that complicate the day, tasks that principals find difficult and/or dislike, and, finally, trouble that can strike as they go about doing their work. The progression in the discussion is from the least to the most serious challenges elementary principals face; the final section presents a brief examination of conflict.

COMPLICATING CONDITIONS

Certain of the conditions under which principals work make that work more challenging than it might otherwise be. Although no single problem is limited to the principalship, the combination of challenges may well be unique. Some of the conditions we will be looking at have already shown up in the previous chapter; they figured in the factors that made some days less than entirely pleasant.

The Scarcity of Time

"What do you do all day long?" people ask my friend the Chicago principal. The questioners point out that since the children are dispersed among classrooms and supervised by teachers, she must surely have a lot of time on her hands. Perhaps memory plays a part in their raising the question; my informal inquiries, including discussion with persons who work in schools, suggest that many have little idea of how their elementary principals spent their time.

There is irony, therefore, in the fact that principals express a lot of anxiety about not having enough time, of feeling constant pressure as they try to complete their work. We mentioned earlier that classroom teachers have designated responsibilities that prevent them from being free to assist the principal in doing organizational jobs. That low "assignability" of staff members contributes to the long list of duties principals have to handle (McPherson, Salley, and Baehr 1975). Empirical studies have pointed out that the principal's day tends to be fractured into numerous activities, which, on average, last only a few minutes (Peterson 1977). This fragmentation of time, although not unique to school managers, is probably exacerbated by the nature of managerial work in schools (Mintzberg 1973). Part of the difficulty lies in the fact that school officials find it difficult to persuade board members and the public at large to spend money on administrative assistance for principals.

What other aspects of the job produce principals' sense of time deprivation? There seem to be several. One is the rigidity of school schedules—the length of the day and number of weeks and the total time schools may operate—are all specified in advance and are extremely resistant to change. Whatever is going to be accomplished has to be done within the rigid parameters of overall schedules set by state authorities and specified by school district authorities. Collective bargaining has added to that rigidity by placing distinct limits on the amount of time that principals can ask teachers to meet outside regular school hours. Other causes grow out of the nature of principal tasks and their definition as public service, both of which limit the amount of time principals can use as they see fit. All compress the working day.

A lack of time flexibility is built into some of the major sets of tasks faced by principals, particularly, for example, in the responsibility to evaluate staff members. This area is highly formalized, an approach that is reinforced by the anxiety of officials to avoid legal action and the need to respect specifics worked out in collective bargaining contracts.[1]

The steps in teacher evaluation illustrate how formalization re-duces the control principals have over their time. Although districts differ in their specific requirements (e.g., how many members of the faculty to evaluate each year), the process normally demands many hours. The prescribed steps must be taken in a set order and, once initiated, must proceed at an appropriate pace: delays complicate communication and add anxiety for those being evalu-ated. Each step takes time—a preparatory conference between the principal and the teacher, observation in the classroom, writing up observations, and a conference to share the evaluation with the teacher. Tension can run high, for the results are entered in the teacher's permanent file. Principals quickly discover how prickly the process can be, leading them to adhere closely to district rules in case teachers who are dissatisfied with their evaluations fault them on procedural grounds (perhaps through the union) or cen-tral officials reprimand them for flouting district policies and prac-tices. These rigidly prescribed sequences can stretch over many days during the academic year, particularly in schools with large faculties and/or in districts with particularly stringent procedures. Principals, as we shall see, express numerous doubts about evalua-tion; some of their dissatisfaction lies in the bureaucratic rigidities involved and the time spent at the expense of activities they con-sider more important.

On Interruption

Although research on managerial time indicates that interactions tend to come fast and often, there are respects in which princi-pals are probably more vulnerable to interruption than is the case in many other organizational settings.[2] Like middle managers in general, it is difficult for principals to resist demands from higher ranked officials; school heads complain that they are sidetracked by sudden deadlines for information and/or requests to attend meet-ings on matters in which they have little interest. In addition, the norms of public service deny them the right to privacy so preva-lent in corporate affairs. Unlike the situation in private sector, it is difficult to erect barriers to limit access from their "customers." Not for them, for example, are the elaborate, recorded responses to telephone calls found in businesses, which constrain access to officers by steering callers to "customer service representatives." In schools, however, to be seen as unresponsive to parents is a serious matter.[3] In addition, many principals maintain an "open door" to teachers, a practice that is consistent with the emphasis we have seen on sustaining the approval and support of faculty members.

One way to underscore the weakness of barriers between principals and the public at large is to consider the scope of potential intervention by "customers" up to and including intervention in the processes of production. There are retail chains (e.g., Sears Roebuck) that control the manufacturing processes of some of the products they sell either through factory ownership or specifications in contracts with suppliers. Such retail firms deal with complaints in a routine fashion, usually by replacing products or refunding the dissatisfied customer's money. They would hardly agree, however, to a retail customer visiting and suggesting changes in the manufacture of, let's say, a washing machine—incredulity would greet any such request. Compare that, however, to the situation of a principal where parents insist that their child be transferred to another class, a demand that penetrates to the core of instructional practice. Granting the request may alienate not only one faculty member but, depending on the circumstances, other teachers as well. Simple rejection of parental requests ("That is none of your business") is not among the responses available to the principal. In fact, a parent who continues to be dissatisfied can appeal to officials in central office. Similar contrasts can be made, of course, to the ability of surgeons and other high-status professionals to restrict client influence on how they do their work.[4]

The Maintenance of Order and Safety

The principal is a front-line supervisor with custodial responsibility (in loco parentis) for hundreds of young children. President Harry Truman's placard saying "the buck stops here" would be appropriate on the principal's desk, particularly in regard to maintaining good order and student safety. The principal serves as backup for teachers who need assistance in maintaining control and who refer individual students for final decisions. There are also occasions when the principal acts as the immediate supervisor of students, such as in the lunchroom or halls and play areas, which may not be supervised by teachers.[5]

Outbursts of student misbehavior can be sudden and unpredictable—effective responses may demand immediate attention and allow little time for deliberation. The same applies, of course, to dealing with accidents in which a student is hurt. The risk of legal liability intensifies official concern, particularly if parents become alarmed and are ready to blame the school for injuries sustained by the children. Other tasks, even when interrupting them is costly, must be put aside. Principal work is marked by such unpredictable urgencies.

It is important to bear in mind the behavioral volatility of children, to recall that they are only gradually socialized into complying with the norms of orderly behavior which can usually be taken for granted among adults. Those charged with supervising children learn that lapses in adult control can produce disorder and that keeping order requires the physical presence of adults. That need results in "pinning down" many staff members and by reducing their mobility, also limiting the range of tasks they might otherwise undertake and preventing the formation of a more refined division of labor. It is another factor that affects the "assignability" of those who report to the principal.

Paperwork

The interviews make it clear that principals see various types of desk work as a constant, unremitting pressure on their time, a pressure many detest. If done at the office, it cuts off contact with teachers and students, but if taken home, affects relationships within the family. Some of the tasks result from the principal being the only (official) manager in the school who consequently has responsibility for overseeing the ordering and distribution of supplies, monitoring cash revenues, etc. Superintendents and boards also expect the principal to report on whatever information they consider relevant and urgent at a particular time—in addition, of course, to maintaining regular records such as attendance figures, which affect state revenues to the district. State and federal surveys are routinely shunted to principals who see such duties as contributing nothing to the instruction of their students. A small number of suburban principals mentioned that they had secretaries or assistants they could entrust with much of the paperwork; nationwide, there was a similar lack of help.[6]

There are subjective costs in having to spend considerable amounts of time doing paperwork—tasks that are not only disliked but that block action on other tasks that are felt to be more urgent, important, or interesting. The load of paperwork also intensifies the principals' sense of too little time.

COMPLEX TASKS

One is hard put to think of any occupation that has no difficult or even distasteful tasks that have to be done. They may be difficult to do well or intrinsically complex. When we bear in mind that school management is fundamentally interactive in nature, it is not surprising that the major complexities that emerge focus on relationships with other people. Two questions that provoked talk about such difficulties will be discussed here; the first asked what aspect of the work is most difficult to do well (Q. 20A) and the second inquired into any mistakes the principal had made during the previous year (Q. 55B). We will also explore responses to the question "Which are of the tasks you do are least enjoyable?" (Q. 20C). Unrewarding tasks are difficult in a particular way; dealing with them requires mobilizing energy without the hope of pleasure and at the expense of tasks that are rewarding.

Challenges at the Core

The most frequent responses dealing with difficult tasks focus on the core of the principal's instructional responsibilities—that is, the formal evaluation and supervision of faculty members (table 6.1). Within that large category, we find two central sources of difficulty: the lack of confidence principals have in the evaluative procedures they are required to use and the resistance teachers show to evaluation and to making whatever changes are proposed by the principal. (Less frequent but closely related responses include

Table 6.1. Most Difficult Task (Q. 20A)

	M	% Total M
A. Evaluation and supervision of teachers		
Weaknesses of evaluation process	31	27%
Dealing with teacher resistance	22	19%
Principal dislikes process	5	4%
Dismissing teachers disturbing	4	4%
Sustaining teacher morale	2	2%
Subtotal	64	56%
B. Other tasks		
Paperwork and "administrivia"	12	11%
Deciding without adequate knowledge	7	6%
Dealing with parents (resistant, angry)	6	5%
Resolving conflicts	5	4%
Living with time constraints	4	4%
Student discipline	3	3%
Miscellaneous (1 mention each)	12	11%
Subtotal	49	44%
Total mentions (N = 107)	113	100%

dismissing teachers, principal dislike of the evaluative process, and sustaining teacher morale.)

Principals mention several problems in evaluating teachers and using the assessments they make to supervise their work. The process, they say, is "too subjective." The appropriate criteria are not clear, and/or there is not enough time to visit classrooms and make solid judgments. ("It's hard to define what you are looking for and to get it across" [29B, Male, 52].) Two kinds of uncertainty are evident—"How do I know what is best?" and "Do I have enough information to make a good judgment?" There are issues, then, in regard to the appropriateness of available standards and doubts about the empirical basis for their judgments.

Some principals felt caught between boards and superintendents who wanted corroboration for possible dismissal and teachers who wanted supportive evaluations; the first called for cool and detailed critiques, the second for more generous appraisals. Other principals saw a contradiction between representing evaluation as pedagogical assistance while, in fact, using it as the basis for retention or dismissal. Some principals rejected the assumption they perceived in evaluative procedures, namely, that there is only one right way to teach. Others reported that central office required them to use forms with specific and limited choices that constrained the quality of their judgments. Principals may, moreover, be required to state conclusions when unsure of their diagnoses; for example, they may not understand why a teacher is having particular problems and what steps might correct them. Recall, however, that principals, whatever their misgivings, have no choice in this matter—they must complete and submit formal evaluations; private reservations must be set aside and formal procedures carried out.

Given the variety of bases for discomfort mentioned by principals, it appears that being required to do formal evaluations imposes interpersonal and emotional "costs" on a substantial number of principals. Yet no respondent called for serious revision of the process or its elimination; it may be that despite those costs, principals see their evaluative responsibilities as supporting their authority in technical and professional realms. (We recall that evaluation received affirmation in the five dilemmas question discussed in chap. 4.) It concretizes the right of the principal to evaluate teacher behavior and to propose changes in their classroom activity; it underlines the important part played by principals in the district "chain of command." In a context of many limits on their authority, it remains valued by principals despite the problems it creates; the responses, taken together, point to considerable ambivalence toward the responsibility to evaluate teachers.

A substantial proportion of the principals' responses (19%) referred to the lack of cooperation shown by teachers when told to make changes in their behavior. The word "threatened" appears often in such responses, with principals varying in how broadly they apply the term to teachers—some generalize broadly while others restrict such references to a few. There are times when teacher resistance is portrayed sympathetically and times when it is not. Assisting teachers with some problems may face built-in difficulties, such as helping teachers to develop more control in the classroom.

I was against ranking teachers when I was a teacher and I still am.
(34B, Male, 35)
    The teacher union protects mediocrity. (24C, Male, 61)
    The more you intercede the more the children disrespect the
teacher. (40B, Female, 50)

Some principals mention the need for tact, the importance of
taking teacher sensitivities into account. Whatever the specifics,
teachers are not portrayed as welcoming evaluation and the supervision growing out of it. One of the challenges facing principals,
therefore, is to exercise their instructional authority in ways that do
not alienate the members of their faculties.

You have to keep a positive rapport with the person you are evaluating. Trying to get adults to change is a hell of a lot harder than
getting children to change. (33A, Male, 49).[7]

The other responses to this question point to the variety of difficulties principals associate with their work. They may disdain the
seemingly endless paperwork and administrative duties they define as trivial, and they are hard-pressed to maintain the energy
to perform tasks that bore them or that seem unimportant. Some
regretted their lack of knowledge: ignorance of cleaning tech-
niques hampered one principal in supervising custodians, a former
physical education teacher found it hard to cope with the academic
curriculum, and another principal who knew little about budget
matters had trouble dealing with the central office business manager. It can be taxing to interact with angry parents or those, at
another extreme, who show little interest in what is happening to
their children. Conflict, time constraints, and discipline problems
round out the list of difficult tasks and situations.
    What general observations can we derive from these responses?
Two appear to be clear. Principals face considerable uncertainty
in the course of their daily activities, uncertainty that makes their
work harder; they are often unsure about the standards they should
use and the reliability or validity of their judgments. The second
overall theme is relational complexity. Teachers can and do fail to
respond to the professional judgments of the principal. Parents

produce unpredicted outbursts while students may exhibit puzzling and/or defiant behavior. Complexities around interaction
account for a large proportion of the difficulties they mention. If
their efforts to resolve problems with parents and subordinates fail,
principals may be left with chronically dissatisfied parents and/or
embittered faculty members, an unhappy and career-threatening
state of affairs. Time and again we see principals emphasize the
importance of good working relationships; at the same time, it is
also evident that they cannot count on them to prevail.[8]

Mistakes

Mistakes are, of course, considerably more likely to occur in difficult rather than easy situations; for that reason, they are cited here
as another indicator of the particular tasks that principals find difficult to perform. Respondents were asked to talk about any mistakes they had made in the recent past. Seventy-one percent were
ready to respond with actions they regretted or actions they wished
they had taken and did not (table 6.2).

The responses to this question are, in interesting ways, similar
to those we just examined. Respondents ready to concede mistakes
link most of them to day-in, day-out relationships; they connected
68% of the mistakes to interactions with others. Of those 61 relational errors, teachers stand out as the major source (32/61 of N =
52%). The latter divide almost equally between employment issues
of hiring and firing (M = 14) and problems that arise in the day-
to-day management of faculty members (M = 18). The following
quotation is a strong instance.

> I have one teacher I think is crappy. I say some things, and weigh it.
> I wish she would take early retirement. I wish it, but I don't say it.
> I put kids in her classroom every year. Would I put my own kid in
> her classroom? No. I've been guilty for 22 years of not being able to
> get rid of bad teachers. (97C, Male, 47)

This respondent is not alone in citing reluctance to let teachers
go as a mistake. In nine of fourteen references to teachers, the principals regretted not having arranged their dismissal; the remaining

Table 6.2. Types of Mistakes (Q. 55B)

	M	% Total M
1. Relational errors		
Teachers		
Managing faculty	18	20
Hiring and firing	14	16
Subtotal	32	36
Noncertified staff		
Hiring and firing	3	3
Parents		
Public relations	8	9
Allocation time and energy	2	2
Subtotal	10	11
Students		
Helped more	7	8
Disciplinary action	2	2
Subtotal	9	10
Central office		
Pushed harder	4	5
Avoided anger	2	2
Informed better	1	1
Subtotal	7	8
Subtotal of relational errors	61	68 (r.e.)
2. Other allocations of time and energy		
Instructional program	10	11
Other	3	3
Subtotal	13	14
3. Career-related regrets	3	3
4. Miscellaneous (1 mention each)	11	13
Grand Total mentions	88	98 (r.e.)
(N = 80/112: 71%)		

five principals mentioned hiring teachers who did not work out. (The three mistakes with noncertified employees were also regrets about waiting too long to dismiss them.) Decisions about employment, and particularly the reluctance to dismiss staff members, can produce remorse. The most frequent regrets arise from omissions, from not acting rather than from acting too boldly; the others were based on poor predictions about how teachers would perform.

The responses classified under "managing faculty" include a variety of mistakes that can be made in supervising teachers. They must be assigned to particular classes, a process that can and does go wrong. There are issues with no clear answers. How should one use one's scarce resources of time and attention? Should one emphasize better performance from teachers, including more training opportunities, or devote more time and effort to increasing rapport with them? One principal may regret not going along with teacher preferences and another regret not having resisted them more strongly. Some principals may rue expressing anger at an uncooperative teacher where others wished they had not ignored the feelings of, and not helping, a new group of teachers displaced from a school that was closed. The perplexing choices involved in exercising authority, in achieving an effective balance between "consideration" and "thrust," to quote terms used by Andrew Halpin (Halpin and Croft 1963), are potential sources of remorse.

The mistakes made with parents consist almost entirely of not according them enough attention or not doing well in relating to them. You can be "too confrontational" said one, a sentiment voiced by two others as well who criticized themselves for being too "testy" and "authoritarian" with parents. Others regret mistakes such as being late in providing information about school changes and being slow to defuse the concerns of some parents. One idea summarizes these responses: the wise principal pays close attention to the parents of students and works hard to keep them well-informed and satisfied. Failure to do so can be costly.

Professional consciences are voiced when principals talk about mistakes with students; while two wish they had been somewhat sterner in disciplinary matters, others regretted occasions when they might have done more to help. Examples include the failure to seek outside expertise in a particular case, not fighting to prevent students from having to compete in an unfair (as she saw it) district competition and, in one tragic case, not trying harder to prevent a student from committing suicide. These mistakes exemplify what can be an important aspect of the principal's moral concerns—the obligation to serve as the defender of, and advocate for, the students in his or her charge.

Mistakes vis-à-vis central office differ. Some say they should have pushed harder against central office decisions; a few regret occasions when they displayed negative feelings toward superordinates and their decisions.

Finally, 14% of those mentions derive from what principals later see as poor judgments in allocating their own time and energy—mostly, insufficient attention devoted to instructional matters. Principals are exposed continuously to the idea that they should exercise "educational leadership," an injunction from authorities who do not necessarily accompany it with permission to slight competing obligations. Some look back, it seems, and blame themselves when they have not met whatever time and energy standards they associate with instructional leadership. One principal's regrets were echoed by others as well:

> Strengths for me are conferences, public relations, communications. Up to this year I have not concentrated on curriculum as much as I should have, perhaps. I want to mesh the two better. I'm not sure if it can be done, but I would like to. (78C, Female, 40)

To summarize, the responses to our two questions on task difficulties undermine any view of the work of elementary principals as straightforward and uncomplicated. The difficulties they described arose in the central responsibilities laid on them, responsibilities, as we have seen, that included aims and relationships they considered important, for example, the oversight and improvement of instruction provided by faculty members. Substantial numbers doubted their own ability to make solid judgments on the quality of teacher performance; similar numbers found teachers did not respond affirmatively to their direction on how to improve their work.

Asked about mistakes they had made, these principals faulted themselves primarily in their managerial decisions in employment matters and where they chose to focus their attention and energy. They were too slow to dismiss ineffective teachers; they made mistakes in how they organized the work of their subordinates. Some did not, as they see it, do a good job in relating to parents and handling their relationship with central office. While none said they put too much emphasis on instructional matters, over a tenth wished they had concentrated more on teaching and learning. Some felt, after the fact, that they had not honored their obligation to take proper care of their students. It seems that recriminations come readily for these men and women—recriminations that grow out of the uncertainties and relational complexities that inhere in their work.

Less Popular Tasks

We turn now to tasks that principals see as undesirable, that is, as "least enjoyable." Table 6.3 presents those responses; there are few

Table 6.3. Least Enjoyable Tasks (Q. 20C)

			M	Subtotals	%M
A. Relational tasks					
Parents:	a)	Angry and/or complaining	16		
	b)	Other problems	7		
				23	19
Students:	a)	Discipline mentioned	18		
	b)	Other problems	4		
				22	18
Central office:	a)	Meetings called	10		
	b)	Other	3		
				13	10
Teachers:	a)	Resist criticism/suggestions	7		
	b)	Other problems	4		
				11	9
Mediating conflict:				6	5
Miscellaneous:				8	6
	Subtotal relational tasks			83	67%
B. Nonrelational tasks					
Paperwork				29	23
"Administrivia"				12	10
	Subtotal nonrelational tasks			41	33
Total mentions (N = 107)				124	100%

surprises as we see many similarities to issues that have come up in examining difficult aspects of principal work. We see numerous references to core relationships that are basic to their daily round.

We note, however, that such relational references stand at the problematic end, that is, when others with whom they must work have, as they see it, failed to live up to the principals' expectations of how they should behave. Other persons have impeded rather than assisted the principal in mobilizing effort to meet school goals. They occur when students present disciplinary issues, when parents disrupt the principal's day with angry outbursts or vigorous complaints and when teachers resist rather than cooperate with the principal. Principals also include those meetings called by central office that make no or limited contribution to the operation of their schools. (Such meetings may also result in new and, at times, unwelcome tasks for principals.) If we think of districts and schools as distinct organizations, it is probably not surprising that principals normally prefer to spend their time dealing with their organization—the school. (Recall that chap. 5 showed it to be the cathected site.)

Some disliked tasks are not primarily interactive in nature. Twenty-three percent of the mentions go to paperwork and an additional 10% to administrative tasks the principals find distasteful—together they amount to a third (33%) of the mentions of least enjoyed tasks. Paperwork (in particular, forms required by federal and state governments), it is said, wastes the principal's time on activities that do nothing to advance the school's well-being and associated deadlines cramp already constrained work schedules. While compliance with such routines rarely brings recognition, tardiness ignites disfavor and the possibility of negative sanctions. The term "administrivia" is usually applied by those who use the term to refer to office and clerical routines, budget work, lunch programs, building maintenance, and student bussing.

ON TROUBLE

We do not use the word "trouble" to refer to trivial difficulties; it carries starker connotations. Much that happens at work can be irritating or even frustrating, but "trouble" normally implies more serious repercussions. It is with such consequences in mind that we asked our respondents to identify and, if possible, give us examples of trouble in their work.

Table 6.4 summarizes the results of our questioning. The headings refer to the source of the trouble identified in the responses and, under each, the number of "stories" told and also the number of simple responses that were given. To be classified as a story, the answer had to have at least some narrative; lacking that, it was classified as a simple statement. Our discussion will rely more heavily on the stories because they tell us more about the dynamics associated with trouble. But first a look at the overall distribution of results.

By far the most frequent source of trouble is associated with adults, not children. Although children may be involved in the events that are described and may be affected by them, the principals rarely cited them as the basic source of the problem. Parents, teachers, central officials, and the principals themselves are mentioned often enough to require distinct categories, whereas children are not. That holds even when the trouble involved injury to a student; such injuries, it seems, are not usually serious. What may turn them into trouble is their potential for legal action by parents against the school district. (Among the miscellaneous responses there are three mentions of trouble linked to students—snowballing, absenteeism, and gang activity.) In these suburban schools, serious difficulties, then, almost always revolved around the actions of grown-ups.

The leading sources of trouble among adults are connected to parents and teachers; together they account for 50% of the mentions of trouble. We begin our discussion by focusing on stories about parents and the way in which they are involved.

Parents

Considering the position of parents in the organizational complex of elementary schools may help us understand why they figure so prominently (29% of mentions) as perceived sources of trouble to principals. They usually have a strong interest in what happens to their children in school; their children spend hundreds of days and thousands of hours there and are much affected by their school

Table 6.4. Sources of Trouble (Q. 52 A)

	M	Subtotals	%M
1. Parents			
Stories	23		
Statements	12		
		35	29
2. Teachers			
Stories	19		
Statements	6		
		25	21
3. Central officials			
Stories	12		
Statements	1		
		13	11
4. Changes			
Stories	9		
Statements	3		
		12	10
5. Accidents/injury			
Stories	4		
Statements	5		
		9	7
6. Self-initiated			
Stories	4		
Statements	1		
		5	4
7. Other			
Stories	0		
Statements	5 (Strike 3, busses 2)	5	4
8. Miscellaneous			
Stories	0		
Statements	17		
		17	14
Total	121		100%

experience. Parents of younger, elementary school children, more-over, are more likely than parents of older students to act as advo-cates for their children, to intervene when they are displeased with events.

Those who govern the schools—board members and superin-tendents alike—see parents as the foremost clients of the district and its schools; as we have observed in earlier chapters, parental views and actions can have serious repercussions for local schools and those who work there. Principals are expected to respect the concerns of board members and superintendents about parental and public opinion in the community at large. In addition, they need and seek parental assistance to help their schools work effec-tively with particular students; some districts make serious efforts to have parents participate as volunteers and share in daily tasks and it is modal in our data for principals to say that their superor-dinates favor parental inclusion (Q. 25B). Generally speaking, sub-urban administrators work hard to acquire the goodwill of parents and to respond actively and carefully when there are indications that it is threatened.

Parents, however, stand outside the internal normative controls that shape the behavior of others (employees and students) in this social system; nor do they share the formal and informal social-ization we find among certified school employees. School people try to influence parental attitudes by urging them to participate in parent-teacher organizations and programs for volunteers. But such attempts do not ensure that most parents will comply with what administrators consider the appropriate times or ways to complain; parents are considerably less constrained by conventions of respect for "observing the chain of command" or other rules of bureaucratic etiquette.

As we saw in chapter 3, parental dissatisfaction can provoke ad-verse reactions from the superintendent and, when they hear about it, members of the board. Such reactions can reduce the standing of the principal and the trust that superordinates are ready to place in him or her; the scope of the principal's working autonomy may be curtailed and/or chances for promotion diminished. Nor is it easy for a principal to conceal parental complaints; the principal is expected to inform central office when there is any chance that the dissatisfaction will escalate.[9] It is also true, of course, that when principals respond favorably to parental wishes (depending on the issue), they may violate teacher expectations of support and produce ill feeling among members of the faculty.

Principals described different kinds of problems they encountered with parents. Some are chronic complainers:

> I have a couple of parents who always bring trouble, they are always finding problems. And they may go to the board or superintendent. (28B, Male, 51)
>
> When I hear "Mrs. Doppy called"—that's trouble. She's a bitchy parent who has complained all the time since kindergarten. I'd get a bad evaluation if she went to the superintendent. That could affect my autonomy. (32C, Male, 46)

Some parents resist school recommendations and/or decisions to place their child in a special education program:

> The parents resisted the special education placement—that is, self-contained learning disabilities. But they wanted special services we didn't have. So the child loses out. The problem is that someone who is not a professional is trying to do a professional's job. (93A, Female, 47)

If there are times (as in the cases above) when parents question the principal's authority, there are other times when parents expect the principal to exercise authority where it does not exist:

> Hostile parents. They want me to settle neighborhood squabbles when legally I have no jurisdiction. They expect me to punish the kids. (30A, Female, 32)

Parents may see their children in ways the school personnel do not:

> This parent overestimated their child. She said we weren't challenging her. [The parent] is very vocal and is a nuisance. I tried to satisfy her while giving her the facts. She made me uneasy with

her nitpicking. I had trouble from her group but luckily it is not a
powerful group. (41A, Female, 59)

That parents can embarrass a principal is evident in the following story.

One parent complained to a neighbor who is on the board about
one incident I had not heard about. Then the board member asked
me about the problem and I had to say I did not know. It made me
look bad. (44B, Male, 32)

The numerous ways in which parents can complicate life for
principals is seen in other situations that are described in the interviews. Domestic difficulties such as divorce can spill over into
the school; one principal told how an accidental encounter she
had with a student's father who was out with "the other woman"
somehow resulted in the mother become enraged with the principal. Principals can become unwittingly involved in family conflicts—and possibly legal action—when a parent picks up a child in
violation of the custody terms of a divorce decree. Others parents
may overreact to situations which, to the principal, fall far short
of disaster; one mentioned the extreme reaction of a parent when
head lice showed up in the school. Some parents may organize to
take action that is not supported by the principal: one principal had
to watch the community (notorious for its racial prejudices) insist
that five African-American children be forced to leave his school
when parents pressured the employer to transfer the fathers of the
minority students to another community. Parents stormed into
one principal's office excited by a rumor that a principal who lost
his position would be reassigned to a teacher position and displace
a local teacher they liked.

Finally, we should note that the number of parents involved in a
particular issue is important. More dissatisfied parents not only mean
more anxiety in central office but may require considerable time and
effort from the principal as he or she works to overcome it:

The parents complained that we were too open with the children,
that there was too much individual freedom and not enough direc-

tion. They said more basic skills were required. The staff and I met with parents at lots of coffee talks and that gave both sides a chance to communicate. (111B, Male, 47)

There are times, however, when such efforts fail:

I recall one time when parents could not be satisfied. They didn't like the school. The previous principal was terrible. We had hours of meetings. There was no solution. (116B, Male, 36)

In short, parents can find a wide variety of matters to displease them. What such complaints have in common, however, is that if the principal is unable to quell the parents' distress and they continue to pursue the issue, the consequences can indeed be "trouble." It is not only that angry parents can be difficult to face, but also that parents who persist in their dissatisfaction can weaken the principal's relationship to those who stand above him or her in the authority system.

Teachers

Teachers come a close second to parents in terms of the frequency with which the respondents link them to trouble. They differ, however, in the ways in which they can introduce turbulence into the principal's work. While parents are depicted as introducing trouble in a variety of ways, the stories about teachers can be summarized in a few categories. One category dominates—10 of 19 focus on uncontrolled or "erratic" behavior, which violates expectations of parents and school administrators. Here are examples:

It's trouble for me if a teacher physically punishes a youngster. I tell teachers each September in the first faculty meeting that I cannot support corporal punishment and will not. If a teacher is getting to the point of losing control, send the kid out . . . If a teacher spanks, I see how weak the instructional situation is; there is a deeper problem than just smacking a kid and I have to remediate with the teacher. And I have an angry parent asking why a professional would slap a kid. (109A, Male, 53)

Teacher abuse of a child. When a child is punished too severely
or incorrectly. [Probe. What happens?] It gets the parents stirred
up—they will hear about it. I have a whole mess of conferences to
deal with that if it happens. (C81, Male, 58)

A poor teacher, an incompetent teacher making mistakes in the
classroom—it bothers me to see poor teachers. Also parents complain to me or the superintendent, it's a pain. The principal is made
to iron out someone else's dumb mistake. You have to support your
staff at the same time you make the parent feel that they have a
right to complain. (8C, Male, 37)

I had a grievance filed by a teacher and threatening letters from
an attorney for depriving someone of the right to work. I called
her to task on her grading as she was going to fail about 80% of
her class, then she changed all the grades to As. I said you can't do
that. The union wanted my letter removed from her file. It wasn't.
(100A, Male, 36)

Other incidents of erratic behavior included an alcoholic teacher
("this school is so small that there are serious repercussions"), an
emotionally disturbed teacher who refused to get help and one
whose use of profanity upset parents. One teacher collected
money for books early in the year and never delivered them; she
was made to reimburse the parents and apologize, but some parents subsequently asked the principal not to assign their children
to her room.

The other major sources of trouble with teachers arise when
they unite to block a principal's initiative (three mentions) or when
internal factions resulting from merged faculties produce factions
that make it difficult to attain consensus on school policies and
practices (two mentions). In two cases, a teacher sought to foment
disunity among faculty members and in one the principal managed
to have the teacher transferred to another school.

Looking back on the two major sources of trouble—parents and
teachers—we find that the incidents mentioned have consequences
not only for the relationship itself but for other important relationships as well. Parent dissatisfaction is feared because it can go to
the principal's bosses and endanger the standing of the principal
and may produce harmful outcomes. Teachers who create trouble

may provoke consequences both outside and inside the school; they attract the attention of parents who, in turn, may take their complaints to higher levels in the school hierarchy. When teacher behavior is flagrantly unacceptable, the principal may be forced to take action that upsets and even alienates other faculty members. Angry teachers who file grievances also bring unfavorable attention to the principal; central officials are anything but eager to deal with hostile action from teacher unions. We can define trouble, then, as a problematic event that is intensified by reverberations that spread from one relationship to others which are important in the interactive setting within which the principal works.[10]

The stories that cite central office as the source of trouble have a similar theme, that is, the action or inaction of the superintendent and staff can hurt the principal's relationship with teachers, students, and parents. Questionable decisions can put the principal in the awkward position of having to deal with a host of problems: John Davidson (interview 11, age 30 —all names are, of course, fictitious), for example, had to cope while teachers and students, forced to attend school while the roof was under repair, underwent falling plaster and other discomforts. Jean Craig's (5A, 51) assistant superintendent failed to inform the parents of a child who was assigned to special education classes; the mother was shocked in September when the child was so assigned. A lack of support can complicate relationships with faculty and parents. Tim O'Brien (83B, 49) lost face when the superintendent did not follow through or help him in dismissing an errant teacher; Walter Jacoby's (87B, 44) superintendent met privately with parents from his school for three months before divulging the content of their discussions to him. In general, a superintendent using authority with a heavy hand can reduce the principal's ability to negotiate with faculty members either collectively or individually; it forces the principal to be hesitant in his or her dealings, to project lack of assurance rather than decisiveness. Restricting the principal's authority over particular in-school functions (e.g., lunch program, special education placement) reduces the principal's ability to resolve issues that come up with parents. The tension between the superintendent and the union that develops during collective bargaining can spill over into the schools; one superintendent refused to allocate personnel to adjust salaries after a strike was over, producing fury among teachers, which was expressed at the school level.

We can move through the remaining sources of trouble with dispatch. The kinds of changes that are mentioned as troublesome deal with major issues such as closing a school and reassigning the faculty and students to other locations—a process that many community members find disturbing. Principals, in turn, have to deal with integrating new faculty members and students; conflicts can arise as faculties with different subcultures disagree on instructional practices and policies. Accidents and injuries to students are clearly problematic, and, as we have seen, carry the threat that parents will undertake legal action; one principal cites an instance where that happened and the result was to use up enormous amounts of time. A few principals talked about problems they brought on themselves; in four such instances, the principal was reprimanded for acting without central office clearance.

The statements alluded to in table 6.4 (categories 7 and 8) displayed the variety of unanticipated problems that came up, of contingencies that ranged from arson fires to floods, from the unexpected death of the superintendent to confusion in bus schedules, from tedious bureaucratic routines to the interpersonal strains among teachers that followed strikes. The various ways in which trouble can come up demonstrate once again that managing elementary schools is hardly an uncomplicated affair.

CONFLICT: THE THREAT TO "SMOOTH"

We have seen (chap. 5) that principals favor those days that move with sufficient "smoothness" that they are able to work on activities of their own choice rather than responding to urgencies imposed on them by others. Unpredicted and disturbing events undermine the equilibrium and calm they seek. Conflict inside and around the school ranks high among the sources of such potential disturbance—conflict that occurs, according to our respondents, with considerable regularity (Q. 30A, B). Most respondents reported that conflict took place both within the groups with whom they worked and in the interaction between members of those groups. We obtained information on what types of conflict made the greatest demands on the attention of the principals and the ways in which they dealt with them.

It comes as no surprise that students clash among themselves; 65% of the principals mentioned that source of conflict. But adults are hardly immune to strife; 64% of principals say that it occurred among the parents of their students and 63% among their faculty members. Student conflict is listed as the largest drain on the principal's time (44%) with teachers not far behind (35%), leaving considerably fewer references to central officials, parents, and fellow principals.

The internal disagreements that threatened the time—and composure—of principals came primarily from students and teachers; as we would expect, principals responded differently to conflict within the two groups. In the case of students, they can punish, impose resolutions, and bring in other authorities such as parents and, when the matter is serious enough, the police. They possess considerably fewer resources to quell battles among their teachers; the main strategy is to mediate as best they can. Given the sensitivity of principals to faculty sentiment, they tread softly through potentially explosive situations. (Imagine the level of tension and possibility for serious schisms when leaders of strong cliques tangle!) Effectiveness as a principal, it seems evident, requires skill in the role of peacekeeper. One might suppose that highly effective principals are not only skilled in resolving conflicts once they have been ignited but have mastered ways to cut down on the frequency of their eruption.

Of the conflicts between groups (Q. 30B), those between parents and teachers dominate; 81% of the principals reported the presence of that particular axis of antagonism. Others were 64% for teacher-central office conflict, 64% for teacher-student conflict, and 57% for conflict between parents and central office. Parent-teacher conflict also dominated the responses to the question asking which kind of conflict demanded the "most attention"; totaling those who cited it both as their first and second choice, it netted 45% of all responses compared with 29% for teacher-student conflict, 13% for teacher-central office conflict, and 12% for conflict between parents and central office. Principals found discord between teachers and parents the most pressing and most distressing.

The principal facing conflict between a parent and a teacher (or parents and a teacher) is in a difficult spot. Given the importance of both parties to the principal, the only desirable outcome is that both emerge from the encounter satisfied with the principal's response. Failure, on the other hand, is symbolized by the teacher who angrily denounces the principal to her or his colleagues or the parent who does so to central office. One of the more distracting aspects of these situations is that although out-and-out battles and subsequent failures in resolution may not occur that frequently, there are, in the course of many of these transactions, points where the principal is unsure about the feelings of those involved and/or is unable to predict what either is likely to do. These events have, in short, a strong potential for distracting the principal due to the uncertainty and associated anxiety they provoke. Principals worry whether a parent is sufficiently aroused to warrant making a call to central office warning them to expect a visit from an angry citizen or whether they will hear from a teacher who is sufficiently provoked to file a formal grievance.

Conflict situations present additional problems for the principal. They are not readily put off, and in fact they can be serious interruptions to the principal's agenda. Effective handling of conflict situations can require considerable time to "establish the facts" of the situation, to gauge the emotions involved, and to find potential bases for resolution. It may be necessary to arrange and conduct a series of conferences with the several parties involved. As in the case of formal evaluation, these steps, having been inaugurated, must be carried through to their conclusion. When the stakes appear high, principals will, of course, devote the time needed, but they are likely to see it as unavoidable maintenance rather than as an investment in school improvement. The rhetoric of educational administrators underscores that view: they often refer to such activities as "fighting fires." All in all, it is not surprising that school principals, unlike some social theorists, are not inclined to extol the essential functions and benefits of conflict in organizational life.

Careers and Satisfaction

The idea of career involves the passage of time and some kind of change. Change can be considered in both the short and long run. It also involves the distinction between "objective" changes, such as movement through distinct statuses in an organization, or "subjective" changes that take place within the person, such as those we identified during socialization (chap. 2). The last few chapters have concentrated on short-run issues, the pleasures and frustrations that principals associate with their day-to-day activities. This chapter, on the other hand, looks at longer-range questions, both subjective and objective. When principals look back on their lifetime career decisions, what feelings of satisfaction and dissatisfaction do they talk about? We will also inquire into issues such as promotion, demotion, and status stability, examining the interplay between objective events and how principals respond to them.

Longer-range issues for principals revolve around their employment in a public bureaucracy and the career contingencies found there. Public sector salaries, for example, are typically lower than those in private, for-profit organizations. What part does income play, then, in the feelings of satisfaction and dissatisfaction reported by principals? Careers in public bureaucracies unfold in a hierarchy consisting of clearly demarcated ranks and chances for promotion to positions with higher income, prestige, and authority. In what ways do hopes for promotion affect principals' feelings about their work? What about disappointment when promotion does not occur? Are there issues specific to the administration of schools that affect principal sentiments about their careers?

The chapter is divided into three sections. The first centers on the discontent principals express toward their financial rewards. The second deals with questions about advancement, satisfaction, and related issues. The data are presented serially, using three decades to organize them. We also incorporate findings from a survey of the principals in the sample conducted eight years after the original interviews. Section three discusses a handful of special factors in school management that have effects on careers in elementary education. The approach here is somewhat different from earlier chapters; more details on individual cases are provided in order to illustrate career processes at work and the ways in which they work together in particular instances. The letters that are part of the identification of respondents—A, B, and C—are explained and their relevance indicated later in this chapter.

ON MONEY AND OTHER COSTS

We begin with data (table 7.1) on how monetary rewards figured in responses to a question that asked respondents to identify the costs involved in the principalship compared with other fields they might have entered (Q. 56). A small proportion, only 7%, said there were no costs, but 93% were ready to respond, some listing more than one cost.

There is a strong central theme in the answers. Low income dominated; it was mentioned by 66% of those who cited costs and constituted 39% of all mentions. References to money were usually linked (two out of three times) to another cost—that the time and effort required were too great (16% of mentions) or that the work was aggravating in some particular way (23%). The messages are clear: being a principal provides too few material rewards. Another message, often connected to the first, is that the work demands too much, requiring too much effort, and the sufferance of too many aggravations. Stating it colloquially, as one did, "It isn't worth the hassle" (Pilot interview 7). The following quotations are also illustrative:

Table 7.1. Costs (Q. 56)

	M	%M
Inadequate rewards		
Income too low	67	39
Limited prestige/recognition	12	7
Opportunities too few	5	3
Work not stimulating	3	2
Insecure employment	2	1
Subtotal	89	52
Aggravations/obstacles		
Work is stressful	8	5
Social isolation	8	5
Insufficient authority	7	4
Insufficient autonomy/discretion	1	1
Excessive pressure	4	2
Trivial tasks	4	2
Interpersonal conflict	4	2
Excessively visible ("fishbowl")	2	1
Legal liability	2	1
Subtotal	40	23
Job demands too great		
Excessive time demands	22	13
Requires too much effort, energy	5	3
	27	16
Miscellaneous (mention)	17	10
Grand Totals	173	101 (r.e.)

N = 102 (110 less 8 no cost responses)

Mean number of mentions among those responding—1.7

Lack of money. And the amount of energy and education it takes don't seem commensurate with the salary. (60C, Male, 38)

Financial remuneration is not that great. It is very difficult to be the man in the middle with so many publics to please. (90B, Male, 49)

Money. My friends make more, spend less time. The drain on my time. (44B, Male, 32)

Being a principal is like living in a fishbowl. There's hardly a
move you make that somebody isn't observing you one way or
another. I could have made more money in something else. (13C,
Male, 50)

Financial. You put in 20% more time. Probably a greater variety
and frequency of criticism. You're vulnerable to community,
teachers, building personnel, superintendent. (35B, Male, 41)

The sense of being underpaid and underrewarded is not all that
rare in the work world, particularly in public service occupations.
Persons in the latter fields, Parsons argued years ago, earn less than
employees in the private sector as a trade-off for the greater security
they receive (Parsons 1967). The widespread dismissals and demotions of principals that accompanied the decline in school-age children during the 1970s must have produced, for many principals, a
feeling of expectations betrayed, of disregard for an implicit contract
between them and society. Illinois principals with teacher tenure
continued, of course, to be assured of employment, at least at the
classroom level. To the extent, however, that they expected security
in their administrative positions, the loss of that assurance reduced
the value of their employment as principals and reduced whatever
compensatory part security played in the rewards from their work.

Interactive patterns of the suburban principalship may also
have contributed to a sense of being underrewarded. Principals
compared their rewards with those obtained by friends in more
lucrative occupations, occupations they may have wanted to enter originally but were unable. Those in more prosperous suburbs
probably compared their incomes with those earned by parents of
their students who, often with less formal schooling then they, had
higher earnings; those families faced fewer difficulties in providing
for their children generally and, in particular, were able to consider
a wider range of alternatives in college choice. Given the strong
emphasis on family life visible among these principals, such difficulties in providing for their children were surely disturbing.[1]

Finally, the organizational context also contributed to the sense
of being underpaid. These principals worked in districts limited to
elementary schooling—specifically, kindergarten through eighth
grade. There were some career advantages in that arrangement;

for example, their superintendents came from similar backgrounds in elementary education; unlike principals in unit districts, they did not report to superintendents whose secondary origins might have resulted in views and orientations less favorable to those with experience in the lower grades. Nor did they have to compete for promotion to central office with anyone with high school standing.

The elementary principals in our sample were, however, disadvantaged in terms of income. Professional salaries in elementary districts in Illinois were lower than those in secondary districts. In unit districts where elementary and secondary grades are subsumed by the district, elementary and secondary teachers and administrators are paid at more similar levels, although the national data on principals' income from 1985 to 2005 show a persistent difference by grade level (U.S. Census Bureau 2007). In 1980, the national means were $25,165 for elementary principals, $27,625 for junior high principals, and $29,207 for senior high principals (U.S. Census Bureau 2001). In 2005, the equivalent figures were $76,182, $81,514, and $86,938 (U.S. Census Bureau 2007). The somewhat higher 1980 incomes reported by our respondents (the mean was $30,880) reflect the financial advantages of working in suburban settings.

Turning to another money question, we can ask whether the sense of being underpaid was all that serious; might it not be a standard complaint, merely one of the things that people in education grouse about as a matter of course? To test for this possibility, we examined the reasons given by the most dissatisfied persons— those who would not reenter the field of education (i.e., become teachers or principals again)—for their views on income (Q. 57A, B). Close to everyone who said they would not choose to teach again gave financial reasons; it was cited by 19 of 21. Two quotations illustrate their responses:

No, I would not teach again. Because of economic frustration. Not being able to keep up with inflation. Not being able to have the life style I want. Others can have the life style they want even though they are in the same age category as I am. If I had it to do over again, I'd go into another profession. (40C, Male, 40)

Because I nearly died—financially—for the 4 or 5 years I was a teacher. I had to work nights, weekends tending bar to make ends

meet. I know an accountant who was the same age and now is making double what I am. [Later, in the same interview.] I am at the top
of my pay and can't go any farther. I want to (117C, Male, 35).

Most of those who said they would not be principals again
or planned to leave education also mentioned low income. (We
will examine other reasons they gave later in the chapter.) Some
referred directly to low salaries; others implied it by saying they
would choose more remunerative occupations such as medicine,
engineering, or corporate management. Only 6 of 19 did not mention low salaries (directly or by implication) in expressing dissatisfaction with their choice of the principalship.[2]

CAREER GRADATIONS

The pyramidal structure of bureaucracies presents those who
work in them with both opportunities and burdens. Those who
attain lower level positions in the administrative structure can improve their lot by moving up to higher ranked positions; most beginners probably expect, or at least hope, for such movement. It
is a mathematical certainty, however, that unless there is vast and
rapid expansion of administrative positions, most will not be promoted as the pyramid narrows upward. Those who benefit from
the possibilities for upward mobility will, of course, be gratified
but for those who hoped to move up and did not, the failure to
achieve the benefits of upward mobility is a disappointment with
which they must cope.

We have data that speaks to the issue of how many principals
sought and were able to move up the hierarchy. The first data set
consists of the aspirations expressed by respondents in the three
age decades of their thirties, forties, and fifties and the differences
between them as they age. We will, for purposes of analysis, treat
the aspirations as age-related phenomena that are repeated (to a sufficiently similar extent to be assumed as continuous) for successive
waves of principals. Most of the respondents (70%) in the 1980 Chicago suburban data started out with the expectation that they would
ultimately move up the district hierarchy or obtain other higher prestige positions (Q. 58B). During their thirties, only two respondents

(5%) expected to retire as principals; that percentage climbed sharply during their forties to 53% and for those in their fifties, 78%. These men and women obviously adjusted their expectations over time, increasingly seeing the principalship as their final position in education, shedding higher ranked alternatives. The data from the Iowa study reveal a similar pattern of reduced aspirations with age.[3]

The second data set was gathered in 1988 through phone calls to the districts in which sample members worked in 1980 and allows us to learn what actually happened to these men and women. Twenty-three percent of those we tracked from their thirties had risen in the system, mostly to superintendent or assistant superintendent positions.[4] The rates of upward mobility in subsequent decades were considerably lower—3% among those in their forties and 3% of those in their 50s. (The two principals in their sixties were included in the fifties group.)

Clearly, upward moves occurred much less often than respondents expected; it is also true that downward moves took place in this period of frequent school closings. By decade, the demotion rate was 10% among the thirties, 5% among the forties, and 3% among the fifties. The net rate of promotion (the difference between promotions and demotions) was positive among the principals in their thirties at 13%, negative among those in their forties with –2%, and zero among principals in their fifties. The gap between what many of these principals expected and what actually happened was substantial.

We turn now to a review of the satisfactions and dissatisfactions registered among the principals by decade, looking for the specific ways in which time affected their feelings toward their work. That will be done decade by decade, focusing on what appear to be the major points at different stages in their work.

A word of explanation before we turn to career satisfaction over the span of the career. The respondents were classified into one of three categories—A, B, and C. Persons in category A are considered definitely satisfied. They said they would repeat the decisions to teach and become principals (expressing no doubt about those decisions) and would not, given the chance, make any changes in their careers (Q. 57C). Those in category B form a sort of "in-between group"; it includes principals who said they

Table 7.2. Satisfaction Group by Decade

(For sources, see text)	A	B	C	Total
Thirties (N)	14	10	13	37
%	38	27	35	100
Forties (N)	9	15	16	40
%	23	38	40	101 (r.e.)
Fifties (N)	11	9	10	30
(Sixties) (N)	1	0	1	2
	12	9	11	32
%	38	28	34	100
Total (N)	35	34	40	109
%	32	31	37	100

would "probably" repeat their occupational choices and also listed changes they wished they had made in their careers. Principals in category C are defined as dissatisfied; they would definitely not repeat the decisions to teach and/or become principals again; many of them also listed career changes they wished they had made.

Table 7.2 shows that there are people in each of the categories in all three decades. There are some differences, however, worth noting. Those in their thirties show a fairly even distribution with a slight emphasis on the satisfied As. In the forties, the proportion in the A group drops and we find relatively high proportions of persons in the B and C categories. The distribution of satisfaction among principals in their fifties is similar to what we see among those in their thirties.

The (Mostly) Hopeful Thirties

Principals in their thirties are special in interesting ways. Many express high optimism about their futures; in fact, hopefuls predominate in this group. A smaller number expressed serious concerns about their future in public education. Before examining internal differences, however, we will examine those in their thirties as a whole.

Of those intending to stay in education, 78% said that they expected to occupy higher status positions before they retired. The usual objectives were central office positions (51%) such as superintendent or assistant superintendent; nine (24%) expected to teach in a college or university. Nine percent were unsure of their ultimate destination while 5% mentioned uncommon possibilities. As mentioned earlier, two expected to retire as principals. A handful (four cases or 11%) expected to leave public education. A substantial proportion of these principals had invested in advanced education to further their mobility goals; forty-three (43%) had earned doctorates or were doing advanced study (certificates of advanced study or doctoral degrees) in local universities.

One of the more striking features of these principals in their thirties was the homogeneity in background of the largest subgroup, those classified as A, the clearly satisfied. Almost exclusively male (93%) and white (93%), they were more likely than the less satisfied principals to come from white collar homes—71% versus 40% for Bs and 46% for Cs. The sample size restricts what we can make of these cases, but they suggest to the writer that higher social origins, carrying greater resources of social capital, probably instill greater confidence that one possesses the necessary interpersonal skills, skills whose importance are so evident in this study. If that is the case, such confidence, we can hypothesize, adds to satisfaction of those engaged in this kind of highly interactive work.

The organizational experiences of those in category A were also likely to support a sense of comfort and optimism. In every instance, they worked for the same superintendents who had appointed them; furthermore, most (86%) had been sponsored in their current district or helped by their former superordinates to move into their current positions. More (79%) placed themselves in the top tier of influentials within the district, compared with 44% and 46% in the B and C subgroups (Q. 29). Three had doctorates and four were doing advanced study.

Eighty-six percent (12 of 14) of the persons in category A expected to move up to higher status positions. It is probably not surprising that these principals saw their futures in such rosy terms—the past had gone well for them, presumably giving them confidence in their abilities and good fortune. Their actual rate of upward mobility, however, was not much higher than that of their less satisfied colleagues. Of those who remained in Illinois, three had moved up to superintendent eight years later; two of those had doctorates. The remaining seven continued to work as principals in the same or another district. No one was demoted.

The principals in category B were somewhat different from those we have just discussed. They were a little less socially homogenous but were similar in having high hopes for the future—seven of ten expected to move up to higher status positions in the hierarchy. Although they expressed some uncertainty about their past choices and (usually) mild regrets about career events, few manifested anything like serious dissatisfaction. Their subsequent careers, however, were somewhat less successful than those in category A; of eight remaining in Illinois, six were principals and one was promoted to assistant superintendent. One was demoted to classroom teacher.

A baker's dozen of the principals were placed in category C, the clearly dissatisfied group. Five of them said although they would not become teachers again, they would, if in education, repeat the decision to become principals. Their reluctance to teach was based, as we have seen, on economic issues; they lamented low salaries and job insecurity. They had not, however, given up hope for other positions. Three aimed at central office, one at college work and another hoped for a principalship "in a more sophisticated district." One, the only woman in the group, had attained the superintendency eight years later.

Contingencies in the Early Years: Problematic Careers

The early years in the principalship present demands that can prove difficult, so difficult, in fact, that some the people facing them wish they were in another line of work. Given their dynamic qualities, these early years merit special attention. Working relationships must be established with those above and below the principal in the authority system. One often hears that "sufficient" authority and discretion are needed to perform as a manager; in education, the reiterated theme that the principal should exercise "educational leadership" carries an expectation of considerable influence over the faculty—influence, as discussed in chapter 4, that is not that easily obtained. Newcomers must learn to do the multiple tasks required, regardless of their initial preferences and/or continuing distaste for some. And some principals, of course, will find the lack of promotion especially hard to accept. We turn next to specific cases of persons in their thirties; they illustrate how the contingencies we have just mentioned (and others) work out in concrete terms.

One man (9C, 38) taught for ten years before being "sponsored" (his word) into a principalship by his principal who was promoted to central office. He chose to move to a richer district two years later to become the first principal of a school that the superintendent had run while also heading the district. "I had to establish the position while the superintendent remained 'a few feet away' in the same building." His efforts fell short of success—"I do not have a principal's job here." Given the chance to do things differently, he would have obtained his doctorate sooner and gone into university work. Eight years later, he was demoted to classroom teacher in the same district. In addition to the obvious problems, this case shows the risks involved in moving in order to ascend the status order among suburban districts—things do not always turn out well.

One of the principals who had trouble gaining influence over his faculty was bitter about his new position (33C, 38). Although he would be ready to teach again, he would not become an elementary principal. "I don't feel I am influencing teachers as much as I thought principals were supposed to. Poor teachers need guidance—that's my job and I'm not influential and I haven't influenced a lot of kids." Critical of central office ("All they care about is public relations"), he tried to spend as much time as he could with the students, whom he enjoyed. Plans to teach high school he mentioned in the interview did not materialize; he still headed the same school eight years later.

The "reality shock" of finding a position different from one's expectations is hardly a rare event; it seems that most people get over it. One female principal (78C, 40) remained unhappy with her assigned tasks, however, even after four years' experience as a principal. This African-American woman had an impressive sixteen-year career in overseeing instruction, from directing Head Start programs to serving in university training programs in two states. Her career choices, however, were constrained by her husband's peripatetic academic career; she landed in Illinois and applied for a principal position in a racially integrated, middle class suburb. Her central complaint was that administrative tasks, given the lack of an assistant, took too much time. "All staff, discipline, purchasing— everything—there was no one to delegate to." She referred to those tasks in explaining why she would not be a principal again. "I want to be able to delegate so I can concentrate on what I want to do." It seems that her specialized and relatively long prior socialization made it difficult for her to accept the multiple and generalist demands of the principalship.

Although disappointment at not being promoted was mentioned oftener by those in their forties, two men who were appointed to the principalship early were dissatisfied during their thirties. One 39-year-old male (36C) was already a principal by 29. He was working on his doctorate and had clear ambitions—first an assistant superintendency and then superintendent. But he would not re-enter education because "There's not enough money." He added, "The principalship is a cushy job but I'm bored." He had made himself visible by high activity in professional associations and held a position of leadership in his church. He allocated 5 of 8 spaces to his work in the life space question (Q. 60A). His frustration at not being promoted was temporary, however, since eight years later he had obtained a central office position in another district. The uneasiness about the future he demonstrated and doubts about his decisions reminded the author of young law firm lawyers he once studied who were uncertain about achieving partnership status (Lortie 1958).

Another young man (8C, age 37) was, to misapply an old phrase, a horse of another color. He said, "I cringe at the prospect of being a principal for the next twenty-five years." Attaining his position had required no special effort; he was asked to apply for a principal position before he even began to search for one; the term "career escalator" is certainly applicable to his early years. He regretted, however, not having done additional university study after being certified, saying that the lack of a doctorate had reduced his promotion chances. Almost inactive in professional affairs, he belonged to no community organizations of any kind. His allocation of space to work on the life space question was among the lowest, two of eight; the two he accorded work equaled the two he allocated to sports and fishing. Eight years later he was principal of the same school. It seems that early and easy promotion did nothing to prepare him for the demands of additional movement up the hierarchy.

The Forties: Affirmations and Regrets

Promotion emerges as a major issue in this decade. Principals confront the likelihood that any earlier aspirations they had to move up the hierarchy turn out, for most, to have been overoptimistic. Our respondents in their thirties seem to have expected promotion almost as a matter of course; we have seen that only a fraction made it. Mobility is even more limited during the forties—only one principal, eight years later, had moved up the ranks. Yet hope dies hard for some, as almost one third (28%) of the men and women in their forties continued to look forward to central office positions.

This age group is somewhat more socially diverse than those in their thirties. (There are a few more women.) The sponsorship rate was 68%, but fewer continued to work for the superintendent who had appointed them—43% versus 100% in the thirties group; many principals in this older category faced new central office regimes, losing whatever advantages were attached to working for bosses who had initially selected them. Hopes of moving up waned and fewer studied, and those studying or holding doctorates declined to 15%. Outcomes eight years later showed the effects of time; 68% worked in the same district, but 13% had retired and 8% had died. Two had left the state.

Although the proportion of clearly satisfied principals is smaller in the forties (23% in category A versus 37%), the men and women in this category are particularly interesting. There is a highly suggestive change in the relationship between the ambition to move up and career satisfaction—they are no longer as closely connected as they were among the younger principals. Of the nine who expressed high career satisfaction, five did not expect to move up; they were satisfied with the prospect of remaining in the principalship until retirement, of continuing work without whatever psychological subsidy would be provided by the expectation of upward mobility. They report pleasure with their work, making statements such as "I can't think of anything I would like more" (79A, Male, 46) and "This is where my talents lie" (19A, Male, 44). One principal who had experienced life in central office remarked, "I missed the direct contact with teachers and students. Up there we talked about reports, not children" (96A, Male, 47). These men remind one of Wolcott's subject, Don, who identified himself as a "career principal" (Wolcott 1973). They had developed firm identities as principals. The interviews leave the impression that daily contact with children, contact that figured so prominently in our earlier chapters, played an important part in the formation of that identification (Barley 1989).

Principals in the B group were less accommodated to the lack of promotion. Those who expressed regrets about their careers lamented not getting doctoral degrees or deciding to stay in districts (usually small) with too few opportunities for promotion. Their ambivalence about their choices showed up in talk about looking forward to retirement or muted displays of enthusiasm about their work.

The principals in category C who said they would not repeat the decision to teach focused on the financial inadequacies of their positions; 9 of 10 centered their comments on inadequacies of income. Although some continued to hope for promotion, plans for a different kind of future began to take shape. Three had plans to enter business upon retirement (sales, insurance, and real estate) and one (32C, Male, 46), seriously alienated, planned to re-enlist in the naval reserve to distract him from the unpleasantness of his work situation.

Those who said they would not be principals again mentioned a variety of reasons. One blamed not getting a doctorate for his failure to get a superintendent's position and resented it (113C, Male, 42). Another, despite being a principal for twelve years, bemoaned his lack of managerial independence (26C, Male, 41). One woman attributed her unwillingness to repeat her choices to the stress she experienced as a principal (110C, Female, 43). A man who had, in his early years, taught English literature in a western university, wished he had followed an academic career instead of entering public education. Referring to professors, he said, "I never thought they would be making that much money" (105C, Male, 48).

The Fifties: The Terminal Decade

The twenty-six men and six women in their fifties and sixties divided almost equally into the three satisfaction categories. The percentage who worked for the same superintendent who hired them dropped to 33%; not one was engaged in advanced graduate study. The largest changes, not surprisingly, lay in their expectations for the future and the actual outcomes of their careers eight years later. Few of these men and women expected to be promoted; 78% expected to retire as principals.[5]

Review of the satisfaction categories of principals in their fifties revealed considerable similarity to those we found in the forties. Men and women in category A emphasized their enjoyment of the work. Those in B who wished they had done things differently in the past regretted, as did those in their forties, staying in districts with too few opportunities or wished they had done more advanced study. All the Cs who said they would not repeat the decision to teach stressed the financial disadvantages of employment in public education.

It may be that dissatisfaction associated with stress occurs later in the career; of the eight who mentioned it, seven were over forty. It shows up in the case of a 59-year-old man who talked about having a severe heart attack two years before the interview—a heart attack that he attributed to his work as principal (95C, 59). Another contingency that occurred in their later years was finding that social change, by broadening opportunities, had lowered their evaluation of the relative advantages of the principalship. One African-American woman (the one who was later promoted to acting superintendent) referred to how such changes affected her views on whether she would repeat the decision to be a principal. "Certainly not. Because there are so many things that are open to black women that weren't open before" (82C, Female, 56).

The one widely shared and distinctive concern of the principals in this older category revolves around a structural feature of careers in public schools—a feature which is more prominent there than in the private sector. (It occurs as well among municipal employees in police forces and fire departments and service men and women in the armed forces.) It was possible for these Illinois principals to retire during their fifties, usually at fifty-five years of age. (The feasibility of actually retiring rested, of course, on savings and other considerations.) This option raised an issue that was special to this phase of the career. The survey done eight years later revealed that the majority had retired (54%) or died (15%).[6]

It is worth noting that suburban principals have some special advantages in switching to other kinds of work late in life. They become acquainted with and are known to literally hundreds of persons because of the numerous occasions on which they interact with adults in the community. Large networks of acquaintances are attractive to sales-oriented companies in insurance and real estate, and principals can make substantial increases in their incomes by working for them.

When interviewed, the principals took diverse stances toward the possibility of retirement. One (74A, Male, 59) of the satisfied men said that he did not want to retire, but others in A group anticipated carrying out specific plans. We were able to learn how plans worked out for most of them in the eight-year follow-up. One respondent had a background in music education and planned to open a shop to repair instruments, but grievously, death prevented realization of that plan (68A, Male, 54). Another man, already engaged in selling real estate part-time, carried out earlier plans to do it full-time (74A, Male, 57). One man with a doctorate (109A, 53) who still hoped for promotion had answered the life space question by allocating as many spaces (3) to his Protestant church as to his job; eight years later he was working as a missionary in Africa.

Some principals who were less satisfied or were dissatisfied with their work looked forward to retirement as a welcome opportunity to undertake other kinds of work or to engage in favored activities such as travel. Some hoped to teach in universities; only one, however, worked in that setting eight years later. It is difficult to assess whether some of the talk about opening a business was more fantasy than reality; for example, two men who mentioned it thought it would give them more managerial control than they currently had but were still in the same school eight years later. They remind one of the study done in the 1950s by Chinoy, who found similar longings for independence among automobile workers (1955). To some extent, the possibility of new forms of employment may act as a safety valve in an occupation that does not produce universally high morale among its members.

SPECIAL FEATURES OF THE CAREER SYSTEM

Careers that unfold in bureaucratic organizations have much in common, regardless of their specific sector or field. Yet there are some ways in which the issues that emerge are shaped by conditions specific to the particular setting. For example, we saw in chapter 2 how state regulation, rare in management careers, presses administrative careers toward localism; we also discussed another special feature of public sector careers, namely, pension systems which allow for comparatively early retirement. We turn now to how other special features found in public education affect careers. Four are considered here—the authority system, career advancement, the involvement of universities, and gender changes in the work force. Ways in which the career system connects to the occupational culture are discussed in the next chapter.

The authority system found in public school districts is, in some respects, unusual in the world of formal organizations. The concentration of authority at the highest levels, with limited powers for lower-level managers, is typical. What is less common is that those who are asked to manage the basic units (i.e., schools) are granted little power to dismiss employees and have scant leverage in the distribution of money rewards. The result, as have seen, is that principals rely heavily on persuasion and relationships backed by the ability to provide resources and support. "Resources" are broadly defined here to include nonmaterial as well as material powers; a principal can play the role of teacher advocate vis-à-vis central office in salary matters and, for example, use discretion in exempting teachers from what is normally prescribed and/or grant particular dispensations as rewards for desired behavior. Providing those incentives assumes agreement, in turn, from central officials who may (or may not) provide the active support or autonomy they entail.

The dependency on central office is, in all likelihood, greater than that found in many organizations where managers have budgets they can control, distinct personnel powers and other forms of managerial independence. The absence of more conventional powers in schools, therefore, requires more cooperation from headquarters than we find where those powers are routinely delegated. If that reasoning be right, resources provided by central office are particularly valuable because of the important effects they have on the ability of principals to manage those who report to them. Principals are caught between two dependencies, requiring greater cooperation from both superordinates and subordinates than is typically the case. The ability to manage "below" rests heavily on the favor of those "above."

Problems associated with that double dependency can be seen in the beginning years of two principals' careers when they sought to become established in the role. One young man who left education after a couple of difficult years as principal (2C, Male, 30) had been, simultaneously, expected to dismiss a handful of teachers (enrolments were dropping) while his superintendent signaled lack of confidence in him by attending all PTO meetings at his school. Another beginner, mentioned above, who was frustrated by his inability to influence teachers and did not want to continue as a principal, also reported receiving no help from central office (33C, Male, 38).

There is another feature of the authority system that is characteristic of school districts; the terrain of the principal's authority is regularly defined by the physical boundaries of the school. But there are situations, usually resulting from limited funds and/or small size, in which the superintendent's office is located in one of the schools. That situation can produce confusion about who is in charge, and unless the superintendent is scrupulous in referring inappropriate (to him) approaches by staff and parents to the principal, principals are likely to complain, sometimes bitterly, about their lack of autonomy. The case described above (9C, Male, 38) is one of several where that was a serious issue for the respondent.

Turning to opportunities for advancement, two factors should be mentioned as more characteristic of public education than other organizations. The first has to do with the number of, and costs of moving to, other locations, the second with not being promoted. Although we do not know how the rate of promotion in school districts compared with that found in other vertical structures, the rate among principals is, I suspect, closer to the low rather than the high end of organizations in general. Except for truly large districts, positions of higher rank are relatively few in school districts. They are limited to a small number of line positions in central office, for suburban central offices are usually small. (That differs from large business firms, for example, where there are specialized executive careers in departments of sales, production, marketing, finance, etc.) The major possibilities are linked to two positions—superintendent and assistant superintendent and, as we have noted, the first requires additional study and certification. Mobility was also reduced by state certification, which limited movement across state lines to those states that had reciprocity agreements with Illinois. Finally, the costs involved in leaving one Illinois employer for another (the loss of district seniority, of special importance in a period of lay-offs, and temporary loss of teacher tenure) also played a part.

The second characteristic has to do with the psychological impact of not being promoted. Such disappointment is hardly unique to school managers. What may give it a special quality, however, is the large part played by sponsorship in the principals' initial promotion to administrative ranks, at least in our suburban districts. A large majority of those appointed from inside the district received personal support from the superintendent and/or other senior officials and most of them worked for several years with the same boss who had supported them earlier. The ease with which they moved up in the early part of their careers probably led them to expect that later steps would be similar: they would continue to be carried up on an "escalator" to higher positions. That did not happen for most of them. It seems likely, therefore, that lack of support and favorable action on the next step could produce greater disappointment than we would find in fields where overt competition (e.g., the tournament process described by Rosenbaum 1989) was greater and sponsorship was less important in the early career.

There are career consequences that flow from the two-step career arrangement for entry to the principalship. One is that the requirement of prior experience in another position carries the risk that transition to the second stage will not work out well. In two instances at least, the principals (78C, Female, 40 and 99C, Male, 38) continued to use preferences rooted in their teaching experience to render negative judgments on their new work; the socialization that took place during teaching impeded the formation of a new identity as principal. It may be that the tendency of some principals to depreciate the more purely administrative aspects of their work (a tendency that the reader may or may not regard as desirable) constitutes a continuation of views formed during their teaching years.

The two-step career arrangement, perhaps ironically (it is based on persons leaving teaching ranks) can contribute to closer relations between principals and teachers. Limiting principal positions to persons who have taught has made for similarity in the social class backgrounds of persons in the two occupations. That similarity helps to avoid schisms that occur when managerial positions go primarily to persons who were able to acquire expensive and protracted educational preparation, creating a gap in a company or business organization between those who manage and those who do not. There is another bond encouraged by young men and women working side by side in schools; although we lack precise data on the number of principals who are married to teachers, it is clear that many are. Perhaps the prevalence of such marriages makes it especially difficult for male principals to project airs of superiority toward teachers.

The state regulation of administrative careers in education requires that candidates for higher positions earn certificates based largely on university study. Those principals who expressed regrets about their careers often wished they that had done more advanced graduate study. Formal requirements for certification increased during the careers of many of the principals while school boards, quite apart from state rules, also raised their expectations; more sought superintendents who not only had the courses certifying them for the position but had fully completed doctoral degrees. This underscores the crucial role played by universities in this occupation; criteria for admission to advanced programs and performance standards within them are added to the other contingencies faced by the principals. Aspirants for promotion are required to meet the expectations of two sets of "career regulators," employers and university personnel. Career advancement, as a consequence, includes a set of potential roadblocks not widely found in formal organizations.[7] In some geographic areas, certificates are awarded by one or a small number of universities, putting aspirants who do not succeed at considerable risk in gaining employment in that area.

In conclusion, elementary education is a leader among those fields requiring college preparation that have, traditionally, been staffed primarily by women. (Other examples include social work, library work, and nursing.) The first waves of women to attain managerial positions after WWII did so after many years as teachers. Their initial decision to teach was made in a context of limited opportunities in the economy at large. As more women have (finally) been able to rise to administrative positions, they, like their female staffs, have become aware of numerous and attractive opportunities that did not exist when they began to teach. Social change has, of course, broadened the range of occupations available to women and, as well, to African Americans; the presence of those alternatives has lessened the perceived value of the rewards earned in schools. Social and economic changes resulting in new opportunities for women are particularly relevant in fields defined largely as women's work. They produce quantitative effects as a higher proportion of persons in those occupations are affected. It can reduce the ability of those occupations to recruit new talent, especially managerial talent.[8]

Although being located in a formal bureaucracy has important effects on the careers of elementary school principals, the findings presented in this chapter underscore the significance of the particulars in that setting. We will focus on special features of the occupation in the two chapters to come, first emphasizing common themes and then ways in which the patterning of interaction in the position contributes to a strong theme in that culture—a tilt toward continuing the status quo.

Reality and Response
A Managerial Subculture

There are ways in which all managers are alike. We have seen, however, that the work of principals is distinctive in a number of mean-
ingful ways. We find features in the context and content of their
work that are relatively infrequent in other managerial settings;
some, in fact, come close to being unique. We consider the likely
consequences of those special features in this chapter and look for
ways in which they contribute to a special occupational culture—a
managerial culture, to be sure, but one with visibly distinctive elements. In order to review the findings from such a cultural perspective, it is necessary to reorder our observations in ways that differ
from the previous presentations. This chapter uses seven categories to summarize the ways in which the work of principals differs,
I believe significantly, from managers in general.

JUNIOR BUT PROMINENT

Rank in hierarchy is always an important aspect of managerial
work; it is not only a matter of income and prestige but is basic
to whatever culture develops within a particular group of managers. In the case of elementary principals, there is a special feature
not widespread among managers in general, namely, an unusual
relationship between subordinate rank and public prominence. On
the one hand, principals are definitely junior executives who lack
policy-setting and financial autonomy; they must act within the

boundaries imposed by the board and superintendent. The scope within which they can take independent action is restricted; violating those boundaries can prove costly for them.

Unlike many subordinate managers, however, principals occupy a highly visible position within a community which is demarcated, in a sense, as "theirs." It is conventional practice to subdivide the school district into "catchment areas" and to assign the families in that area to a particular school. It is common for individual "buildings" to acquire strong identities; many, if not most, evoke the commitment and loyalty of staff and students over the years. Principals head up distinctive organizations; they are the "boss" to staff members, oversee students who may not be aware of other district officials and are approached first by parents and other community members on school matters. Although subordinate in the official hierarchy, the principal is "in charge" of an important local institution with its own specific public or constituency. Although the public served is smaller than the superintendent's, it is no less real. The principal is a public figure and, as we shall see in the following section, no less vulnerable to the peculiarities and preferences of his or her particular constituency. The public aspects of their work play an important part in the formation of the culture of principals.

It is also important, however, to bear the subordinate status of the principal in mind when we examine that culture. The conservative tilt found there will become increasingly evident as we review our findings. The tendency toward continuity rather than change reflects, in addition to its other origins, the limited scope for action possessed by members of this occupation. Principals are fully aware that they have little power to institute major changes. As we saw in chapter 5, they can make changes and feel pride when they succeed. But the scope of the changes they make and others they might consider will be determined not solely (or even primarily) by their personal preferences but by what is acceptable and perhaps desired by those who stand above them in the organizational hierarchy. They are not agents who are free to initiate change when and where they see the need. Furthermore, as will become apparent in the final chapter, significant changes in their own position will most likely originate outside schools and school districts.

THE FISHBOWL

The first definition of "private" in the *American Heritage Dictionary* (3rd edition) reads, "secluded from the sight, presence or intrusion of others"; the fourth is "belonging to a particular person or persons, as opposed to the public or the government." The definitions point up a distinction that has significance in the study of management, namely, the differences between private and public. The seclusion of the private stands in opposition to the openness required from persons in the public sector; private ownership differs from the communal nature of what is public and the implication, in a democratic society, that those doing public work are held accountable to the public. We begin with the latter issue, developing observations introduced earlier in the book.

There are structural differences that set principals apart not only from managers in the private sector but, in addition, from the thousands of other managers employed by federal, state, and local governments. Principals stand at the more "exposed" end of the public service continuum. They are nearby and highly visible; schools engage many families in the area and provide services requiring protracted and regular contact with school personnel. Taxes for schools, compared with other local services, are relatively high. Citizens, acting as elected board members, respond to local concerns; actions by principals and others, if they raise doubts about the effectiveness of their stewardship, can provoke employer disapproval.

Principals make their decisions without the protection of a rightful claim to privacy. Considerable transparency is expected in their interactions with those around them; norms of openness make it difficult for principals to conceal potentially embarrassing actions or interactions. Openness also makes differences in outlook between individuals and groups explicit, a condition more likely to foster than dampen conflict. Actions and decisions, moreover, are evaluated in terms of the equal treatment expected in the public sector. Although moralistic expectations of teachers and principals are not as strong as they were in Waller's day, some apparently linger on ("You have to be as pure as Caesar's wife" [1A, Male, 35]). It is, to put it mildly, difficult to avoid criticism when occupying a position with such characteristics; it is no surprise when principals complain about "working in a fishbowl."

We have discussed some of the consequences that flow from the accountability and exposed position of principals. Members of the public, particularly parents, expect immediate and full attention; as a result, principals have difficulty maintaining control over their time: they are eminently interruptible. The ability to finish an undertaking marks a day as good, for principals live with the particular uncertainty that results from not knowing whether they will be able to complete their plans. Is it not probable that facing such constant uncertainty will promote tentativeness rather than decisiveness among principals? It does seem likely, in any event, to discourage engagement in some of the longer-range projects that principals might otherwise undertake. It presses them toward short-range action and a short-range outlook.

There are, I believe, other consequences that arise from personal vulnerability. One is a tendency for principals to act in conventional and unchallenging ways, to lean toward caution rather than taking risks. We have seen that they place enormous emphasis on the quality of their relationships with all those with whom they work and monitor their performance by paying close attention to feedback from them. Striving to obtain such general approval is likely to encourage behavior with few sharp edges, to favor action widely seen as correct. Parents, for example, can and do differ in their preferences; it seems that principals, to the extent they can, look for and focus on what is shared, seeking the common denominator. It is easier to perceive incentives for caution than boldness under such circumstances.

Other themes fit with an emphasis on moving carefully and, as far as possible, consensually. We recall that principals see their superordinates as favoring calm, as detesting what they label "boat rocking." Things should be "smooth." Principals are expected to stay within the boundaries established by district policy and, in fact, to check constantly to make sure they are familiar with that policy. There is protection for school administrators, of course, in adhering to bureaucratic policies and procedures because it supports solidarity among officials by presenting a common front and a shared rationale to members of the public and subordinates alike.

Many, many hours spent with the interview data have left the writer, however, with the strong impression that although these principals respected the limits imposed on them by their employing organizations, reliance on bureaucratic processes did not play the major part in their response to their high exposure and accountability. The central commitment, it appears to me, was to build and sustain warm and mutually supportive relationships wherever and whenever they could. The central strategy can be described as building broad coalitions among parents and teachers and central officials, of working to create reservoirs of goodwill to buttress them for whatever confrontations might arise. Although emphases were not identical (e.g., a few placed emphasis on relating to parents, more principals emphasized closeness to teachers) the common, underlying theme was the desire to form and preserve positive relationships with *everyone*—superordinates, subordinates, and persons outside the authority system.

Although it may not be surprising that the drive to please all—to ensure harmony—will reduce efforts at change, it is useful to illustrate ways in which it does take place. The difficulties provoked by conflict have been discussed in earlier parts of this work, leading principals to rely heavily on mediating various kinds of controversy that arise within and between various groups. (A high-cost example is conflict between teachers and parents, conflict that can be intensified by factors we discuss in the next section.) There are two ways in which heavy use of mediation favors continuation of the status quo.

The first is the likely content of mediated solutions. The divergent views of two parties in opposition define the parameters for the emergence of a compromise solution and the mediator normally works to find an acceptable midpoint. (The word mediation derives from the Latin *medius* for "middle"; *Shorter Oxford English Dictionary*, 3rd edition.) Thus solutions, standing between alternatives favored by others, tend toward compromises that are unlikely to differ significantly from ideas that have prevailed in the past; familiar rather than innovative ideas are more likely to occur. The accumulation of mediated decisions, over time, tends to favor what has been.

The second relevant feature in mediation is that it places the principal in a position of limited authority through its deference to the views and preferences of those contesting an issue. Where arbitrators can impose solutions of their own derivation, mediators operate within the framework others are willing to consider and ultimately accept. The balance of interests represented by the "settlement" rests essentially on the values of the parties involved. Although success as a mediator may produce appreciation, it is not likely to raise the principal's standing as an agent of change. A principal's reputation as an effective mediator may well produce greater reliance on mediation, leaving the authority of the principal's position unchanged.

AN EMOTIONALLY CHARGED SETTING

The relationship between school people and their clientele is complex and emotionally charged. We have noted above that the contacts between schools and families are numerous and protracted and there is a lasting quality to whatever relationships develop. It is also true that the relationships between schools and those they serve have greater emotional intensity than one finds elsewhere, a point I wish to develop here. Principals head organizations that reach into families in powerful and unusual ways, circumstances that are highly consequential for them and the subculture they have formed.

The school makes claims on children made by no other organization. Buttressed by state authority, it incorporates the children into itself and subjects them to its authority, authority that essentially displaces the family's over many daytime hours—and for years on end. They also reach outside school-based schedules to assign homework outside school hours and to promote extracurricular activities that affect how time can be scheduled in the home. The time children spend under the direct control of school authorities has increased in recent years as both parents have, increasingly, worked outside the home. There has been widespread development of programs before and after school.

The parents of students are asked to extend considerable trust toward schools and those who work in them. Upon enrolling their children, they not only give up control over their daily behavior for hours on end, but are expected to accept the legitimacy and rule of the social order instituted and operated by the school. School personnel define the nature of acceptable and desirable performance by the children in school and what merits praise or censure; those definitions can create reputations for individual children that transcend school boundaries. Teachers and principals can impose punishments on children in order to reinforce the system of rules and procedures they have developed. As Everett Hughes pointed out years ago, school people are the only persons outside the kinship group authorized to punish one's children (Hughes 1958). But parents can and do question not only the severity of punishments but may also challenge the fairness of the rules and even the values on which they are based. Disciplinary events, in short, can produce weakened adherence to the hegemony claimed by the school district. Principals discern that parental trust can be a delicate thing and that how they monitor the behavior of teachers, and of themselves, can reinforce or threaten that trust (Bryk and Schneider 2002).

Although suburban school districts make efforts to inform their communities about school activities and student progress through publications, web sites, and periodic reports from teachers, much of the information received by parents comes from the children themselves. Parents of young students may have difficulty knowing how much to credit, and in what particulars, their children's reports on school events. As far as teacher reports to parents are concerned, parents are at a disadvantage in that few of them possess as much knowledge as school people on what is "normal" for children of a given age. School personnel grade the child's performance and, over time, their decisions act to classify the child's abilities. There is a claim (implicit or explicit) to "know" the child in ways the parent does not. Although such commonplaces of school life are very familiar, we should not overlook how much they ask of families and the stake that families may have in how schools define their children. Schools routinely expect parents to extend trust and a readiness to comply that we find in few other organizational settings.

There is another aspect of the emotional relationship between families and elementary schools that is also unusual. In the normal course of events, children are likely to disclose aspects of family life that would not emerge at other times and in other places. For example, the compositions written by grade school children (and their talk) are unavoidably autobiographical, regularly disclosing family events and the like without the more sophisticated "editing" done by more mature students. Such communications can be seen by some families as threatening boundaries of privacy they wish preserved. Families are forced to trust teachers, counselors, and other individuals to respect such boundaries by exercising tact and discretion about family "revelations." (Some school people may fail in this regard, perhaps signaling to parents, possibly with the best of intentions, awareness of particular family issues.) Some families may have areas of strong sensitivity that produce anxiety regardless of the care school personnel take in observing privacy norms. Perceived "violations" of such norms (accurate or not) can produce hostility, perhaps shielded behind other complaints, with which the principal will have to cope. Particularly effective principals, one expects, will be adept at reading what may lie behind expressions of parental displeasure. (On displacement of complaints, see Roethlisberger and Dickson 1966.)

Schools, then, make demands of their clientele that are not found elsewhere, demands which some parents can find difficult to accept. Parents are asked to "go along" with decisions made by teachers and other staff members and, if displeased, to accept the principal's authority to act as "appellate court." Making these arrangements work falls largely to the principal; she or he is motivated to learn how to "cool out" dissatisfied parents, to deal with their discontent in ways that prevent further escalation and, if possible, enhance parental satisfaction (Clark 1960). (Recall the major part played by relationships with parents in the principals' discussion of "trouble.") The pressure on principals to build and sustain positive relationships with parents—their adult clientele—is a constant and influential force in their work lives.[1] Becoming and serving as an elementary principal in suburbia means learning to take relationships with the families of students very seriously.

WITHIN CONSTRAINED AUTHORITY

As we saw in our earlier discussion about principals and their authority vis-à-vis teachers, the management of schools differs sharply from what prevails in most hierarchical organizations. Principals are asked to establish leadership over faculties with a dearth of formal incentives and sanctions. Teachers who have yet to achieve tenure, of course, have stronger career reasons to seek the approval of the principal and pay close attention to his or her directives.[2] Principals are asked to establish their leadership over the tenured majority of faculty members without relying on substantial financial motivations or clear-cut power over their continued employment.

The peculiar circumstances that mark the authority system in these schools have resulted in beliefs and practices that emphasize the establishment of personal relationships with teachers, of earning their confidence over time, and exerting influence through consultation and the provision of needed support. If authority that is based largely on financial rewards and threats of dismissal can be described as "hard," these principals espouse views which, standing at the other end, we have called "soft." "Persuasion" and "cooperation" are relevant and appropriate terms, "command and obey" considerably less so.

There are strong indications that our principals considered gaining and holding leadership over their faculties a major challenge in their work. Influencing teachers was most often mentioned as the most difficult and important thing they had to learn to do as beginners. The leading source of mistakes they mentioned revolved around relationships with teachers and, in particular, not being sufficiently firm with teachers whose competence was questionable. Principals included teacher resistance to their initiatives among the difficulties they encountered in their work. Yet even when discussing such matters, it was unusual for them to connect those issues to a need for greater formal powers over teachers. Although responses to one question showed that some felt their authority was too limited, the majority of the principals (70%) denied that "tenure and contractual arrangements today make it almost impossible for principals to have real influence over faculty" (Q. 24A). All in all, most of these principals, despite the challenges they face in their relationships with teachers, did not press for increases in their formal authority. For example, it is interesting that when they compare their positions with those in private management, they complain very frequently about differences in income and infrequently about differences in managerial prerogatives. Why are they not more inclined to express concern about the weakness of their formal powers over teachers? I believe that two considerations are part of the explanation: the two-step career and the greater-than-apparent leverage available within the soft management approach.

The requirement that principals serve first as teachers means that they were exposed for several years to experiences teachers undergo and to the ethos they share. It seems likely that they felt the same resentment other teachers felt when principals, as they saw it, were excessively controlling or insufficiently supportive of their work in the classroom; teachers see at least some autonomy and support as essential in *their* management role, that is, handling groups of students. It is noteworthy that in talking about what they had to learn to become principals, they did not mention any sea change in their views on the need for teachers to have leeway in how they taught (table 2.6). Having worked as teachers made it possible for them to either internalize values and norms held by most teachers or, at the very least, to appreciate their significance.

The conservative aspects of reliance on soft management are evident in that principals agree, in essence, to working within the framework of teacher dispositions whose culture is itself marked by technical conservatism (Lortie 1975). The challenges they put forth are, apparently, relatively gentle; working within teacher-set agendas, for example, gives teachers considerable ability to use their working premises as the basis for discussion. But I believe that the processes involved in soft management can exert considerably more influence than those accustomed to stronger managerial authority may realize. I see two reasons for why this is so. The first revolves around the uncertainties teachers experience and their subsequent need for reassurance. The second stems from other vulnerabilities in teaching to which principals can respond in supportive ways. In short, principal leadership can emerge from effective use of the authority they do possess.

Along with granting favors that make life easier for the teachers who receive them, principals emphasized the importance of praise, recorded or ephemeral, in rewarding teachers (chap. 4). Praise is important, I believe, because psychic rewards play such a critical part in teaching, rewards based on the belief that one is effectively reaching students (Lortie 1975). But the endemic uncertainties built into judging the quality of one's teaching threaten the ability of teachers to get those satisfactions from their work. The situation is exacerbated by the relative isolation of teachers and the lack of feedback and reassurance from other adults and the limited opportunity to observe others and compare one's efforts with theirs.' Principals can fill that gap by giving teachers the sense that their work is efficacious; under such circumstances, praise from the principal can take on special powers of reassurance. One likely outcome is that teachers, enabled to feel better about themselves, become more receptive to the principal's ideas and initiatives.

Another basis for increased teacher responsiveness to principal leadership lies in the buffering and protective functions they can perform. Teachers in suburban schools are also vulnerable to parental displeasure; principals can buffer teachers, especially when parental behavior exceeds normal expectations. (Some principals develop explicit policies for processing parental complaints that produce more predictability, and less anxiety, for all involved.) Administrative functions based in central office (e.g., leaves, salary details, special assignments) may be complicated for teachers and difficult for them to handle without assistance. Principals can build allegiance by serving as their advocates in those dealings with higher authority. One way principals can "get close" to teachers, then, is to serve their interests and build trust over time by shielding them from parents and assisting them with central officials. Principals who "loan" their authority to teachers in such ways increase the interest that teachers have in the preservation of that authority: they develop a stake in its viability. A system of exchange relationships can be formed that protects and benefits teachers while strengthening the claims of the principal to their loyalty and compliance.

The authority principals possess may not permit them to express the authoritarian views one hears among managers in the private sector or allow them to act with the boldness those views imply. Those authority resources do not, based on what we see in our data, leave most principals feeling that they are handicapped by inadequate authority. It seems highly likely that, overall, their socialization and experience in the position have prepared them to live and act within the particular constraints found in their position.[3]

DIFFUSE GOALS: UNCERTAINTY NUMBER ONE

Organizations differ in the ways in which those who operate them go about deciding whether they are—or are not—effective. The goals of not-for-profit organizations (private and public) are somewhat more difficult to identify and to "prioritize." Americans have difficulties in identifying and ranking educational goals and additional difficulties in connecting them to the evaluation of managerial decisions and performance. One of the major problems lies in the tendency in our society to "pile on" functions for schools to undertake. Uncertainty in objectives that must be absorbed and dealt with one way or another is found throughout.[4]

Our concern here is with the ways in which goals figure in the work lives of the principals. How are principals affected by their multiplicity and vagueness?

We can gain some insight into principal thinking by examining the considerations they emphasized when talking about how those "above" them evaluated their performance. They stressed two sets of considerations, that they were held accountable, they said, for both student learning and the satisfaction of those around them. That duality ran throughout the data. We see that the district, however, absorbed some of the uncertainty in those goals when its officials insisted that they be accomplished within the context of district policies and procedures. In terms Simon introduced years ago, the value premises for their action were articulated by higher authority (1947). We are reminded that bureaucratic characteristics play a significant part in the day-to-day operations of school districts.

Principals, however, still have to guide their own behavior within those boundaries and monitor how well they are doing. How did our respondents tell whether the goals of student learning and producing satisfaction were realized? As we saw, they relied primarily on feedback from those with whom they work on a day-to-day basis—teachers, parents, central officials, and others (70%); a much smaller proportion (19%) said they observed and assessed the performance of those under their supervision (table 5.6). They oriented themselves primarily, then, on the basis of what other persons said. The result was that they found it difficult to be confident in their own evaluations of their performance; 86% said that was the case (table 5.6). They found it hard to trust what others said and what they themselves thought.

It seems clear that these principals had to tolerate considerable uncertainty about their efficacy as they went about doing their work. Relying on others to attest to the quality of their performance, in addition to its unreliability, tended to fuse the two major goals of advancing student learning and producing satisfactions. Principals were aware, one presumes, that those persons who were satisfied with their situation would be more likely to provide favorable feedback in general and discontented persons less so. When we recall that principals frequently helped teachers to absorb the uncertainties that arose in their work, the need to deal simultaneously with their own qualms must have been, at times, a source of considerable strain.

Finally, whatever uncertainties principals experienced about their efficacy were not, for most of them, offset by the career system. Doubts can, presumably, be stilled by promotion, a public announcement of competence. The rarity of its occurrence among the principals in our sample meant that few of these men and women received that kind of reassurance about their performance.

SHAKY PREMISES: UNCERTAINTY NUMBER TWO

As noted earlier, school work is marked by considerable uncertainty in the knowledge base on which its managers must work. Those involved in studying and teaching educational administration have long expressed serious concern about the state of knowledge in the field (Miskel 1990, Elmore 2007). How does uncertainty about cause and effect, to use Thompson's (1967) phrase, show up in the daily work of the elementary principal?

Teachers absorb the lion's share of what we might call "routine problems" in handling students. The more intractable problems, however, are shunted up the hierarchy and deposited in the principals' domain. Principals are expected to find effective ways to discipline errant students within the particulars of district policy and legal constraints and to resolve the more persistent and puzzling cases. Although teachers tend to turn primarily to their peers for technical advice, some take their instructional perplexities to the principal; principal responses, whether intended to do so or not, can be seen as authoritative statements that are binding on faculty members in general. Principals can, in short, find themselves setting precedents without planning to; once in place, they may have no choice but to live with them for at least some time to come.

It is not difficult to find examples of decisions that principals must make without being able to rely on clear-cut solutions. They must "sign off" on the placement of students in various kinds of special education programs—a complex process, which, in addition to presenting demanding intellectual challenges, requires them to deal with family members and staff who are likely to hold and express different viewpoints. When central office focuses on school totals in standardized tests, principals are pressed to figure out what teacher placements will work best for the school's results as a whole, a less-than-simple process. They may find it necessary to reallocate the amount of time to different subjects within the school day without having reliable knowledge about the effects of alternative allocations. They authorize the composition of classrooms and the internal distribution of students who learn at different rates (Barr and Dreeben 1983). It falls to principals to choose among new and inexperienced applicants for teaching positions and to decide who should be recommended for tenure. They are expected to do accurate evaluations of teacher performance despite the strong doubts many have about the reliability of the process itself.

There is irony in the fact that they express their gravest doubts about tasks that stand at the core of their responsibilities—the supervision and evaluation of teachers. There are some managerial responsibilities in schools that can be approached using computational strategies based on precisely stated objectives and familiar means. One can plan bus routes or calculate the nutritional value of school lunches, for example, in demonstrably efficient ways; such calculable types of decisions, however, are likely to appear marginal to many school administrators who are concerned with the complexities of instructional improvement, not what they term "administrivia." (The cognitive advantage found in some administrative tasks may present some principals a "temptation to focus on lesser problems," a possibility that would require observational data to ascertain how frequently it occurs. Don, in Wolcott's book, appeared to be inordinately preoccupied with differences between floor waxes [Wolcott 1973].)

There are other specifics that reflect points of uncertainty identified by Thompson (1967). For students to learn, they must be ready and willing to do so, an example of the "dynamism of objects" cited by Thompson. Although some experts argue that things work better when educators believe and act as if student motivation can be manipulated (it is, presumably, to some extent), assertions that the characteristics the students bring with them do not affect school outcomes are very rarely heard among educators. Nor are schools free from competition from other sources that affect what students do and learn. Families are universally recognized as major contributors; few deny the power of mass media (e.g., television and video games). In his monumental history of American education, Cremin has argued persuasively that schools are but one of our society's educative influences (Cremin 1970).

What consequences for principals flow from the lack of knowledge of cause and effect? How does it affect principals in their work?

One obvious consequence is that it reduces the self-confidence and sense of mastery experienced by elementary school principals. Their readiness to admit to problems in knowing how to deal with the core of their instructional responsibilities indicates a lack of arrogance, to put in mildly. As we have seen, they have been ready to rely on the observations of others and to seek feedback from others. Most appear reluctant to make firm judgments on important matters without such consultation; it plays a key part, in fact, in how they monitor their own performance.

There is an organizational result from the problem of knowledge and the readiness to consult and confer with others. We turn once more to Thompson, who attributes specific effects to the limited knowledge of cause-effect relationships. He has a series of propositions which say, in essence, that limited knowledge results in larger dominant coalitions and the representation of the core technology in the dominant coalition. Hence the numerous committees, made up of teachers, administrators, and community members, that we find in schools and school districts—structures underscoring public participation. We have commented that such reliance on public participation is seen to have political advantages; it is one way to cope with the emotional intensity of relationships with families. It also appears to be related to limitations in both pedagogical and managerial knowledge, including some with neither educational experience nor professional preparation, which seems to underscore the point.[5] (As Selznick's original work on cooptation made clear, inclusion of interested parties in decision-making slows the rate and scope of change [Selznick 1949].)

Finally, the difficulty of knowing when and how managerial actions affect instruction is probably the source of the delight principals express in engaging in teaching activities in the classroom. Whatever its longer-range uncertainties, teaching can allow one to feel directly engaged in the core purposes of school. Principals seeking out teaching activities might be seen as "reverting to the known" or "reverting to the direct." When they teach or assist others in teaching, principals relish the concreteness and directness of face-to-face, instructional contact with students. Such contact ranks high among the rewards they receive on a day-to-day basis.

CAREER PROCESSES

The theme of conservatism is supported by the career processes we have examined in our earlier chapters. We have observed that employers of principals and principals themselves have shown a strong preference for relying on what they believe worked well in the past. Employers select the persons they know best; principals, in the main, stay with familiar situations. We can recapitulate the career data from that point of view.

Careers in bureaucracies unfold in a sequence of positions of increasing prestige and authority: to succeed is to "move up" a pre-existing set of offices. In the bureaucracy of public schools, each change in job title requires specific types of experience and university study that can be transformed into "certificates." Formal regulation plays a major part in career movements in this field; that regulation moves the composition of the occupation toward cultural homogeneity, particularly within each state.

In general, the number of positions in each stratum (and, therefore, the number of potential vacancies) is based on demographic

considerations such as the birth rate and the age distribution of children in different communities. Their numbers are the critical factor
in how many people are employed in public schools. The ratio of
teachers and administrators to students in the suburbs we studied
is relatively similar from one community to another, although differences in district wealth seem to play some part. The dominance
of demographic considerations means that school officials can do
relatively little to expand the number and kinds of administrative
vacancies in their districts. (Although obtaining grants from governments and foundations is an exception, the duration and effects of
such income sources are normally temporary and limited.) School
districts differ sharply from businesses (and, at times, nonprofit organizations) in the lesser part played by enterprise in affecting managerial employment within the organization. The lesser significance
of that kind of enterprise may, in fact, have contributed to the limited enterprise we see in the career system. (We note some changes
taking place in this regard in the next chapter.)

The careers of principals in our sample followed a distinct
pattern. First, initial geographic mobility into the suburbs was
important because few principals were born and grew up there.
Two-thirds (65%), however, began their careers as teachers in suburbia. Migration to suburban districts is perhaps the single most
important type of enterprise shown by the principals in our sample. Second, promotion to principal took place primarily (68%)
within the same district in which respondents taught or served as
low-ranking administrators. There is a common pattern exhibited
in these appointments as employers and principals both exercised
caution, preferring individuals and locations already well known to
them. (In 1980, those chosen were primarily white men, particularly in the higher income districts.)

Seventy-seven percent of principals remained in the same district in which they were initially appointed principal. The main
pattern was to stay put, with relatively few seeking to improve
their situation by moving to other districts; the latter, a minority,
were ready to take the risks (tenure and seniority loss) involved
in changing districts (Crow 1985). A small number, primarily during their thirties, moved up to higher-ranked positions in new districts. If we define enterprise in terms of such risk-taking, it was

clearly a minor rather than major theme in these data. Stability dominated.

Promotion to principal was regulated in informal as well as formal ways. The modal pattern was to receive assistance from persons of higher rank, either by being sponsored internally or by getting help in finding a position elsewhere; relatively few of the principals we studied got their positions through aggressive searches or other strictly personal efforts. Speaking generally, we can say that "insidership" was a major factor in promotion to principal; informal processes such as favoring persons with suburban experience and direct help from school administrators augmented certification requirements in localizing the career system.

To the extent that we can say that these career patterns expressed the values of those running suburban school districts, the tilt was toward maintaining the organizational status quo rather than looking for opportunities for change; there was little discernible effort to change schools by seeking out different kinds of choices. Over and over again, those governing these organizations chose to hire those already familiar to them, clearly preferring the comfort of the known to the potential discomfort of the unknown.

Decisions made by principals and district officials have accumulated over years to create and maintain a social system that lacks the dynamism associated with new kinds of people doing new kinds of things. If the subculture of principals displays a readiness to accept the status quo rather than trying to reshape it in novel ways, that theme reflects processes that result in some persons rather than others being prepared in the universities and selected for the occupation. It may well be true that members of the American public at large have generally shown scant interest in seeing major changes in the public schools. To the extent that is true, they have participated in building and sustaining a work system that reflects their preferences. Specifically, the recruitment of persons to, and placement in, elementary school principalships have displayed little impulse toward fostering change.

I have characterized the culture of elementary principals in suburbia as leaning toward the ways of the past rather than the search for beneficial change. The situation today, as we shall see in the next chapter, is replete with challenges from actual and potential changes in the context and workings of public schools. Some ideas on various outcomes that might result from the interaction of those challenges and the work life of elementary principals are presented. Serious collisions between the ways of the past and the demands of the future may take place. As I hope I make clear, learning what really happens in the years ahead will require serious and sustained inquiry.

An Uncertain Future

> Educational methods run through fashions. Fads in methods of
> teaching arise, are advocated with great emphasis, have their
> run, decline and disappear.
> —Sumner 1906, p. 131.

Change can be a trying topic in the study of public education. As
Sumner noted a century ago, in education there is always something new (or thought to be new) in the air—something novel
that may ultimately vanish or become a relatively minor part
of the scene. As we saw in chapter 1, there are components of
public schools today with origins in colonial America while major changes (e.g., the emergence of an administrative structure)
developed over several decades in the nineteenth and early twentieth centuries; in structural terms, education has changed at a
glacial pace. Projected changes occur against this background of
structural stability, suggesting that, in any given period, there will
be less rather than more change in school districts and schools.
Schools are enacted institutions that have accumulated the moss
of legal decisions and traditions over many decades—the past be-
queaths an inertial cast to the entire field. (For example, we have
noted a conservative tilt in the culture of elementary principals.)
Yet despite the slow pace, change of some kind is inevitable and
will eventually become part of the system. The intellectual challenge is to study trends that may prove lasting and to conduct

sensitive inquiry as they unfold; this chapter is an effort to contribute to that formidable task.

Our examination will include two questions. First, what has
happened since the Chicago and Iowa data (1980 and 1988) and the
national findings (1998) were produced? Second, what changes are
likely to occur in the future? Some information on the first question is available in a brief survey of internet sites in the 59 suburban districts in our sample. Consideration of the second question
is based on trends found in a variety of studies including ours. Any
strong predictions on what aspects of the current scene are likely
to vanish, remain as they are, or expand are, of course, likely to
miss the mark. I believe, however, that thinking seriously about
alternative futures is valuable, not only to alert policymakers to
alternatives but to stimulate relevant research; it can help us decide
what to watch for as events unfold.

The chapter is divided into three sections. After some introduc-
tory comments reviewing change and stability since 1980, the first
major section examines one of two important changes—the shift
in gender composition. The second section examines other recent
trends—differentiated programs, the expanded use of computers,
and greater competition for students—and their potential effects
on the management of elementary schools in the future. The
chapter ends with an exploration of high stakes, mandated testing
and its potential effects on schools and principals. Current trends
do not all point in the same direction; one can, therefore, envisage
somewhat different futures for this managerial position.

INTRODUCTORY COMMENTS ON CHANGE AND STABILITY

Two special features of the subculture reviewed in chapter 8 have
undergone visible changes since the 1980s—the career system (specifically, gender) and the diffuse nature of educational goals. The
subordination and public prominence continue. The fishbowl, constrained authority, an emotionally charged setting, and technical
uncertainty have apparently undergone only minor changes. We
will take a quick look at the latter before turning to changes that
are more pronounced.

It is difficult to find any clear evidence of significant change in five of the cultural themes. In regard to the subordinate position of the principal, one anonymous reader has suggested that if anything, heavy emphasis on testing has increased central office domination and, subsequently, the subordination of the principal—an hypothesis well worth testing. I believe that the work of suburban principals has become more rather than less visible and exposed (the fishbowl) in the last few years; for example, test results and other kinds of local school information have become increasingly available with the spread of district web sites. There is no indication that parents or other community members have become less interested in what happens in the schools. The media, local and national, continue to draw attention to what they perceive as problems in the schools. (My impression is that the important part played by schooling in the distribution of life chances has received increased media attention in recent years.) Nor have we seen widespread changes in the power position of teachers in suburban schools or a significant increase in the authority of the principal; that relationship, in addition to being embedded in tradition and law, continues to be constrained by processes of collective bargaining between districts and teachers.

The conditions that produce an emotionally charged relationship with adult clients prevail today as they have for many decades. In fact, as new types of options in schooling have emerged, the sense of entitlement among parents has probably risen and increased their readiness to challenge school officials. As far as technical uncertainty is concerned, educational research has added to the knowledge base for school administrators, but I am unaware of any notable break-throughs that have changed the daily decision-making of principals. What has happened, it seems, is that the choices available for consideration by principals and school districts have been augmented by various kinds of innovations and research findings (Biddle and Saha 2002). It is entirely possible, of course, that one or more of those innovations (or other ideas under development today) will prove to be highly significant in the future.

Most of the characteristics we identified as basic to the culture of the principalship have not changed in any significant way. That persistence suggests that the culture continues much as it has in the past. We turn now, however, to areas in which change is taking place. Research is obviously needed to determine in what ways, if any, these changes are altering, or will alter, the culture of the occupation.

CHANGES IN GENDER COMPOSITION

The workings and outcomes of the career system have changed markedly since the 1980s. The social composition of the occupation in the suburbs we studied has shifted from primarily male to primarily female. In 1980, women were a minority in the principalship in those suburbs—15% in the Chicago suburban sample and 10% in the Iowa sample. A recent survey using the Internet indicates that the percentage of women principals in suburban schools around Chicago is now well over 60%. National data from the late years of the twentieth century pointed to a similar but less dramatic shift.[1]

The sharp increase in women elementary principals raises questions about several aspects of the occupation. First, it suggests changes in how persons enter the position. For example, has the increase resulted from limits on the superintendent's ability to sponsor persons for the position? For example, there has been widespread discussion favoring broadening the ways in which principals are selected, such as using ad hoc committees that include community members and teachers along with board members (U.S. Office of Educational Research and Improvement Services 1987). Have such broader approaches been adopted in suburbs and favored hiring more women? Once adopted, have they affected decisions in other ways; for example, do recent choices reflect the same insistence on prior experience in suburban settings that is evident in our data?

Where ad hoc committees have not been used, have superintendents and school boards, faced with more female applicants with certification credentials, decided that past practices that favored men were no longer acceptable?[2] What happens today to practices of like hiring like when women move up and become superintendents? Are they less likely to favor persons of the same gender than their male predecessors? If sponsorship in general plays a less central role in hiring principals, do neophyte principals today receive less support from central officials who, having played a less critical role in their selection, have a smaller stake in their success? The importance of sponsorship in the past becomes more obvious when we consider its possible replacement; changes in that one component of the career system may reverberate to affect other parts of the career system and the day-to-day operations of school districts.

It will take time for recently appointed women to make the career choices that will show how much the changed gender balance affects other aspects of the career system. If women are similar to the men in our study in preferring, initially, to make low-risk decisions and do not, subsequently, make more moves across district lines, two aspects of that system—its stability and its localism—will probably persist. (In that case, careers will continue to dampen rather than stimulate the flow of new ideas across district lines.)

Estimating ways in which gender change will affect other aspects of the occupation is difficult; one cannot assume, for example, that differences in orientation between the genders will continue once women have achieved numerical parity or dominance. For example, as the gap closes between the length of time men and women teach before being appointed to the principalship, the greater engagement in instructional matters among female principals that prevailed in the past (many were initially promoted to the principalship after instructional supervision positions in central office as well as after long experience in elementary teaching) will probably decrease as their career lines and work socialization approximate those experienced by men (Meskin 1981).

Although it is difficult to project organizational changes that will result from the shift to women as modal members of the occupation, a few speculations may be suggestive for future research. One possible effect lies in the relationship of principals and teachers. Women teachers in the past have not, to any significant degree, aimed to move up the hierarchy. Since most elementary teachers were (and continue to be) women, facilitating promotion was not an important incentive available to principals. The shift to more women principals, however, indicates that more women teachers have already and will, we expect, continue to be interested in being promoted to principal. If so, it will augment the material incentives available to principals and buttress their authority with ambitious members of the faculty.

Another possible effect of gender change is economic. To what extent, if any, will women principals (particularly those who are married) continue to express less concern than men about the size of their salaries? (See chap. 7.) Will women be as likely as their male colleagues to compare their incomes unfavorably with private sector managers? If not, will they express more satisfaction with their career choices? The societal context is relevant here: it may be that the relationship between gender and the breadwinner role will change as more and more women in our society bring substantial earnings to their families or are the sole breadwinners. If so, gender differences in regard to money may decline.

Recent years have seen the emergence of a feminist conception of how organizations should operate—a conception that has been put into operation in some organizations (Alter 2007). In those elementary school districts where women occupy the majority of administrative positions, some superintendents and principals may try to move their districts toward more "democratic" and less bureaucratic norms than has been the case under male dominance. As Alter puts it, "the distinctive characteristic of feminist organizations is that they are collectives, whereby all members have equal voice in the decisions of the organization, and the organization proceeds only after consensus is reached." The issue is, of course, how much change of that kind can take place given the formal powers of school boards and the manifold controls from state and federal governments; one might watch, however, for indications that relationships between central office and school personnel are moving toward a less hierarchical style of operation when both levels are staffed by women.

The change in the principalship to an occupation numerically dominated by women will undoubtedly have consequences for the occupation and for school organization. At this point, however, major changes in the structure of school districts will probably not be among them; to date, the increased upward mobility of women in professions and corporations does not appear to have produced large-scale changes in their social systems. Early predictions about the likely effects of women's liberation in the 1960s included the prediction that employer regimes would become more flexible and less demanding; my impression is that the former has taken place more often than the latter. It is true, of course, that the expansion of opportunities for women remains—in historical terms—relatively recent; continuing research is clearly needed on how shifts in gender affect organizational operations in general and schools in particular.

PROGRAMMATIC, TECHNOLOGICAL, AND COMPETITIVE TRENDS

When we examine recent events that have taken place in schools, additional trends, if they continue to develop, appear likely to have substantial effects on the management of school districts and schools. Those effects may, by changing managerial tasks, require different knowledge and abilities from principals. We will look at several trends—program differentiation, greater reliance on computers, and the changed competitive environment of public schools—from that point of view. Such projections are obviously speculative but, I believe, have at least two major advantages in that they can signal potentially useful lines of inquiry to research scholars and alert those preparing school administrators to new issues and demands their students may confront in practice.[3]

Program Individualization

The historic pattern for organizing instruction in grade schools is, as the term implies, rooted in the grades through which students move annually. The age of the student is usually correlated with the grade because entry into school systems is usually based on reaching a stipulated age. In the language of organizational analysis, the students are "batched" and treated to standardized curricula as they move through the various grades (Woodward 1965). In later years, they have choices in what courses they can take, a situation which is rare up to and including grade 6.

The "technology" of instruction based on this kind of batching has been challenged somewhat in recent years by developments in the field of special education. This was not initially the case as students designated as "special" were separated into their own groups. More recently, however, there has been considerable movement toward including special education students in "regular" classrooms for at least part of the time they spend in school. The placement and programs of such students have revolved around the IEP (individualized educational program) developed in "staffings" (conferences) attended by designated school personnel and chaired (in the states with which the author is familiar) by the principal. Parents are also involved. Any particular program becomes official only after the principal has "signed off" in approval.

Several trends are increasing the scope and significance of special education. There is the tendency, for example, for the list of special designations to increase as society discovers (apparently) new problems. Categories in learning deficiencies become refined by psychologists and lead to new subspecialties taught in universities. Demands for higher performance from students built into state tests may produce larger numbers who fail, which, in turn, may increase the population of special education students. It seems to be a sector in schools which keeps expanding.

Whether it continues to expand or not, ideas and practices in special education that are already present may have broader effects on how schools are organized. Parents of students who are not categorized as "special" may question the additional assistance received by students who are so classified and demand more for their children. In fact, programs for especially talented or creative children are not required under the legislation that mandates special education; it is an instance where parental demands have emulated the example set by special education. It is conceivable that elementary education will incorporate increasing elements of the "intensive" technology of which the hospital is a crucial example— treatment is based on the condition of the patient (Thompson 1967). Each patient undergoes a particular and specific program of medical and/or surgical care. What aspects of special education may prove to be important when and if elementary schools move in that direction?

One characteristic of special education that seems potentially significant in more general ways is the idea of the individualized education program. The logic of that approach places the individual child in the foreground and conceptualizes the school as an arena of potentially valuable learning experiences. One could project that logic into a dizzying array of possible arrangements involving various combinations of technological, organizational, and human resources both inside a conventional schoolhouse and outside it in the community at large. Knowing that schools do not change all that rapidly, however, we might do better to speculate on the basis of actualities that are already present. Let us use current practices in special education, therefore, as existing instances of individualization in elementary education and as potential models for its further development. We will concentrate on their likely effects on the principalship.

The principal plays a significant role in the development of the plan for each special education student. Although other staff members (normally specialists are included) may contribute much, the principal's responsibility is manifest in the signature attesting to his or her approval. There are three implications of that responsibility that I wish to examine.

First, participation in this way expands one's instructional responsibilities. Central officials, worried about legal risks, tend to focus their attention on and monitor compliance with required procedures, leaving substantive matters primarily to those closest to those involved. To the degree that special education approaches expand their influence, therefore, principals will probably shape a larger part of the instruction experienced by their students. (The same will apply, of course, if individualization increases in other ways as well as in special education.) This produces a larger terrain in which principals, rather than central officials, exercise instructional leadership.

The second implication of the principal's involvement with special education students is that it expands the area in which she or he makes decisions under conditions of uncertainty. Although there is growing knowledge and experience in the field of special education and its subspecialties, practitioners are often required to rely on trial and error. The sheer presence of uncertainty in making such public and consequential decisions adds to the potential for stress built into the principal's work.[4]

The third implication of the principal's major role in staffing for individualized instruction is also psychological in nature. A leadership role in staffing individual children increases the principal's personal involvement in the fate of students. That involvement can stimulate more identification with particular children and emotional engagement with them. Feelings of joy or sadness will arise as events unfold and decisions either work to help the child or not; there is an increase in what we might call the "emotional load" of the principal's work.

Although the extent to which individualization will increase in the future is not clear, we assume that special education programs are here to stay. This in itself creates a managerial challenge that is easily overlooked when we reflect on the work of the principal. The logic of individualized instruction that supports special education programming does not always rest comfortably alongside the logic of conventional student batching. The latter focuses on programs that yield the best results with groups of students, results increasingly assessed through test results. One thinks about them in terms of standard operating procedures and equality in resource distribution. Neither standardization nor equality in distribution are central to individualization because its emphasis is on which particular activities are best for a particular child at a particular time and place. As an example of intensive technology, judgments made in special education press against bureaucratic procedures and logic. It falls to the principal to cope with problems that arise when these divergent approaches collide and to find the best balance between special and regular programs that can be worked out.

Finally, two somewhat opposing sets of demands are being made on principals at the same time. While being asked to focus more effectively on the problems of the individual student, they are also being asked to increase the collective performance of school groups on mandated tests, a topic we will consider below. That is a high and possibly unrealistic challenge; should consideration be given to providing them with more assistance from persons with expertise in these different demands? Given the importance of close observation in clinical decisions, should such persons be located at the school level rather than central office?

Computers

As in the case of other new approaches to teaching, computers have been hailed as potentially revolutionary. Some say that such predictions remind them of the initially high expectations for television followed by later reports that "school basements are filled with TV sets." Cuban has pointed out, with considerable persuasiveness, that technological innovations have often had superficial rather than deep effects; wisdom suggests that one should avoid making rash predictions about their likely effects (Cuban 2001). But when we reflect on the widespread changes that computers have brought about in society at large, it is difficult to discount the potential they have for changing schooling.

Broad predictions about the development of computerized instruction, however, are beyond the scope of this study. I wish to limit myself to how the principal's position might be affected by increased reliance on computers and its possible effects on how they, and perhaps others, conceptualize school administration. I will also speculate about one specific way in which computer technology might develop.

Computers had already added to the instructional responsibilities of the suburban principals during the 1980s. For example, some were developing "learning centers" equipped with computers and staffed by teachers familiar with their use. A national report (NAESP 1988) revealed that principals were anxious then about their lack of knowledge about computers and some were critical of their districts for not providing them with more training in using them for instruction.

What has happened in the past is often useful in thinking about future possibilities. Important in this regard is McGee's comprehensive study of the contribution made by principals in the introduction and development of computer-assisted instruction in the suburbs around Chicago (McGee 1985). Two of the findings are particularly relevant here. The first is that there was considerable variation in the rate and spread of computer usage in the suburban school districts in the random sample drawn by McGee. The second finding is that the best explanation for those differences turned out to be managerial actions taken by individual principals. Management at the school level was the strategic component in the development of this innovation; its adoption and potential effectiveness hinged on the principal solving problems of coordination, scheduling, and other managerial issues. Instructional efficacy, the possibility of which required that students make substantial use of computers, hinged on the quality and quantity of principal action. Assuming that the findings will prove relevant in other settings, the vital contribution of principals in this domain will probably become more visible in the years ahead.

It is obvious that any extensive change in a school's program requires managerial involvement; it may be less obvious, however, that the managerial action that matters most in instruction with computers takes place at the local school site. Its location there adds visibility and credibility to the principal as the official who advances instruction by planning and managing computerized instruction; at the same time, reliance on centrally devised plans declines. In short, effective programs based on the use of computers highlight the importance of the instructional decisions made and actions carried out by principals.

We can hypothesize that in addition to underscoring the important role of principals in computer-related instruction, the significance of managerial actions in conducting effective programs of computer-assisted instruction will affect perceptions about the relevance of managerial processes in general, perceptual changes which, in turn, will increase their standing within school administration. As their significance to instruction becomes increasingly clear, principals may define fewer managerial tasks as mere "administrivia." Although the ability to relate to teachers and to perceive student needs remain vital, more than purely interpersonal abilities are involved in managing technology. Specifically managerial kinds of cognition and action are also critical—skills in planning, identifying effective sequences of training and assignment, coordination of events through time, deployment of appropriate resources, attention to procedures for follow-up and reinforcement, and the like all come into play. These are not minor clerical tasks. They are essentials in the conduct of instruction that effectively integrate the use of computers and the human agency of staff members.

There are properties of computer-assisted instruction that raise broad questions about educational values in our society, which, one assumes, will be dealt with in the groups and institutions making educational policy. One such issue arises from differences among innovations, which vary in the extent to which individual students can use them "on their own" and pace their own progress. Computers with that capacity allow students to move ahead at different (sometimes very different) rates of progress, thus allowing and even encouraging differentiation in what is learned. School board members and state officials (and, these days, federal functionaries) will make decisions on how much they will foster or restrict such differentiation.

The dominant structures in place today exercise considerable constraint on such differentiation. For example, grade structures that are linked to the age of students have persisted over many decades, a persistence that suggests strong resistance to allowing students to move at other than a preordained pace though a bounded curriculum. The entire structure is reinforced by a system of related supports, supports that include largely similar curricula, widely used textbooks, an increasingly influential testing regime, and, of course, admission requirements in higher education.

Will those governing schools choose to allow computers to advance differentiation in what students learn? Discovering how to operate elementary schools without the established grade format (and without related categorical procedures) would require the creation of new, flexible, and challenging arrangements at the local and district level—organizational construction of a high order of intellectual and political demand. One wonders: how much differentiation in student learning is American society ready to seek or tolerate? How rigid are the established forms used to classify and process students? Would greater differentiation be defined as a threat to equality?

It is possible, though far from a sure thing, that decisions could be made to favor considerably more differentiation. Changes of that nature, with associated changes in teaching and learning, could stimulate new ways to organize schools. To make strongly differentiated programs work, sophisticated and novel allocations of teacher and student time would be required. Expanded use of computers would press against conventions of grading and the progression of students at a predetermined rate, away from what some advocates of flexibility call "lock-step" movement. (Could the largely similar "lecturing" format that Goodlad [1984] found in his national survey of classrooms gradually give way to new approaches?) There is, I believe, potential for enormous change in instruction using modern technology *if and when* those who govern schools decide to use it to its maximum capacity to permit students to learn at decidedly different rates with decidedly different outcomes. (I remain skeptical, however, that such will happen.)

Competition

By 1998 the increases in competition facing public elementary schools were sufficiently large to attract the attention of their national organization (NAESP 1998). Public schools had, of course, encountered competition from religious and private secular schools for many decades. The last years of the twentieth century and the early years of the twenty-first, however, have seen sharp growth in sources of competition, including home schooling, "Christian" schools, not-for-profit charter schools, and for-profit voucher-based businesses. In some locales, public schools, working under new arrangements for choice within districts, began to compete with each other. The scale of competition for students in elementary education has obviously changed.

That competition has affected the work of many public school principals is evident in the NAESP 1998 study. Doud and Keller, its authors, asked respondents in a question listing eleven different areas of responsibility to say whether their involvement had increased, decreased, or stayed the same in each area over the previous three years. The choice marked by the greatest change was "Marketing/ Politics, etc., to Generate Support for School and Education"; 70% said their involvement had increased, 28.7% said there was no change, and 1.3% said it decreased. The authors speculated that "the pressures generated by school choice and dwindling financial support for public education" may be partial explanations for that finding. ("Dwindling financial support" received no further mention or documentation in the report.) Whether factors other than increased competition figured in the responses, it is clear that most principals see themselves under increasing pressure to protect and advance the interests of their schools. Fewer principals can count on the mandatory and automatic assignment of students based on geographic location to provide them with a clientele; the position today requires an increasingly proactive stance from more and more of those who occupy it.

Assuming that competition for students is not going to decrease and may well increase in the years ahead, more suburban principals (as well as elsewhere) will be engaged in "marketing," broadly defined. They will pay closer attention to gauging the preferences of local families and devising ways to meet them. Strategies will presumably be shaped by the kind of competition they face; in larger suburban districts offering internal choices, for example, they will be involved not only in creating desirable images for their schools but will try to influence policies and practices that affect competition, such as the location and size of school boundaries, admission criteria, how racial categories are defined and implemented, and the like. (They will probably have an eye on the potential performance of students in state and other tests.) Principals in districts confronting charter or for-profit schools may match the competition with promotional activities such as attractive brochures and web sites not unlike those produced by advertising agencies for business firms and, increasingly, private colleges. Where enterprise previously played a lesser role in principal careers, the qualities involved (e.g., assertiveness, taking risks) will probably figure more prominently in the future as those hiring principals for public elementary schools become increasingly interested in the entrepreneurial potential of the candidates. Success in competitive situations may become more important, and some may be ready to hire (presumably certified) persons with experience in charter and for-profit schools. We may, in short, see a shift away from the high stability observed in our data to somewhat greater dynamism in the career system of elementary principals. Career factors may become less important in sustaining cultural conservatism.

Increasing internal competition between schools in the same district is likely to affect relationships within the district; one is the quality of collegial relationships among principals. The principals in our sample, when asked about the kinds of help they received from others, gave interesting answers when talking about their peers (Q. 26A–C). While they sought policy and overall direction from central officials and information about students from teachers, the kinds of help they wanted from other principals were less restricted and stretched across a wide range of possible topics. They defined good colleagues, moreover, as persons who were willing to share their ideas, to help whenever asked. (Sometimes collaboration extended to agreeing how they would, acting jointly, choose to define and implement initiatives from central officials, asserting peer solidarity in the face of central authority.) Might reduced consultation and trust among principals reduce their effectiveness?

More internal competition for students among schools could result in less cooperation among principals and reduce the emotional support they provide for each other. Increased social distance among principals could also slow the diffusion of new ideas. Such effects are likely to depend on the extent to which different schools do in fact compete for the same students; schools might conceivably become differentiated enough that each occupies a distinct niche within the population of potential students. That degree of school specialization could, of course, reduce rather than increase interpersonal competition among principals.

Some competitors to public schools offer potential clients the image of a less bureaucratic, more responsive, and accessible organization taking care of their children; charter schools, for example, proffer those presumed advantages. Such circumstances might lead districts to allow individual schools greater flexibility to meet such competition. They may, in fact, allow and even encourage schools to occupy different niches to challenge the competition, necessarily weakening central controls over curriculum and other areas.[5]

It seems that when we engage in such speculation, one of the outcomes is the emergence of new and complex demands on those who manage schools. Following Thompson, it might be useful to think in terms of administrative processes in general and make fewer assumptions about the future based on the current division of managerial labor (Thompson 1967).[6]

Finally, a word about consequences and complications that could arise if competition increases decentralization to the school level. A larger decision load would probably influence principals to share more of those decisions with teachers; if local decisions become more consequential (e.g., involve significant proportions of the school budget), teachers may well show greater interest in school-wide affairs. (That interest was evident in four Chicago schools I studied during the period that featured decentralization including greater discretion in the school budget.) One recalls, however, that the way in which teaching work is structured places important limitations on the time availability of teachers to work on organizational issues. Increased engagement in school affairs by a limited number of teachers may produce a subgroup whose members acquire more experience and become something of an internal "political" cadre.

One of the requirements faced by schools in the public sector is the need to provide for the review and legitimation of their actions by public representatives. If autonomy is sought from the authority system of the school district, one would expect arrangements to be made for local community members (presumably including parents) to take on such responsibilities.

Moving toward greater internal school autonomy would require solution of institution building challenges. First, acceptable ways to divide responsibility for surveillance of a single unit when it is financially dependent on another (i.e., the school depending on taxes collected by the district) would have to be worked out. This is a current issue in the charter school movement. Second, there is the need to recruit volunteers to assume governance responsibility and to devote sufficient time at each school; overall, decentralization will require a large increase in the number of citizens willing to be highly involved in local school governance. New ways to specify the responsibilities of district board members in a decentralized system are also needed because they are normally reluctant to accept responsibility for the actions of subordinates over whom they have no direct authority. Can exceptions from liability, for example, be formulated to protect (and facilitate recruitment of) citizens to serve at the central board level in a truly decentralized district format?

A Common Theme

Although there are potentially different lines of development within each of the trends we have reviewed, one important characteristic is found in each trend, including the trends we did not explore in detail, more heterogeneity in the community and in the division of labor. That characteristic is the need for principals to cope with increasing complexity of different kinds. Program individualization presses the principal deeper into instructional decision-making about individual students and the uncertainties that prevail there. Greater use of computers for instruction intensifies the managerial responsibilities of the principal, binding managerial decisions more closely to the effectiveness of the instructional program. Competition among schools requires the principal to present the school in the most favorable light and to attract students who might otherwise go elsewhere, calling for qualities of personal enterprise which have not been prominent in the past. An increasingly heterogeneous context expands the need to develop and exercise (already important) diplomatic skills both inside and around the school. A more refined division of labor increases similar complexities in the supervision of staff.

I know of no way to be sure which of these trends will become more important and which will not. But the possibility seems high that at least one, and perhaps more, will persist and require significant changes in school management and the demands it makes on those in the principal's office. Each is likely to increase the complexity of those demands in one way or another—intellectually, emotionally, and/or in terms of interactional abilities. That seems evident even before we turn, as we will next, to developments that are already complicating the work of principals—the advent of high-stakes testing.

HIGH-STAKES TESTING

The term "high-stakes testing" has been applied in recent years to the widespread and consequential standardized tests fostered by states and the federal government. That term implies a major change in the significance of such tests, not only in their broadened use but in the part they play in warranting state and federal intervention in local district school operations (Conley 2003). People who run schools today (of necessity) pay considerably more attention to standardized test scores than they did in the 1980s. The general tendency of suburban students (with some exceptions) to have higher scores means that more serious and dramatic consequences such as external intervention are less likely to occur in suburban schools. That is not to say, however, that they do not have important effects in suburbia as well—they can and do.

The focus of this chapter is on possible changes in the elementary school principalship. Overall school operations are already influenced and could be altered significantly in the future as state and federal governments exercise and, quite possibly, increase various kinds of pressure on school districts. A full exploration of those possibilities lies beyond the purview of this book; readers interested in them are advised to look to other sources for relevant views and information (Conley 2003, House 1998). The focus here is on the likely effects of mandatory testing on the statement and implementation of instructional goals. Although there is less than full agreement about the extent to which curricula have been affected by high-stakes testing, I expect that Campbell's law pointing to the powerful effects of reliance on a single quantitative measure will prove to be correct. the attention of teachers and administrators will be influenced by what is tested and what is not and the specific demands that the relevant tests make (Nichols and Berliner 2007).

The hypothesis I wish to present states that there are two distinct ways in which high-stakes testing affects the work of principals. On the one hand, increased emphasis on achievement testing can *reduce* uncertainty about educational goals. On the other, it can *increase* uncertainty in other aspects of school management, in particular, the conduct of vital relationships. These mixed outcomes offer significant opportunities for research with significant implications for policy. We will explore this terrain by identifying possible uncertainties on both sides—effects on goal specificity and effects on achieving harmony in key relationships.

Statements about educational goals in the United States have tended to consist of long lists of desirable outcomes. Those outcomes, usually stated in general and abstract terms, are so diffuse that they are difficult to use as working criteria in assessing the success or failure of educational programs; furthermore, statements of priority are usually absent. Their range is enormous, encompassing personal, social, economic, political, and moral spheres. The generality leaves room for a variety of evaluative judgments, a variety that allows for the expression of different interests and multiple perspectives by diverse individuals and groups.

Heavy reliance on standardized tests in order to evaluate district and school performance is different. It replaces vagueness with specificity, focuses attention on a reduced number of goals, and provides what supporters of testing consider to be objective measures for what are otherwise subjective and imprecise judgments. The measurements permit quantitative comparisons between schools and school districts and among different parts of those institutions. The central concern is with the cognitive goals that proponents believe are accurately measured by pencil and paper tests. There are, of course, other kinds of goals that are not normally evaluated using such, including goals that center on physical, social, and emotional maturation. They are not included in the high-stakes testing regime.

The use of standardized testing to characterize educational effectiveness can reduce uncertainty about goals for school authorities. It becomes possible to identify areas of success and failure in meeting specified objectives in those subjects in which students are tested. The curricula and persons involved can be pinpointed in efforts to improve performance. One presumes that the definition of "student learning" by principals becomes less personal and variegated when testing dominates assessments. Numbers and percentages reinforce attention to specific cognitive goals and the extent to which the school as a whole, and subgroups within it, achieve them. Unless such information is regularly supplemented by other kinds of evaluative procedures, the test results can become the "working goals" of the schools.

There may be many ways in which the reduction of goal uncertainty brought about by high-stakes testing can be experienced and, in some respects, welcomed by principals. I will mention a few here, essentially for illustrative purposes.

The sources of the testing regime are important. That they originate in state and federal governments can serve useful purposes for principals, depending on how members of their constituencies react. That state and federal authority lies behind the tests will be important to some citizens as a source of legitimation, buttressing their acceptability. When that is the case, the amount of "consensus work" required of the principal declines as he or she can point to the authority (and special expertise) that supports the testing. Any added legitimacy to school activities reduces potential conflict, a decided advantage in the eyes of most principals. On the other hand, individuals around the principal may be unimpressed by the origins of the testing, perhaps even objecting to attendant losses in local district and/or school autonomy. But even in those instances, principals can deflect criticism by pointing to "outside" influences which, given the law, must be obeyed.

Relying on test results as an indicator of school effectiveness is intellectually useful for principals; as in educational research, the results provide a "dependent variable" to use in evaluating alternative policies and practices. Making decisions is facilitated when one can support them with data; having such data in hand also makes them considerably easier to defend. Gathering data and relating them to test scores are not, of course, without costs in time and effort. But, as we have seen in American schools where Japanese conceptions of "quality management" have been adopted, there are men and women in the principalship who are ready to do that kind of inquiry and decision-making. There is another potential advantage. To the extent that such inquiry spreads throughout schools in general, principals will be able to connect their own practices with results based on testing that they encounter in the professional literature and at professional meetings.

We have observed the difficulties principals experience in evaluating the quality of their faculty members. The evaluation of beginners being considered for tenure is a case in point. Although they may claim they are not using test results to evaluate individual teachers, one is entitled, I think, to considerable skepticism about such denials when superintendents and school boards are faced with decisions about granting lifetime tenure to staff members. Test results provide those who govern the school district with data independent of the principal's observations, reducing, at least to some extent, a responsibility which, handled alone, can be emotionally taxing for principals.

A final example. Relying on test results as indicators of student learning reduces the dependence of principals on feedback from teachers and parents and even central officials. The desirability of freedom from those observations depends, of course, on results from the tests. Although poor results are clearly undesirable, most outcomes will probably move toward a somewhat "average" center, which includes strong as well as weak results. When that occurs, the tests can offset the damage done by those whose criticisms are extreme. That can include, for example, parents, perhaps few in number yet nonetheless loud, who are never satisfied with what they see in the school.

Turning to the less positive side for principals, high stakes testing can produce considerable tension and discomfort in their relationships with the adults who matter so much in their daily work—teachers and parents.

One of the ways in which this can happen revolves around the different meanings that test results can have for different groups in the school district. Board members may see test results differently from those who work in schools or are the parents of the students. Although board members and superintendents are held accountable for overall district performance, they are not "on the spot" to the same extent as principals and teachers whose instructional units are measured and compared. In fact, the ways in which apex members will work to improve the overall standing of the district will probably include singling out and concentrating on those units whose scores hold down the average. The constituents of board members include persons in the community who are not parents along with those who are; many will be influenced by the emphasis the media place on test scores as indicators of district performance.

The views of teachers and parents on what matters may be considerably more complex than those condensed in a set of test scores. To the extent that this occurs, principals will, more than ever, be "in the middle." They may find themselves trying to carry out policies and practices based on a conception of school performance that does not match that of those who are so important to them—teachers and parents. We begin with teachers.

Although classroom teachers accept responsibility for conveying curricular content to their students, many add other goals that give extra meaning to their work. Those goals may involve untested objectives such as helping a child connect to school, inculcating morals, or fostering habits that may lead to lifelong reading. Time and attention to such goals are reduced when there is considerable pressure to concentrate heavily on student test performance. When that results in reducing teacher rewards, the principal may be seen as less supportive, threatening the relationship and the ability of the principal to provide instructional leadership. Or what of those teachers whose subjects (music, art, physical education) play no part in the testing regime and gain no public attention? Is it not likely that at least some will find that depreciating? More concretely, how should a principal deal with that widely regarded, veteran teacher who chooses to ignore the tests and continue to teach as she always has?

We have noted that principals derive rewards from their skills as managers who keep things smooth, handle issues in ways that please others and cope effectively with potential threats to the unity of the school. Continued and pronounced emphasis on the principal's function as producer of higher test scores can deflect attention from his or her managerial prowess unless central office makes the effort to offset possibly lopsided evaluation of the principal's performance. Might principals suggest the use of measures that take other goals and proficiencies into account? For example, what about indicators of good climate, effective discipline, improved attendance, strong participation in extracurricular activities and/or astute use of scarce money and supplies?[7]

Using achievement tests to evaluate how things are going can sidestep the more traditional reliance that those at the top have placed in reports from their subordinates. The latter has consisted of teachers reporting to principals and principals to central office. It is probably true that the independence of test results carries fewer risks of distortion based on self-interest. But weakening the process of reporting also entails risks; it can result in losing information that is not contained in tests and the insights of professional advice based on firsthand contact with students. In addition, whatever gains in morale have come from these opportunities for teachers and principals to have a say in the direction schools take are also placed at risk.

Discussion about testing and parental views often remark that realtors and others use local results to influence the purchase of homes in one community over another. It is assumed, presumably accurately, that home purchasers want to locate where there are "good schools" for their children. When we move closer to the reality of tests, parents, and actual schools, however, the situation becomes somewhat more complicated.

School districts whose officials pay close attention to the results of tests do so in terms that do not necessarily match those valued by parents. They are relying on an apparatus with an internal logic that classifies students and depicts their development strictly in terms of that logic. There are at least two kinds of potential difficulties with parents.

The first issue is that tests differentiate students in terms of ability, underlining differences among them; all tests produce winners and losers, and the more serious the testing, the stronger the distinction between them. Parents of students who do not fare well take small satisfaction from a school "doing well" in its overall ranking because their primary concern is with what happens to their own children. Some will press teachers and school officials to do whatever they can to help their particular children do better, adding to the load of expectations experienced by school personnel. Such pressure may make a constructive difference when and if staff members are lax in their efforts, but what if they are in fact working as hard and well as they know how? Given the limits of pedagogical knowledge and differences in ability and motivation among students, tests will probably produce a degree of ineffective, unnecessary, and perhaps, at times, harmful pressure that is hard to estimate.

The second difficulty arises from the focus of achievement testing on one aspect of child development—testable cognitive learning. Unless officials and teachers show interest in other kinds of child development that parents care about, parents may feel that their rightful concerns are being ignored. Is Mary's energy excessive? Is Mario isolated from other kids? Is Tom being bullied by other kids? The interactive complexities principals face when parents are dissatisfied increase when such concerns are overshadowed by heavy emphasis on test scores. There is the possibility, already alluded to, that central officials emphasize outcomes different from those wanted by parents in a particular school, a serious matter for any principal who is caught between various people, all of whom can affect his or her career.

There are complex issues in how goals are affected and the principal's role played out when there is marked emphasis on achievement testing. Principals and those who govern them will probably differ in how they define and cope with that emphasis. There are thorny questions of value involved; the closer we look at the possible repercussions, the more basic questions of educational philosophy come to the fore, confronting us with challenges we have not encountered in the past. Sociological thinking and research cannot resolve those questions of value; in a democracy they can only be resolved by sustained, widespread, and informed discussion. But a crucial ingredient required for that level of discussion, I believe, is the availability of realistic, accurate, and unbiased inquiry into and reliable description of what is actually happening in the schools. Major changes in the operation of organizations carry unintended as well as intended consequences— high-stakes testing is such a change. It merits close and very serious examination from scholars, practitioners, and the general public in the years ahead.

SUMMARY

This chapter has reviewed a variety of trends, ranging from gender changes through programmatic, technological, and competitive trends, and, finally, high-stakes testing. Each presents specific challenges to the traditional organization of schools and affects the position and tasks of the principal. They can move that work in divergent directions, some shaping it one way, others another. But none seem to make the work simpler, for all involve greater complexity and the uncertainty that accompanies it.

One conclusion seems clear for those who are engaged, one way or another, in selecting and preparing persons to take on these increasingly difficult positions. Those responsibilities have never been easy and I, as one former participant in preparing persons for the position, have never felt anything like complete satisfaction about our approaches to the task. It always seemed to me that we simply did not know enough to do the job we should.

The challenges are greater today. Principals will have to have a firmer grasp of how their decisions affect students and what they learn. They will have to expect and, encountering them, master emotional hazards that cannot be avoided. Their diplomatic skills will have to be sharp and steady as potential occasions for conflict will probably increase. And, perhaps most difficult and most important to acquire, they will have to possess a sense of direction and be guided by educational goals that provide coherence in their daily work.

The Interview, the Fact Sheet, and the Sample

This appendix contains three kinds of information on the methods used with the Chicago suburban respondents. The first is the interview done with all members of the sample, the second lists the variables obtained from them through a self-administered questionnaire called the "fact sheet." The third is a brief description of the sample; additional information is presented in chapter 1.

THE COMPLETE INTERVIEW–CHICAGO SUBURBS

The spaces allowed to transcribe the open-ended responses are omitted in the following replication of the suburban interviews.

Brackets are used to indicate instructions to the interviewer. The interviews lasted, on the average, around two and one half hours.

First, I'd like to ask you a few questions about your career in education.

1. How long did you teach—or do other work—before becoming a principal. _____ years (total)

2. When did you first become a principal. _____ (Date)

3. Please tell me about that school—what kind was it and where was it? Level, grades _____ Place: community and school district _____ Number of students _____

4. What positions have you held since? [Skip if in first position.] Level: grades _____ Place: community and school district _____ Number of students _____

5. A. Going back some in time, when did you make the definite
        decision to become a teacher? During grade school _____
        During high school _____ During college _____
        After college _____

    B. You probably considered other lines of work seriously. How
        did teaching emerge as your choice? [Probe: first or second
        choice?]

    C. When you decided to enter teaching, did you expect to stay in
        it or did you expect to move into administration or other work?
        [or, for women, other?] Expected to stay in teaching _____
        Expected to move up _____* [Only after probing] Plan
        vague at the time _____

    D. *If expected to move up, did that expectation play a part in
        your decision to teach?

6. When you decided to become a principal, you probably expected
    it to be better than what you were doing at the time (teaching,
    supervising, etc.). In what ways did you think it would be better?
    [Probe for 3 or 4, note comments on realization but do not probe.]

7. What were the circumstances when you received your first
    appointment as a principal—

    A. Were you looking around at the time?

    B. Did anyone give you a hand?

8. A. Principals have told us that they had to learn a good deal on the
        job during the first year or two: what were the most important
        things you had to learn?

    B. What persons were the most helpful to you during that early
        learning period?

9. A. People sometimes say that their parents' work, even if different
        from theirs, prepared them for their occupations. Do you think
        your father's work helped you, in any way, for your role as a
        school principal? Yes _____ No _____

    B. Did your mother work outside the home while you were
        growing up? Yes _____* No _____*If yes, did
        your mother's work help you, in any way, for your role as a
        school principal?

    I'd like to ask you a few questions about the school you head—
    some are on the fact sheet, but these may help me to understand
    your situation better . . .

10. First, the students . . .
   A. How many students are enrolled in your school this year? _____
   B. What about the social background of the students? Which group occurs most frequently? What is the second most frequent? (Hand card #1) No. 1 _____ No. 2 _____ (Note any comments on distribution)
   C. How about the education of the parents? What level is most frequent? Which level is the second most frequent? No. 1 _____ No. 2 _____
   D. What proportions of the students fall into the following groups? White _____ Black _____ Oriental _____ Hispanic _____ Other _____
   E. What ethnic and religious groups predominate among the white students? (Don't force listing) 1. _____ 2. _____ 3. _____
   F. What special characteristics do your students have which you would mention to another principal in describing your school?
   G. Where do most of your students fall on national achievement tests? Above the national average _____ At the national average _____ Below the national average _____
11. A. How many adults work regularly in your school? That is, teachers, specialists, administrators, aides, secretaries—everyone? _____ (Total)
   B. If you were to describe your faculty to another principal, what three or four adjectives would you use to describe them?
   C. What is the average age of your professional staff? Years _____ Probe: Is there much variation?
12. Please imagine a traditional elementary school in which instruction consists of a group of teachers, each of whom works with one class, and a principal who supervises the school. There are no specialized classes, no special programs, and no teaming—or anything like that at all. (Hand card #2)
   A. Please tell me those features on the card which are present in your school. (Interviewer circles 1–17)
   B. Are there any other ways in which your school is different from the traditional school I described?
13. Every school operates in a "community" made up of parents and others who take an interest in school affairs. (Hand card #3)

Here's a card with several dimensions describing a community, with opposites at each end. Please pick a number along the line which best describes your immediate *school* community. In thinking about it, compare it with all the communities you know about.)

A. Responsive to us at school   1 2 3 4 5 6   Unresponsive
B. Assertive in making demands   1 2 3 4 5 6   Not assertive
C. Predictable in their reactions   1 2 3 4 5 6   Unpredictable
D. Alike in their expectations   1 2 3 4 5 6   Not alike
E. Eager to participate in school   1 2 3 4 5 6   Not eager to
   affairs   Participate

14. Has your school or its community undergone any important changes in the last two or three years? No important changes _____ Some or one important change(s) _____* What were those changes?

15. Is your school special in any ways you have not yet mentioned?

16. A. What 4 or 5 tasks consume the largest blocks of your time?
    B. What tasks do you most like to emphasize?
    C. In general, do you think the time you spend in various tasks is appropriate or not appropriate? Yes _____
       No _____* Why?

17. A. What do you watch to tell how well you are doing as a principal?
    B. What difficulties do you encounter in evaluating your performance?

18. How would you describe a really good day—you know, the kind that leaves you feeling great about how things are going? (Probe with bad day contrast if needed.)

19. A. If you could magically find ten hours more per week to spend on hour work (magically in that it would not take away from your private life), how would you spend the time? What *single* activity would you be most likely to use it on?
    (Hand card #4) B. If hour choices were limited to those on this card, which would be your first and second choices? (Interviewer circles 1–7 for first and second choices.)

20. Of the tasks you do, which would you consider to be—
    A. The most difficult—that is, the hardest to do well?
    B. The most fun?
    C. The least enjoyable?

21. What resources, other than your own skills and knowledge, are most important in helping you to get the job done? Resources can be either tangible or intangible.

22. There are some dilemmas, we understand, in supervising a faculty—some tough choices which come up where a principal has to trade off one good thing for another. Obviously, you won't do the same thing in each instance, but I'd like to mention some of these problems and ask you to say what you *tend* to do or think about them.

   1. You may believe that a particular decision will improve the effectiveness of your school but also believe that it could endanger your relationship with the teachers. When and if that happens, would you tend to take the action or hold off in the interests of staff morale and your relationship to the faculty? Take the action _____ Hold off for morale _____

   2. Thorough evaluation of teacher performance by the principal improves instruction, say some, while others argue that emphasis on evaluation makes the principal too distant from the faculty. Which comes closer to you opinion? Evaluation is important _____ Evaluation increases distance _____

   3. Some principals say that including teachers in many school decisions (including budget, etc.) increases their commitment and the quality of their work. Others say that it reduces efficiency, slows things up, and so on, and is not worth the time and effort. Which comes closer to your view of things? Should include teacher in a wide range _____ Should emphasize efficiency _____

   4. Principals differ in how closely they think they can or should supervise classroom instruction. Some report that they provide detailed and specific guidance while others prefer to give teachers latitude to use their judgment. In general, which approach do you favor? Detailed, specific guidance _____ Latitude for teachers _____

   5. In school-wide matters, some principals favor the use of clear, definite and written rules for teachers wherever possible while others favor a more informal, case-by-case approach to things. Which come closer to your style? Use of rules _____ Case-by-case approach _____

6. Compared to other principals you know, are there any other characteristic ways in which you relate to your faculty—ways not mentioned in this question?

23. Here are some ways in which principals in elementary schools try to improve instruction in their schools. (Hand card #5)
   A. Would you tell me which approach is the most valuable to you? Why? If it's not on the list, please describe it.
   B. What is the second most useful approach? Why?

24. Some people say that tenure and contractual arrangements today make it almost impossible for principals to have real influence over faculty.
   A. Do you agree? Yes _____ No _____
   B. Since you can't give teachers more pay, in what ways can you reward desirable teacher actions?

25. A. How important do you think it is to include members of the community—especially parents—in school affairs? Other than having a parent and teacher organization, for example, do you think it useful to get parents involved in school matters? Yes _____ No _____ (Probe how it is helpful or not helpful.)
   B. How do your school board members and superintendent feel about the question of community and parental involvement in school affairs? Do they encourage you and other principals to do much of that? Yes _____ No _____ Why?

26. A. You probably seek the advice of other persons from time to time to help you deal with problems that come up. What or who are the most important sources of advice to you in your day-to-day work? 1. _____ (relationship to principal _____ Kind of advice or problem (Three spaces provided.)
   B. What kinds of problem are you likely to get help from (each in turn)?
   C. Who is your single most important source of advice?

27. Do the principals in this district work together closely or do they tend to keep pretty much to themselves? Work together closely _____ Stay to themselves _____ (Probe for way in which work together)

28. How often do you talk to other principals—either at their initiative or yours—about common problems or to share and ask for advice?

Never _____ Times per week _____ Times per
month _____

29. Principals tells us that their differ in the amount of influence they
have within the school district. Where would you place yourself in
comparative influence on district affairs—in the top, middle or
lower third? Top third _____ Middle third _____
Lower third _____

30. As we all know too well, the groups one works with don't always
get along too well either internally or with one another.

A. We assume internal conflicts occur from time to time within
each of the following groups:

Teachers   Yes _____ No _____
Parents   Yes _____ No _____
Students   Yes _____ No _____
Principals   Yes _____ No _____
Central office   Yes _____ No _____

a) Which of these internal conflicts occur in your school
or district? Let's review each. (Interviewer—check yes
or no) b) Which requires the largest amount of your
attention? _____ c) What action do you take to
deal with that kind of conflict?

B. Conflicts also can arise between groups: Between—

Parents and central office   Yes _____ No _____
Parents and teachers   Yes _____ No _____
Teachers and central office   Yes _____ No _____
Teachers and students   Yes _____ No _____

a) Which of these inter-group conflicts occur in this school or
district? Let's review each. (Check yes or no) b) Which
requires the largest amount of your attention? _____
c) What kind of action do you take when conflicts of that
kind occur? d) Is there another of these conflicts which
requires your attention? Which one? _____

31. Let's turn to the school district in which your school is located.

A. How many schools are in this district? _____
All elementary Yes _____ No _____
How many not? _____

B. With which central office people do you work on a day-to-day
basis? 1. _____ 2. _____ (etc.)

C. How long has the superintendent occupied his
    position? _____
D. Was he hired from within the district? Yes _____
    No _____
E. Did your superintendent hire you? Yes _____
    No _____
F. Is the superintendent's background in elementary education?
    Yes _____ No _____

32. Communication patterns differ from one school district to another.
    In your district, how do things work?
    A. First, how many written reports, on the average, do you submit
       to central office each month? _____ per month
    B. Are any of those reports other than routine statistical reports?
       Do they require you to write about school events in any detail?
       All statistical _____ Other _____* What are those
       reports like? How often?
    C. On the average, how many meeting—meetings called by
       central office—do you attend per month? (Include district
       committees) _____ per month
    D. (1) In the average week, how many phone conversations do you
           have with people in central office. _____ per week
       (2) Most of these conversations are with which officials?
           _____ _____ _____
       (3) What percentage, would you estimate, do you
           initiate? _____%
    E. How many visits from central office persons does your
       school receive in the average month? _____ per
       month _____ by superintendent specifically
    F. What other ways than those we have asked about do you let
       central office know what is happening in your school? (Probe
       for all)
    G. What other ways does central office use to let you know what
       is expected of you and your school?

33. Some principals have said that it was difficult to learn what matters
    they should discuss with central office and which they should
    deal with independently. If you were responsible for training a
    new principal in your district, what would you recommend in this
    respect? What should the new principal be *sure* to talk to central
    office about?

34. As you know, there is constant discussion about how centralized or decentralized school districts should be. Would you please help me to get a picture of how your school district locates decisions at different levels of the organization? We'll cover several aspects of the school affairs and then I'll ask your overall view of this problem.

    A. As far as budget preparation is concerned, do you participate by submitting requests for your school or do you receive a per capita allocation? Submit requests _____ Per capita basis _____ How does that work? (Confirm acceptance of different amounts to different schools.)

    B. What discretion do you have over spending money once the budget has been set? (Own special fund? Yes _____ No _____) (Able to transfer from one item or category to another? Yes _____ No _____

35. A. When you hire someone—a teacher or another person—can you pretty much count on getting the person you want or is it necessary for you to compromise? Yes, get whom I want _____ Need to compromise _____

    B. Are you ever forced to accept someone doubtful into your school on transfer? Yes _____ No _____

    C. Are you ever forced to let someone go you think is okay? Not including reduction-in-force firing. Yes _____ No _____

36. A. As a principal, have you had the opportunity to influence any collective bargaining contracts that have been negotiated? Is it enough? Yes, enough _____ Yes, but not enough _____ No opportunity to influence _____

    B. Once the contract is settled, do you have sufficient freedom to deal with teacher matters? Yes, enough freedom _____ No, not enough freedom _____

37. As far as evaluating teachers in concerned, does central office expect all principals to go about it in a standardized way, using similar forms, visiting patterns and so on? Or are you allowed considerable discretion regarding this matter? Which comes closer? Same approach required _____ Discretion allowed _____

38. Let's turn now to curriculum and how it's handled in your district. I want to ask about four subjects and how the curriculum is organized for each. Now as far as (mathematics)(etc.) is concerned:

A. Are there written, specific objectives authorized by central office for each grade in your school?
B. Are those objectives linked to any regular standardized test such as the Iowa or Stanford? Are those objectives linked to a criterion-referenced test?
C. Is there district-wide adoption of the same textbook in (mathematics)? (Note if there is more than one adopted textbook.) Subject name, objectives (Yes _____, No _____), testing (standardized or criterion-referenced, textbook (Yes _____, No _____) asked and recorded for mathematics, reading, science and social studies.

39. Compared to what you know of school districts, where would you place yours in the question of what is expected by the teacher in teaching content? Would you say that they are expected to stick closely to the prescribed curriculum or are they allowed to use their own judgment? (Hand card #6) (Interviewer circles)
A. Stick to prescribed curriculum 1 2 3 4 5 6 Use own judgment
B. Do they? Please rate what teachers actually do.
Stick to prescribed curriculum 1 2 3 4 5 6 Use own judgment

40. A. Do you feel that you are expected—by central office—to implement a particular kind of classroom organization?
Yes _____* No _____ * Do you do it?
Yes _____ No _____
B. Do your have preferences of your own on classroom organization? And do you try to influence teachers in this regard? Preference: Yes _____* No _____
*Do you try to influence? Yes _____ No _____

41. A. In your situation, in which area of your work would you most like greater freedom? Why?
B. In general, is _____ (previous response) the most important area for a principal to have autonomy in? Or is something else a more important area?

42. From what you know about school districts in general, how would you describe your school district? In general, are decisions centralized in central office or decentralized to the individual schools? (Hand card #7 with choices below)
Centralized in central office 1 2 3 4 5 6 Decentralized to individual schools.

43. Do you think that the situation is the same for all schools and principals or are some supervised more closely than others? Same _____ Different _____* What seems to account for the differences?

44. Political realities differ from one district to another. In yours, for example—

   A. What do you think is the relative influence of the board of education compared to the superintendent? Board more powerful _____, Superintendent more powerful _____, Equal power.

   B. Is it your impression that the board works together well or is it divided on important issues? United, works well _____ Divided on important issues _____* *What are the major divisions?

   C. Does the district community give strong support to the school district or are there any problems in this respect? Strong support _____ Any problems _____* *What are the problems?

45. We have found some differences in the ways central office wields its authority over the principals in a district. In some districts, central office issues many rules and directives to principals, trying to control principals largely through what the principal is told to do and not to do. In other districts, the principal is given considerable leeway over how he or she does things, provided the results of his or her work meet central office standards for the principal and the school.

   A. In your situation, would you say that central office makes high, medium or low use of rules and directives regarding your work? High _____* Medium _____* Low _____ *If high or medium, what are the most important rules and directives?

   B. How about controlling through watching results and giving you feedback about them? Would you say that central office makes high, medium or low use of that approach? High _____ Medium _____ Low _____ What are the most important results that are watched? (Get 3 or 4 results)

46. A. Does your school district have a detailed, written description of your responsibilities as a principal or a manual which does

the same thing? Yes _____* No _____ *Are you
expected to adhere to that description? Yes _____
No _____

B. Does your district have a regular system for the formal
training of principals or send you and others to seminars
and institutes for that purpose? No, neither _____
Yes, internal _____ * Days in last two years _____
Yes, external _____** **Days in last two years _____

C. Does your superintendent use any formal system of
management such as MBO or PPBES or anything like that?
Yes _____* No _____ *What is that system? Does
it really affect things? How?

47. A. What do you think is most important to central office when
they evaluate your performance as a principal? (Specifics)
Anything else? (Probe for 3 or 4)

B. What source of information do you think has the greatest
effect on the evaluation of your performance made by the
superintendent? (Specifics) Anything else?

C. In your district, what difference does it make whether you
get a good evaluation or not? (Probe salary increases if not
mentioned.)

D. Have any principals been let go in your district within the last
four or five years? Yes _____* No _____ *Why
were they let go?

48. Are principals expected to push for resources for their schools in
your district? Would it help them to get government grants or fire
up the parents' group or push hard for the school in general? (If
any doubt, ask if it could hurt)

B. As far as the distribution of resources within the school
district is concerned, do some schools get more than others?
Yes _____* No _____ *Why do some get more?

49. There may have been times when central office wanted one thing
for your school and you and the faculty thought something else
was better. Can you give me an example of such an occasion and
explain how it worked out?

50. A. From your perspective as head of a school, in what ways does
central office help you to get the job done?

B. What might they do to help you get the job done better?

51. What kinds of things can central office people—the superintendent or others—do, or not do, to make your job harder? (Probe specific examples)

52. A. From your point of view as a principal, what kind of event spells trouble? Would you give me an example of something that was trouble for you within the last year or so? (Probe what outcomes worried respondent)

    B. Do you ever find it necessary to trade off something desirable in order to avoid trouble? Yes _____* No _____ *Can you give me an example?

53. We all like to have good reputations with those around us. In just a word or two, what kind of reputation would you like to have with: A) Students B) Teachers C) Parents D) Other principals E) The superintendent and his staff.

    F. Which of these reputations do you value most? (Get first and second) No. 1 _____ No. 2 _____

54. As specifically as you can, please tell me what the main satisfactions are for you in your work as a principal? (Probe: which is most important?)

55. A. Thinking back over the last year or so, what work achievement is the source of greatest pride for you? (Probe basis of pride)

    B. Looking back over the same period, is there anything you did not do but wish you had done or anything you wish you hadn't? I'm asking, you could say, for any mistake of omission or commission which you now regret. (Probe: why was that a mistake?)

56. What costs or disadvantages do you associate with the principalship compared to alternative careers you might have followed?

57. A. If you had it to do over again, would you enter teaching? Yes _____ No _____* *Why not?

    B. Would you become a principal if you had it to do over again? Certainly would _____ Probably would _____ Probably not _____* Certainty not _____* *Why not?

    C. If you had it to do over again, what changes might you make in the specifics of the career? For example, would you come to work in this district or this school? No changes _____ Another district _____ Another school in this district _____* *Why?

58. A. What is the next step you would like to take in your career? (Probe why attractive)
    B. What kind of position would you like to attain before you retire? (Probe why attractive)

59. What would another district have to offer to entice you away? To a principal's job. .
    A. First, how about salary? How many thousands per year would constitute "an offer you couldn't refuse?" Assume this offer was from an otherwise similar district) Thousands per year more _____
    B. What other attractions would lead you to take a principal's position in another district?
    C. What other questions would you ask about the school district in considering their offer? What would you want to know about the superintendent and central office staff?

60. (Hand card #8)(Circle divided into 8 sections) Let's say this circle represents your total "life space"—all your major interests and activities. How many pieces of the pie would you say "belong" to your work as a principal?
    A. Pieces out of 8 _____
    B. What other interests take up spaces? _____ to _____, _____ to _____, _____ to _____

61. Would you please let us know your income for the past year?
    A. Respondent's salary _____
    B. Spouse's income if working _____
    C. Any additional income you made last year _____

Thank you very much for your cooperation in this interview.

FACT SHEET

The following data were obtained in a self-administered questionnaire left with the respondent who was asked to mail in the completed form. To save space I have listed the information rather than using the original fact sheet. Telephone follow-up calls were made to respondents who did not return the forms and the data were obtained over the telephone.

1. Job titles and numbers of persons employed in central office.
2. Assessed valuation of the district. (1979–80)
3. Per capita expenditure per student. (1979–80)

4. Checklist of occupational groups and which most common and second most common in the district. (Census categories)

5. Description of persons in district in terms of similarity versus difference and identification of important differences.

6. Is there a collective bargaining unit for teachers and if so which one?

7. Predominant ethnic and religious groups in the district as a whole.

8. Number of persons working in the school in each of several categories such as classroom teachers, aides, clerks, etc.

9. Principal's year of birth.

10. Kind of community (e.g., from open country to large city) in which respondent spent most of the years before high school graduation.

11. State in which principal grew up or name of foreign country.

12. Ordinal position within the family at age sixteen, older and younger siblings and gender.

13. Father's occupation and kind of employing organization when respondent sixteen years of age.

14. If mother employed outside the home, kind of work done.

15. Father's schooling.

16. Mother's schooling.

17. Undergraduate college from which graduated.

18. Study done since college graduation.

19. Location of graduate study.

20. Current enrolment in degree program, where and for what degree.

21. Synopsis of positions held as teacher—district name, grades and subjects, number of years in each position.

21. Synopsis of administrative positions before first principalship— district name, position title, school name and level, and length of time in each.

22. With what religious group is respondent affiliated?

23. Frequency of attendance at religious services.

24. Does respondent identify with a particular ethnic or national group? If yes, which?

25. Marital status.

26. Number of children.

27. List of professional organizations to which belonged and level of activity in each.

28. Other kinds of organizations including hobby or athletic groups and level of activity in each.

THE SAMPLE

The sample was drawn (with the expert advice of Professor Larry Hedges) from 60 districts in three counties surrounding Chicago. Information on the districts and the names of principals were obtained from lists provided by county officials. Given the importance of size in organizational relationships, we decided to stratify the districts by the number of principals in each and selected respondents proportionally. Two principals were drawn, at random, from each of the districts. Ninety-four percent (113) of the 120 persons generated in that process agreed to participate in the study. Since two of those who did not participate were in one district, the sample consists of 59 districts. Although it is not a large sample, it appears to be representative; the statistical results, as presented in the text, frequently match those found in studies based on a larger number of cases of suburban principals in particular and elementary principals in general in other locations and the nation at large.

The resulting sample is diverse. (Additional information is presented in chaps. 1 and 2.) For example, districts range in size from 2 to 28 schools and, in contrast to any image of suburbs as uniform in social composition, they vary in many of their socioeconomic characteristics. The schools, in turn, also differ in the occupations of the parents, the number of students, and the experience of their principals, the latter ranging from a few months to 32 years. The principals were primarily white (84%) males, with no Hispanic or Asian principals. The number of women in this sample (16%) differs markedly from what prevails today, a difference discussed at some length in chapter 9.

The Iowa Data and
Community Differences

Robert J. Vittengl completed his dissertation at Iowa State University in 1984. It was entitled "The Iowa School Principal: A Sociological Perspective." It was based on a large sample of Iowa elementary principals during February 1983, in which "all 640 of Iowa's public elementary school principals received a survey instrument." Responses came from 451 of those, or 70%. This section of the book lists some of the questions he asked, focusing on those that are similar enough to allow direct comparison with the Chicago area data. (The categories do not, however, always coincide with the codes developed for the Chicago suburban data.) The marginal responses to the questions are also included; the items included deal primarily with sentiments reported here in chapters 5 and 6 and, to a lesser extent, career data found in chapters 2 and 7.

The Iowa data contribute in several ways. First, the sample is larger than the Chicago area study, allowing us to check the distribution of themes in a larger, more inclusive group and the extent to which they are similar to or different from the Chicago suburban data. Second, the districts in Iowa are unit districts, a circumstance which permits comparison with Illinois principals working in elementary districts. Finally, we were able to analyze the Iowa sample to find differences between suburban principals and those working in urban and rural settings; there is a brief discussion of those differences in the final section of this appendix. The sample, being relatively large, permitted the use of chi-square tests to check the statistical significance of the observed differences. They are presented here primarily to provide leads for future research.

THE QUESTIONS AND RESPONSES

24. At what age are you planning to retire from education? _____
    Years ($\bar{X}$ = 61.7, Mode: 65)

25. Listed below are several descriptors that principals have used to tell
    us how they spend a good deal of their time. Please tell us which
    three of these *responsibilities* you believe are the *most important for
    you in your job.* Place a "1" beside the responsibility you believe
    is the most important, a "2" beside that which is second most
    important, and a "3" beside the third most important.
    _____ A. Building Manager
    _____ B. Control Student Behavior
    _____ C. Curriculum Development
    _____ D. Emphasize Student Achievement
    _____ E. Morale Builder
    _____ F. Personnel Manager
    _____ G. School-Community Relations
    _____ H. Supervision of Instruction/Teachers
    Responses:
    Number 1: Top choice. H (53%), A (22%), C (8%)
    Number 2: 2nd choice. H (20.5), C (20.5), D (15%)
    Number 3. 3rd choice. G (24%), C (18%), A (14%)

26. Which do you consider to be the *most difficult* to do well?
        Letter _____ H (58%), C (18%), G (6%)
    Which do you consider to be the *most enjoyable?*
        Letter _____ D (23%), G (19%), E (18%)
    Which do you consider to be the *least enjoyable?*
        Letter _____ B (46%), H (23%), A (10%)

29. We're interested in knowing what for you would constitute a *really
    good day*—the kind that leaves you feeling great about how things
    are going. Listed below are several things principals have told us
    that are often found on their good days. Please circle the number
    which best corresponds to your feeling about each statement.
    Would not be   1 2 3 4 5 6   Would be
    a part of a good   a part of a good
    day for me   day for me
    [Note: In this and other similar questions the numbers 1 through 6
    were included in each particular choice.]

A. A day I don't have to see any children for disciplinary purposes. $\overline{X}$ = 4.8, S.D. = 1.34 [Rank tied number 2.]

B. A day which allows me to work at my desk without interruption for a couple of hours. $\overline{X}$ = 3.6, S.D. = 1.4

C. A day in which I'm provided with some new educational challenge. $\overline{X}$ = 4.8, S.D. = 1.04 [Rank tied number 2.]

D. A day in which I move about and interact with the children. $\overline{X}$ = 5.5, S.D. = .91 [Rank number 1.]

E. A day which I meet with other principals to discuss matters of mutual concern. $\overline{X}$ = 4.3, S.D. = 1.2

F. A day when I observe in the classrooms. $\overline{X}$ = 4.7, S.D. = 1.1

G. A day when I have an evaluation conference and can offer suggestions for improvement to teachers. $\overline{X}$ = 4.5, S.D. = 1.2

H. A day when I have a staff meeting. $\overline{X}$ = 3.96, S.D. = 1.02

I. Other. [Responses not available.]

30. Elementary school principals have told us that while they are usually satisfied with their jobs, there are occasions when they feel *unfulfilled or frustrated* in their role as an elementary principal. Listed below are several reasons principals have given as to why they feel unfulfilled or frustrated. Please circle the number which best corresponds to your feelings about each statement.

No problem/not   1   2   3   4   5   6   Significant problem/
true for me   very true for me

A. I'm seldom told I'm doing a good job. M = 3.3, S.D. = 1.5

B. I have little opportunity to keep abreast of new developments in education. $\overline{X}$ = 3.0, S.D. = 1.3

C. I don't have enough opportunity to interact with teachers. $\overline{X}$ – 2.9, S.D. – 1.4

D. There seem to be so many interruptions, I'm seldom able to start and end a task as quickly as I would like. $\overline{X}$ = 3.99, S.D. = 1.4 [Rank Number 1]

E. I don't have enough contact with students. $\overline{X}$ = 3.2, S.D. = 1.5

F. Working with people is very imprecise. $\overline{X}$ = 2.9, S.D. = 1.3

G. I have to spend an inordinate amount of time managing student behavior. $\overline{X}$ = 2. 5, S.D. 1.3

H. I have to spend an inordinate amount of time dealing with incompetent staff. $\overline{X}$ = 2.2, S.D. = 1.1

I. I'm forced to spend an inordinate amount of time dealing with a myriad of bureaucratic paperwork. $\overline{X}$ = 3.7, S.D. = 1.4 [Rank number 2.]

J. They don't pay me what I'm worth. $\overline{X}$ = 2.8, S.D. = 1.5

K. The job I do as a principal is generally unrecognized by my boss. $\overline{X}$ = 2.8, S.D. = 1.5

L. I'm responsible for more than one building. It's difficult to keep them running smoothly and occasionally I'm in the wrong place at the wrong time. $\overline{X}$ = 3.5, S.D. 1.8

M. My boss expects too much from me. $\overline{X}$ = 2.1, S.D. 1.2

N. Many parents in my building's attendance area have unrealistic expectations for their children. $\overline{X}$ = 2.4, S.D. = 1.2

O. There seldom seems to be enough money to buy the things we need at our school. $\overline{X}$ = 2.8, S.D. 1.5

P. Our school children seem to be accomplishing quite a lot and very few people seem to appreciate it. $\overline{X}$ = 3.1, S.D. = 1.3

Q. I am assigned extra duties which have little to do with what a principal should be doing. $\overline{X}$ = 2.3, S.D.= 1.4

R. Our district seems to have its priorities turned around—too much emphasis is placed at the secondary level. $\overline{X}$ = 3.3, S.D. = 1.7

33. Do you consider the elementary school principalship your final occupational goal? Yes (63.9%) *No (36.1%)
*If no, which position is your ultimate goal? (Check one only) Elementary teacher (.06%), Secondary teacher (0), College teacher (12.4%), Secondary Principal (1.3%), Supervisor or member of central office staff (8.5%), Director of elementary education (16.3%), Assistant superintendent of schools (3.9%), Superintendent of schools (27.5%), Other (29.4%) (Total 99.4% r.e.)

35. Some principals have told us that they would like to have greater *freedom/autonomy* in certain areas. Listed below are a few of those items. Please circle the number which best corresponds to your feeling in each area.

| Have plenty of freedom/ autonomy | 1 2 3 4 5 6 | Would like much greater freedom/autonomy |

	$\overline{X}$	S.D.
A. Use of monies within your building(s)	2.7	1.6
B. Interviewing and hiring staff for your building(s)	2.5	1.7
C. Dismissal of staff in your building(s)	2.8	1.7
D. Evaluation of teachers	1.8	1.3
E. Implementation of particular classroom organizational patterns (self-contained, departmentalization, etc.)	2.2	1.2
F. Selection of curriculum materials	2.5	1.4

Of those listed above, A through F, which one do you feel Is the *most important* for a principal *to have great freedom/autonomy in?*
A. 9.7%, B. 54.8%, C. 5.8%, D. 14.5%, E. 10.1%, F. 5.1%

36. Elementary school principals have shared with us several ways in which they were rewarded or recognized for doing a good job as a principal. Please examine each of the following and indicate *how you would feel about being recognized/rewarded in that manner.* Please circle the appropriate number.

Would mean very   1 2 3 4 5 6   Would mean a
little to me   great deal to me

	Mean	S.D.
A. Receiving a substantial increase in salary	4.6	1.3
B. Having the students in your building/s increase their scores on a standardized achievement test by a significant amount.	4.9	1.1
C. Have a mother write you a letter thanking you for all you've done for her child.	5.2	.9
D. Having the school board tell you they like the idea you've presented and, yes, you can have the $5000 to implement it in your school.	5.0	1.1
E. Having the media contact you and ask to come to interview you about something special that's going on in your school.	4.1	1.3
F. Seeing a child who was having social and academic problems begin to improve probably because of something you did.	5.6	.65 [Rank no. 1]
G. Receiving a handwritten note from your boss thanking you for the fine way you handled a problem for him/her.	5.2	.96

H. Having your boss suggest that you've been   4.5   1.4
    working very hard and s/he thinks you should
    make plans to take a week off and go to a
    national convention all expenses paid.

I. Being formally recognized by a local civic   4.5   1.4
    organization as an outstanding educator.

J. Finally getting your staff to pull together   5.3   .9
    on something on which they were previously
    polarized.   [Rank no. 2]

K. Having your boss seek out your opinion on   5.1   .9
    a perplexing educational problem because
    s/he believes you're on top of it.

40. If you could magically find ten more hours per week to spend on
    your work (magically in that it would not take away from your
    private life), how would you spend the time? What *single* activity
    would you be most likely to use it on? Check just one.

	N	%
Engage in discussion with other principals dealing with principal problems.	45	10.0
Improve management procedures in my office.	15	3.3
Join with central office people on districtwide matters.	7	1.6
Meet and work with parents and others in the community.	25	5.6
Spend time in contact with students.	131	29.2
[Rank no. 2]		
Study and inquire into new research bearing on my work.	42	9.4
Work with teachers on instructional matters.	178	39.6
[Rank no. 1]		
Other	6	1.3

41. Listed below are things principals have told us they see as *costs
    or disadvantages associated with the principalship* when compared
    to alternative careers they might have followed. Please circle the
    number which best corresponds to the degree of disadvantage you
    attach to each factor when you think of other careers you might
    have pursued. [Note: Mean presented by gender as well as for total
    group.)

    No disadvantage   1   2   3   4   5   6   A great disadvantage

	Mean	Males	Females
A. Salary	2.0	2.1	1.7
B. Being a "public servant"	2.0	2.0	1.9
C. Not enough freedom / autonomy	1.7	1.7	1.6
D. Little real power	1.7	1.7	1.8
E. Little recognition	1.7	1.7	1.6
F. Little personal satisfaction	1.4	1.4	1.3
G. Limited number of relationships with other adults	1.6	1.6	1.5

SUBURBAN, CITY, AND RURAL DIFFERENCES

Iowa respondents were asked, in question 18, "how would you characterize the community which your school serves?" The rural choice dominated with 51.8% (232), urban second with 31.7% (142), and suburban third with 16.5% (74). Michael Selzer, a valued consultant, cross-tabulated community type with all other survey variables, including chi-squares, producing 123 tables. (Tests of significance were not done in 19 instances.) In order to get an overall impression of the extensiveness of community effects on the responses of these principals, I estimated how many significant tables we would expect using .05 level of significance (6 cases) and compared it to the actual number of significant tables (24), yielding a difference of 18 cases. In percentage terms, 19.5% were significant compared to the 5% we would expect from chance as the .05 level, a difference of 14.5%. Community location, therefore, is apparently exercising some influence on the working life of these Iowa principals; we will examine the significant differences here in the hope that identifying them may help in future research on the ways in which district setting affects the occupation. Although I will discuss only tables marked by an acceptable, and often high, level of statistical significance, I will take a few liberties in projecting possible overall differences between different locations of school districts and the situation of elementary principals in them by discussing possible meanings of the observed differences. Again, the intention is heuristic, not confirmatory.

First, I observed that the responses of suburban principals were usually midway between those given by city and rural principals, a tendency that I suspect is in large part due to the fact that suburban districts are usually smaller than urban and larger than rural districts. Size tends to produce differences quite apart from territorial location. Although the questionnaire did not ask for the number of schools or students in the respondents' districts, Vittengl, probably using data from other sources, presented a series of 24 tables comparing the largest 15 districts with the rest, finding significant differences (ranging from the .05 level to .0001) in 15 instances. Although these tables were appended to the thesis and received little or no attention in the text, they strongly suggest that size of district is a variable that merits attention; it also suggests that future research should be designed, if possible, to separate out the effects of size and district location. The same appendix in Vittengl's report contains 16 analyses of variance comparing the 3 types of communities, 7 of which are significant with findings similar to those I will discuss below; I will mention the foregoing when they overlap with the Iowa tables produced in Chicago.

Second, the most striking differences in the responses are between the city principals and those located elsewhere. Urban answers tend, unlike the suburban, to stand at one end or the other of the distribution; we will describe those that are statistically significant. They reflect the characteristics of large-scale, city districts familiar to students of school organization. City principals complained more often about having to spend time on discipline (significant in my percentage tables [.000] and the Iowa analysis of variance [.01]; problems of student compliance with school rules is more commonly associated with city schools). Paperwork, a bane for principals in general, gets significantly more mentions from the city principals (.000). To the problematic tasks suggested by those differences, we find the wish for more autonomy and greater influence; that is evident in regard to hiring personnel (.000), dismissing staff (.000), and in the selection of curriculum (.000 in my table, .01 in Iowa 35F described above). Urban principals have more complaints, then, about the tasks they face and the extent to which the structure in which they work hampers their efforts to assemble a staff of their choice and to influence the nature of the curriculum.

Extending the foregoing findings, we may reasonably hypothesize that managing urban elementary schools, particularly in matters of instruction, is the most difficult and demanding of the three types. Yet despite the plausibility of that hypothesis, it is not safe to assume that running such schools makes for less satisfying careers if we credit the data on repeating career choices as indicators of such satisfaction. In two questions, respondents were asked whether they would repeat the teacher and principal decisions. In regard to the teaching decisions, the percentages ran as follows: 89% of city, 78% of suburban, and 77% of rural principals said yes (.16). In the question on repeating the principalship, four choices were given—certainly no, probably no, probably yes, and certainly yes (.96). Combining the yeses, the city percentage was 87, the suburban and rural responses were both 90. These indicators of largely similar levels of satisfaction (particularly in the choice of the principalship) raise interesting questions for future research. Are the rewards that require discretion in managing instruction of less importance than other kinds of rewards? Does working with city children bring greater rewards linked to service to others? Do socioeconomic differences among parents, acting as reference groups for principals, tend to equalize the meanings attached to material benefits? Might social backgrounds of the principals differ in ways that affect what they expect from their careers?

Principals working in rural areas were considerably less likely to complain about inadequate managerial powers. They stood at the low end in wanting more influence in hiring staff, dismissing them, or selecting curriculum. One gets the impression that they had, comparatively, more opportunities to have their preferences make a difference. That impression is supported by the data on how they perceive their standing in terms of influence within their districts; significantly larger numbers of rural principals locate themselves in the top third in affecting districtwide policy; differences stand at the .000 level in both my crosstabulation and Vittengl's analysis of variance. (It is likely, of course, that if we had data on district size it would also prove to be influential as was the case among the suburban districts in the Chicago sample where principals in smaller districts reported a higher sense of influence.)

One point where rural principals indicated dissatisfaction with their role set is vis-à-vis parents: at the .000 level in my calculations, they were less inclined than suburban or urban principals to say that parents should be "very active" in school affairs. (Q. 43D asked "what level of involvement would you choose for the parents of your ideal elementary school?" Substantially more were ready to select "moderately active" or "relatively inactive.") The same difference appears in Vittengl at the .01 level. Are there special reasons why engagement by parents in rural communities is more problematic for elementary principals? For example, do neighborhood relationships in these small communities favor parental interventions which principals resent?

Although the number of statistically strong differences is limited, the variations suggest that city and rural principals locate their difficulties in dissimilar areas. Urban principals express more concerns than their rural colleagues; furthermore, they locate their dissatisfactions around issues *within* their districts and schools. They regret the lack of discretion they have, the amount of paperwork, and their numerous disciplinary duties. Rural principals have fewer complaints overall and do not complain that much about internal matters. They focus their concerns on persons outside the formal structure, the parents of their students.

Individuals who enter the principalship in rural settings are considerably more likely to cite salary as a major reason for that decision; they do so 60% of the time compared with 39% of city and 42% of suburban principals (.000). I would guess that this is due to fewer salaried opportunities in rural communities; the relative scarcity of salaried employment in small towns and farm areas may, in fact, affect the principal's standing. One might expect that salary levels are, in local terms, relatively high and in that way add to one's prestige. But being employed may, in contrast to owning small businesses and farms, have the opposite effect, reducing the principal's prestige. Are status issues related in some way to problems that principals fear will occur when parents are heavily involved in school affairs?

The responses from suburban principals in Iowa do not stand out as sharply as those provided by their rural and city colleagues. A few differences, however, are suggestive. We noted that Chicago area principals rated the evaluation and supervision of teachers as their most important responsibility and, at the same time, indicated that it was problematic for them in various ways. For example, it led the list of tasks (table 6.1) ranked as most difficult, a response also found in the Iowa study. When we compare communities in Iowa, however, it shows up, significantly, among suburban principals as their "most enjoyable" task considerably less frequently than it does among their peers who work in other kinds of communities (.000). It is also cited as "least enjoyable" more often, but not at a significant level.

Although these data are hardly overwhelming, they raise a question about whether the emphasis we found on complexities of evaluation and supervision are less marked in cities and farm communities. Are there ways in which the relationship between principals and their faculties are particularly complicated in suburban districts? Suburban districts are generally better equipped, economically, to compete for young teachers from stronger colleges and for experienced teachers who have demonstrated their competence elsewhere; we saw that Chicago suburbs were able to draw their principals-to-be from smaller communities in Illinois and adjoining states. Are teachers who are made aware of their desirability in the marketplace more inclined to challenge those who are expected to manage them? We have seen that school officials in our suburbs take the demands of parents very seriously; do those demands press principals to exercise more (potentially unpopular) controls over faculty members?

Comparatively few principals in Iowa were women in the early 1980s—10% overall. But suburban districts in Iowa were even more resistant to hiring women—4% compared with 8% in rural districts and 18% in the cities (.002). The dominance of male recruitment to the principal position implies that mentoring and sponsorship by superintendents (themselves male) were particularly powerful mechanisms in the suburbs, at least in comparison with larger and more impersonal city districts. One wonders whether suburbs in Iowa and elsewhere have seen the same enormous expansion of women principals that has taken place in recent years in the Chicago metropolitan area. The high proportion of rural principalships in the case of Iowa may mean that the percentage of women principals has increased at a slower pace.

There are indications that the suburban principals in the Iowa sample were somewhat more ambitious than their peers in other locations. Although their expectations on entering the principalship did not differ significantly from others', a higher percentage who expected to move up selected the higher position—the superintendency. First, let us examine the level of expectation in general.

Almost all the beginners (three years or less experience) in the Illinois sample expected to end their careers in positions other than the principalship; expectations for promotion among Iowa beginners were lower. 42% expected to end their careers as principals. (It showed a similar gradient to that observed in our study in chap. 7, rising to 87% among those with 17 or more years of experience.) How might we account for the much lower initial expectation of promotion in Iowa?

The hypothesis I would put forward is that in unit districts, persons working in elementary administration see their opportunities for promotion as more limited than in those where elementary schools are organized separately. Superintendents are often drawn from secondary rather than elementary schools; the prestige system generally works to favor those working with older rather than younger students. But in the suburbs we studied around Chicago, almost every superintendent had a background in elementary education. Beginning principals in elementary districts worked with persons with the same background they would present to boards in future years; it was seen as realistic, other considerations aside, to hope for that ultimate position or a central office position occupied by persons who also had backgrounds in elementary districts.

Returning to the comparison within Iowa, we find that overall, regardless of level of experience, 37% expected to do something other than remain principals, that is, 34% of city, 34% of suburban, and 40% of rural principals (.475). When we examine those expecting to become superintendents, 40% of suburban versus 11% of urban and 29% of rural principals had that goal in mind (.01). It is also suggestive that suburban principals were considerably more likely to have done more than 25 hours of graduate work in the last 5 years: 21% versus 6% for urban principals and 11% for rural principals (.01). These Iowa differences raise the question of whether suburban principals are in general more ambitious than those working in cities or rural settings. In Iowa, the fathers of suburban principals were more likely to have some college or more education compared with others, suggesting that perhaps their social origins, being higher, led them to have higher occupational aspirations (not significant: 23% vs. 14% city and 17% rural).

Finally, the suburban principals indicated stronger preferences for innovation in thinking about their ideal elementary school. Asked about the general curricular focus of that school, they were more likely to choose a number closer to "innovative/experimental" at one end (6) than "traditional/basic" at the other (1). If we select positions 5 and 6 as indicating a preference for innovation, suburban principals registered 25%, urban 20%, and rural 10% (.003 Warning re cell size). I suspect strongly that this preference reflects their more extensive graduate study along with whatever tendencies suburban schools have to place a greater emphasis on change than schools in rural settings do.

What can we say, then, that is especially true of suburban principals in Iowa? One is that they found their supervisory relationships with teachers somewhat more difficult and somewhat less enjoyable than principals in cities and rural communities. A second is that more harbor hopes of moving up into the superintendency and central office positions; they stood ready, furthermore, to do the extra study that would make such promotion likely. In both states, there was considerable resistance to hiring women, but more so in Iowa. Finally, the suburban principals were readier to favor schools with more innovative programs. I suspect that the latter readiness reflected the high aspirations (and possibly greater sophistication) of the parents of their students.

{ **Notes** }

CHAPTER 1

1. Working single-room schoolhouses are rare today, but along with unused railway stations, surviving school buildings show up as shops selling gifts, antiques, and the like. One wonders what part continued awareness of such schools plays in the American imagination: does it support a public image that depicts teachers and students as critical components of schools while ignoring the role of administrators?

2. Collective bargaining was the rule in the districts in this study; 87% had teachers represented by either the Illinois Education Association or the American Federation of Teachers.

3. The development of grades within elementary schools also favored the gradual standardization of curriculum that spread throughout the country in succeeding decades—a standardization that spread despite a stated insistence on the importance of local control.

4. Certified personnel working in schools without regular teaching assignments find themselves pressed into helping the principal. An example was provided the author in a personal communication from Carl Milofsky about school psychologists who "visited" schools on a regular basis and were often pressed into providing the principal with various kinds of advice on topics not normally considered part of their duties.

5. Few women were appointed to elementary principalships in the initial decades after its emergence; the picture becomes less clear after the turn of the century when more women were selected during the early decades (Meskin 1981). The period immediately following WWII saw an expansion of suburban schools with new appointments heavily dominated by men. Sharp increases in the number of women principals, especially in

elementary schools, took place beginning in the 1980s and grew in subsequent decades.

6. In a widely reprinted article, DiMaggio and Powell (2007, but originally published in 1983) list several predictors to "institutional isomorphism" defined as "homogeneity in organizational forms and structures." Those predictors are found, to a remarkable degree, in public schools and help to explain the widespread diffusion of the standard model.

7. A few respondents commented that drops in enrolment were sometimes used by superintendents who wanted to dismiss a principal for other reasons.

CHAPTER 2

1. The NEA study, based on a national sample, drew more farmers than we would expect in a suburban sample. There are other differences in the categories that make the data less than fully comparable, but those data can be said, at the very least, to indicate a general resemblance between the two groups.

2. There are interesting gender and racial differences in place origins within the sample. Eight of the 19 women (42%) compared with 27% of the men originated in Chicago; the African Americans (7) of both genders listed under "other US" were almost entirely from Southern states.

3. Another indicator of principal caution in taking risks is the readiness to change districts—moving involves loss of tenure as a teacher and seniority in the district. All in all, few sample members displayed such enterprise in their careers. Twenty-nine percent worked in only one district and few others moved once they had become principals; 77% stayed in the same district in which they were originally promoted to principal. The weak job market, as mentioned in the previous chapter, also contributed to that stability.

4. Principals who were sponsored were more likely to receive help from administrators during their beginning years as principals, indicating that for most of them sponsorship was a continuing relationship. Among those promoted internally, 63% of the sponsored reported such help while 37% did not. Of those who were not sponsored, 25% were helped later and 75% were not. The term "sponsored" is used to refer to persons receiving help for internal promotion and when help resulted in a position in another district, the term used is "assisted across district lines."

5. The classification of districts by socioeconomic status was based on calculations using 1980 Census data. Districts were ranked in terms of mean household income, percentage white collar and the percentage who graduated from college; the mean of the three ranks was subsequently used to array the entire distribution. The overall distribution of ranked districts was

then divided into three close-to-equal subgroups labeled low, middle, and high status. There was a marked tendency toward geographic clustering. Low-status districts were predominantly south and southwest of Chicago proper, middle-status west, and high-status north and northwest. The mean percentage of African-American students in all schools was 23% in low-status, 4.9% in middle-status, and 2.8% in high-status.

6. Respondents are identified by number, level of satisfaction, gender, and age. For a fuller explanation, see chap. 7.

7. When teachers and others (e.g., parents, clerical, and other subordinate staff members) choose to tolerate inexperienced principals—and when they do not—could prove to be a useful topic for further research. It is a type of informal and unofficial screening that may exercise considerable influence on who stays in and who leaves principal ranks.

CHAPTER 3

1. It is difficult to know how the "distinctness" of schools and classrooms is related to the history and prior existence of "schools" and "classrooms" before districts were "assembled" during the nineteenth century. As we observed earlier, both predated school districts. And, of course, schools (frequently private and/or religious) and classrooms have roots in European history.

2. The legislation governing Illinois schools—the Illinois School Code (2007)—expresses both the subordinate and superordinate position of the principal. For example, it states, "The principal shall assume administrative responsibilities and instructional leadership, under the supervision of the superintendent, and in accordance with reasonable rules and regulations of the board, for the planning, operation and evaluation of the educational program of the attendance area to which he or she is assigned." Revisions in the code since 1980 have increased the emphasis on the improvement of instruction as the principal's responsibility. "School boards shall specify in their formal job description for princials that his or her primary responsibility is the improvement of instruction. A majority of the time spent by a principal shall be spent on curriculum and staff development through both formal and informal activities, establishing clear lines of communication regarding school goals, accomplishments, practices and policies with parents and teachers." A related sentence reads, "School boards shall ensure that their principals are evaluated on their instructional leadership ability and their ability to maintain a positive education and learning climate."

3. Although independently governed, elementary school districts in the suburbs were aligned with particular high school districts. The latter sought, through various coordinative arrangements, to bring about instructional standardization so that students from various districts were more or less uniformly prepared for entry to a designated high school. Thus decisions

made about the formal curriculum were subject to influences by high school districts as well as state and other sources of influence.

4. The 1978 NAESP report asked principals to describe the division of authority in hiring staff. Presented with four degrees of influence, 43% chose "I have all the authority I need. The central office will not assign a teacher to my school over my objections." Another 38% chose "I don't have as much authority as I would like but the central office does listen to me. In disagreements over personnel, I win more frequently than I lose." The remaining 19% chose responses that described little or no influence. It appears that our respondents had more influence than those in the national sample, perhaps because they worked in elementary districts and/or worked in suburban districts of limited size.

5. Both district and school sizes are important factors in this matter. The 1978 NAESP report discussed the distribution of "administrative teams" made up of central officials and principals. Overall, 68% said their districts had such teams; principal membership, however, was distributed unevenly, with more principals of small schools (79%) and from generally small rural districts (86%) dominating. They were found least often (56%) in urban settings. Size also played a part in our sample. In a few tiny districts, jobs normally performed by central officials were assigned as part-time duties for principals; for example, one might serve as curriculum director, another concentrate on personnel. At the larger end, respondents reported that they interacted more often with assistant superintendents and less often with the superintendent when compared with those in smaller districts.

6. Although the 1978 NAESP report did not include a question on sources in the evaluation of principals, the 1998 report did. It reported that 41% of principals in the national sample included teachers among those whose views were sought about their performance.

7. There are indications in the data that principals in some districts "work together" informally to present a united front on the issues provoked by the unequal powers of superintendents and principals. This might prove to be a rewarding topic for future research into the organizational dynamics of school districts. One might compare them with situations where principals decide to use more formal approaches such as unionization, an approach that was not mentioned by our suburban school principals.

8. One should not overlook the implicit praise of self in saying one has enough autonomy; it can imply that one is trusted by superordinates and, by further implication, is highly competent.

9. The concern with hiring staff was echoed in the data gathered in Iowa. Asked what areas they considered "most important to have great freedom/ autonomy in," 55% chose "interviewing and hiring staff" from a list of six alternatives. Teacher evaluation was a distant second with 15% of the vote.

CHAPTER 4

1. Judith Little, using transcripts of conversation between a teacher and a sophisticated advisor, described their failure to communicate because the frameworks they employed were different. The intimate knowledge the classroom teacher had of the students did not get communicated and the two talked past each other (Little, personal communication, July, 2007).

2. The two responses showing disagreement (numbers 5 and 1), the use of rules versus case-by-case deciding (49% vs. 51%) and acting versus holding off for morale (60% vs. 41%), point to interesting differences in the use of authority and merit, I believe, consideration in future research on differences in leadership styles. The dilemma labeled number 2 is ignored here, for although 87% is indeed a highly modal response, I realized later that it differed from the other parts of the question in not representing a genuine choice, because doing and submitting evaluations is an unavoidable obligation, making opposition to doing it chimerical.

3. Sackney, after quoting from work done by both Bridges and Owens, states "The dilemma for the principal is to decide when to involve the staff in decision making and when to exclude them" (Sackney 1980).

CHAPTER 6

1. Another formalized area is special education placement, which is closely regulated by federal and state law. Principals must "sign off" on the disposition of each student involved and must make sure that the proper procedures have been observed; "staffing" involves specialists and others in formal meetings, usually along with the principal. The steps involved are somewhat fewer than in evaluation and come into play as placement issues arise, not as a stipulated number each year. They have the special complexity, however, of requiring the participation of parents who can be extremely sensitive about the classification of the child and the program that it specifies.

2. This problem has continued to beset elementary principals. "Fragmentation of my time" was the top "concern" (72%) of respondents in the 1998 NAESP study, leading the second ranked problem (lack of financial resources) by 16%.

3. In the question asking respondents to discuss the content of the reputation they wanted with others, being seen as "responsive" led the list vis-à-vis parents with 46% of the mentions (Q. 53C).

4. The concern shown by Iowa principals (1980) about interruptions and paperwork is evident in their responses to a question asking them about "occasions when they feel unfulfilled or frustrated in their role." Interruptions ranked number one and paperwork number two of the eighteen choices offered (see appendix B, Q. 30).

5. The time spent on discipline figured prominently in the 1998 NAESP report. It received a ranking of third most demanding of twelve possible uses of time.

6. NAESP reported in 1978 that 19.5% of the principals had assistants, mainly in the large urban schools. The numbers in the 1998 report were nearly identical.

7. Madeline Hunter, a prominent and influential professor at the University of California Los Angeles, was a popular speaker at administrative meetings during the period. In one presentation I heard, she focused on the problem of offsetting teacher resistance to supervision, advising listeners to surround any critical comments with copious supplies of praise.

8. The Iowa study asked respondents to rate the difficulty of a list of eight task areas (appendix B, Q. 26); 58% selected the option marked "supervision of instruction / teacher evaluation," a modal response very close to that seen in table 6.1.

9. Respondents were asked how they would advise a new principal on deciding when to talk to central office (Q. 33). A minority of principals (14%) would urge avoiding contact unless it could not be avoided. For example, one said, "Stay away. Go only under unusual circumstances" (103A, Female, 64) Much larger numbers (86%) were ready to approach central office on various issues to get advice before acting. A substantial proportion (46%) emphasized letting central office know if there was a chance that they would become involved, most likely by a parent calling or a teacher initiating a grievance. They emphasized that central office should never be embarrassed, that they should always be prepared for complaints. As one respondent made clear, such notification is a moral obligation, a point reminiscent of Bosk's work on hospital residents and supervising physicians (Bosk 1979). "Problems that have the potential of coming to the attention of central office, such as a difficult conference with a parent or teacher in which I made a decision which they didn't like. Also, any time you goof—being honest and above board is necessary for self-preservation" (13B, Male, 50).

10. Such reverberations are more likely in compact social systems where cooperating parties are socially and geographically close to each other, where the words "neighborhood" and even "village" catch the flavor of daily relationships. It may be especially true of elementary schools where children ("the real neighbors") draw families together, particularly in suburban and other relatively small communities; families are less likely to know each other in cities and their generally larger elementary schools.

CHAPTER 7

1. As in other studies, most of the principals, by a wide margin, were married (89%) and had children (93%). In Iowa, the respective figures were

92% and 91%. Answers on the life space question (Q. 60A) showed that involvement in family life, based on the number of sectors assigned, was a close second to work.

2. Within the sample group, differences in salary were only weakly associated with the three satisfaction categories, with a linear difference of 1.8 thousand dollars (5.8% of the mean) across the means of categories A, B, and C; see below for an explanation of the categories. As suggested above, the emphasis on low salaries in the data probably lies heavily on the average earnings of principals within the educational hierarchy and differences between those earnings and managerial salaries in other sectors. In regard to the first, recent Illinois data replicate national data showing that elementary principals continue to earn less than principals at other levels and officials in the central office. Elementary principals stand at the bottom of the income hierarchy within administrative ranks in public schools (2006 Illinois Association of School Boards, 11th annual salary survey). Although it is difficult to find comparable data over time comparing elementary principals, say, with managers in the private sector, I have encountered nothing to indicate that their relative position has improved since 1980.

3. In Iowa, expecting to remain in the principalship, versus moving up the hierarchy, increased sharply with greater experience (appendix B, Q. 33). Citing the principalship as the final goal went from 42% among the beginners (1 to 3 years) to 89% among the veterans (17 years and over; chi-square level of significance .000).

4. The dynamism of the thirties was evident in other ways. Of the ten principals who left the state, eight were in their thirties; three of the four who had plans to leave education were also in that category. Things slow down considerably when these suburban principals reach forty, and after that, careers were generally very stable.

5. One, however, did get promoted—an African-American woman had become acting superintendent of her district (82C, 56). It is both ironic and sad that one principal who was forced after 1980 to return to the classroom talked about how much he enjoyed being a principal (46C, 50).

6. Principals answering the NAESP survey in 1998, asked when they planned to retire, projected a mean age of 57.

7. The possession of advanced degrees may lead some older principals to hope for promotion well beyond the time when it is likely; two principals in their fifties with doctorates (102A, Male, 52 and 109A, Male, 53) continued to expect appointment to superintendent positions which neither, eight years later, had achieved.

8. One wonders about the future. As more and more women realize that managerial positions are open to them in a wide variety of fields and—a critical point—decide earlier in life to aim for such positions, how

will educational administration fare in the competition for newcomers? In a sense, educational administration has become subsidized, as teaching was in earlier years, by the limits on what women could reasonably aspire to. Will the attractiveness initially associated with the novelty of increased managerial opportunities in schools wear off as the higher incomes and higher prestige in managing corporations, hospitals, or universities become more accessible to women? Will the two-step requirements in public education disadvantage it in competing with fields where one can aim for executive work immediately after graduation from college or university?

CHAPTER 8

1. Central officials, reflecting their own concerns with parental opinion, encourage principals to include parents in school affairs. Asked what their superintendents thought about parental involvement in the schools, 80% of respondents (Q. 25A, B) said they favored it and a substantial proportion, 62%, agreed with them. There are, of course, risks in any such approach, essentially a strategy of cooptation; one is that principals may have to deal with "special requests" from parents who contribute much time and effort to school affairs. Responding to such requests may threaten a principal's reputation for honoring universalistic standards that assert that all parents should receive equal treatment. Another risk is that parents, encouraged to voice their opinions, may do so to an irritating extent. Some principals believed there should be a clear line between parental and professional decision domains and resisted parental inclusion in ways that blurred the distinction.

2. Some respondents concentrated their attention on untenured teachers, who were less likely to resist teaching suggestions, apparently enjoying the opportunities they presented for educational leadership. Helping them succeed, moreover, provided relatively tangible psychic rewards.

3. The NAESP reports for both 1978 and 1998 present responses on the general authority principals felt they possessed and whether it was commensurate with the degree to which they were held responsible if things went wrong. Nationally, 80% answered affirmatively in 1978; in 1998, 72% said yes nationally and 75% gave affirmative responses in suburban districts.

4. Today there are those in high places who want to treat standardized achievement testing as the single bottom line for schools and school districts. "High-stakes tests" have become part of the educational apparatus of states and the federal government. Interest in test scores was not pronounced, however, at the time our data were gathered. Although the districts gathered standardized data, they did not, as we have noted, appear prominently in the responses of the suburban principals. As we shall see in the next chapter, the pressures to pay attention to high-stakes tests have increased in recent

years. That can be, as I shall point out, associated with some reduction in the uncertainty of educational goals.

5. The limited development in what we can call "clinical" research and knowledge in the practice of school management may be related, to some degree, to the major part played in decision-making by persons outside the occupation. Boards of education, for example, make final decisions over the full range of school affairs. Investment in developing such knowledge may be discouraged by the belief that it will not be used extensively by school boards, or, for that matter, federal and state legislatures. I am indebted to Fred Lighthall for pointing out we should not overlook, when considering the dearth of such research, the heavy time demands of clinical research and the difficulty professors have in fitting them into the promotion schedules and policies of universities.

CHAPTER 9

1. The 1998 NAESP report states that overall, 41.9% of its respondents were women, and 64.5% of those with fewer than 5 years of experience were women; 47% of suburban respondents were women. The NCES reported that between 1987–88 and 1993–94, the percentage of women in elementary school principalships increased from 30.1% to 41.1% compared with 9.4% among secondary principals at the earlier date and 13.8% at the later. Should more recent data indicate that the Chicago area is somewhat exceptional in the rate of increase of female elementary principals, it may be that the rate in the Chicago area has been facilitated by the separation of elementary and secondary education into separate districts.

2. Professors teaching educational administration in several universities have told the author that they observed something which he had as well, namely, that there was a marked increase in the number of women applying and being accepted to their programs during the last two decades of the twentieth century. As the gender composition of available candidates changed, there were obviously more opportunities—in addition to increased social pressure—for districts to hire women with the required credentials.

3. There is one trend which is important and yet unlikely, as I see it, to make novel demands on principals. However, by intensifying current demands for diplomatic capacities such as sensitivity to cultural differences and the ability to lead different kinds of individuals toward harmony, it may well increase the complexity of the work. I refer to the trend toward heterogeneity in the population of suburbs and increasing specialization within school work, two kinds of diversity which are growing in importance. The first derives from new population groups (e.g., ethnic, racial, and socioeconomic) moving into suburbs and the second to the increased division of labor in schools.

Cultural diversity requires principals to be aware of a wider range of differences among the families they serve and to be skilled in unifying the student population (Crow, Hausman, and Scribner 2002). They may, in addition, find it necessary to help teachers deal with new kinds of students. (In instances where similarities are seen between district changes and realities found in city schools, there may be a tendency to open recruitment of suburban principals to persons with experience in urban districts.)

Internal differentiation leads to differences in orientation in which more employees lose sight of wider realities as they "get into" their particular functions (Lawrence and Lorsch 1967). Increased differences in outlook require principals to spend more time and effort focusing on the common objectives that unite rather than separate school personnel. Principals are also called on to discover what newly emerging specialties can contribute to the overall school program.

4. One wonders what will happen if families whose children are not classified as special education students demand more individual programming. What knowledge would be brought to bear under those circumstances? It is possible that policymakers will press school practitioners into programs that require more know-how than they in fact possess. Could this run the risk of undermining public trust in schools and their officials?

5. Although the example of urban systems may not carry great weight for those governing suburban districts, it is worth noting that New York City Schools have undertaken a structural change in which a fifth of their principals are granted enhanced authority over budget, staff, and instruction and more autonomy vis-à-vis central officials; the new principal powers are linked to a two-year trial period to meet performance targets with the possibility of being dismissed if they are not met. The experiment is taking place despite conflict with the principals' union over a contract that expired three years before the project. See "Back to School in a System Being Remade," *New York Times*, Sept. 5, 2006, p. A20.

6. The author observed while doing research on Chicago schools that some, as part of grant-based programs, hired specialist teachers to head particular projects such as enhanced reading and/or math programs. In some cases, this resulted in the emergence of administrative teams composed of such persons working with the principal and his or her assistant principals. The city schools were, of course, larger than those studied in the suburbs and more likely to rely on outside grants from government and foundations. It is possible that increased program differentiation in suburban schools might move them, despite those dissimilarities, to somewhat similar arrangements. We also note that some scholars in educational administration favor "distributed leadership," which, among other things, entails greater participation of and reliance upon staff members in school governance (Spillane 2006, Jacobson and Leithwood 2007).

7. One possible response of persons inside the educational system might be to press for supplementing achievement tests with other kinds of systematic information. Schooled to think in terms of multiple goals (e.g., Bloom's typology), they might attempt to counter a monolithic definition of school effectiveness by pressing for the use of measures other than the high-stakes tests in current use.

An example of that possibility is the work by Nichols and Berliner, who identify the costs that have resulted from heavy reliance on high-stakes testing (2007). They propose a mixed system of school evaluation based on formative assessments, an inspectorate, end-of-course examinations, and performance assessments of various kinds. Principals might press for measures that more directly evaluate the extent to which they manage their schools effectively and harmoniously.

{ Bibliography }

Abbott, Andrew. 1988. *The System of Professions*. Chicago: University of Chicago Press.

Alter, Catherine. 2007. "Bureaucracy and Democracy in Organizations: Revisiting Feminist Organizations." Chap. 7 in Amy Wharton, ed., *The Sociology of Organizations*. Los Angeles: Roxbury.

Arthur, Michael B., Douglas T. Hall, and Barbara S. Lawrence. 1989. *Handbook of Career Theory*. Cambridge: Cambridge University Press.

Au, Wayne. 2007. "High-Stakes Testing and Curricular Control: A Qualitative Metasynthesis." *Educational Researcher* 36, no. 5 (June–July): 258–67.

Bacharach, Samuel B., and Edward J. Lawler. 1980. *Power and Politics in Organizations*. San Francisco: Jossey-Bass.

Bailyn, Bernard. 1960. *Education in the Forming of American Society*. Chapel Hill: University of North Carolina Press.

Barley, Stephen R. 1989. "Careers, Identities, and Institutions: The Legacy of the Chicago School of Sociology." In M. B. Arthur, Douglas Hall, and Barbara Lawrence, eds., *Handbook of Career Theory*. Cambridge: Cambridge University Press.

Barnard, Chester I. 1950. *The Functions of the Executive*. 8th printing. Cambridge, MA: Harvard University Press.

Barr, Rebecca, and Robert Dreeben. 1983. *How Schools Work*. Chicago: University of Chicago Press.

Becker, Howard S., et al. 1968. *Institutions and the Person: Papers presented to Everett C. Hughes*. Chicago: Aldine Publishing Co.

Biddle, Bruce, and Lawrence J. Saha. 2002. *The Untested Accusation*. Stamford, CT: Ablex Publishing.

Bidwell, C. 1965. "The School as a Formal Organization." In James G. March, ed., *Handbook of Organizations*. Chicago: Rand McNally.

Bizar, Marilyn, and Rebecca Barr, eds. 2000. *School Leadership in Times of Urban Reform.* Mahwah, NJ: Lawrence Erlbaum Associates.

Black, John A., and Fenwick W. English. 1986. *What They Don't Tell You in Schools of Education about School Administration.* Lancaster, PA: Technomic Publishing Co.

Blau, Peter. 1956. *Bureaucracy in Modern Society.* New York: Random House.

Blau, Peter, and W. Richard Scott. 1962. *Formal Organizations.* San Francisco: Chandler.

Bloom, B. S., et al. 1956. *Taxonomy of Educational Objectives.* New York: Longmans, Green and Co.

Blount, Jackie M. 1998. *Destined to Rule the Schools: Women and the Superintendency, 1873–1995.* Albany: State University of New York.

Blumberg, Arthur. 1985. *The School Superintendent: Living with Conflict.* New York: Teachers College Press, Columbia University.

Blumberg, Arthur, and William Greenfield, 1979. *The Effective Principal: Perspectives on School Leadership.* Boston: Allyn and Bacon.

Bolman, Lee G., and Terrence E. Deal. 1991. *Reframing Organizations: Artistry, Choice and Leadership.* San Francisco: Jossey-Bass Publishers.

Boris-Schacter, Sheryl, and Sondra Langer. 2006. *Balanced Leadership: How Effective Principals Manage Their Work.* New York: Teachers College Press, Columbia University.

Bosk, C. 1979. *Forgive and Remember.* Chicago: University of Chicago Press.

Bossert, Steven T. 1979. *Tasks and Social Relationships in Classrooms.* New York: Cambridge University Press.

Bridges, Edwin M. 1978. "The Principalship as a Career." In D. A. Erickson and T. Reller, eds., *The Principalship in Metropolitan Schools.* Berkeley, CA: McCutchan Publishing.

———. 1986. *The Incompetent Teacher.* Philadelphia: Falmer Press.

———. 1990. *Managing the Incompetent Teacher.* 2nd ed. Eugene: Eric Clearinghouse on Educational Management, University of Oregon.

Brinton, Mary C., and Victor Nee, eds. 1998. *The New Institutionalism in Sociology.* New York: Russell Sage Foundation.

Brookover, W. B., et al. 1973. *Elementary School Environment and School Achievement.* East Lansing: Michigan State University.

———. 1979. *School Social Systems and Student Achievement: Schools Can Make a Difference.* New York: Praeger Publishers.

Bryk, Anthony, et al. 1993. *A View from the Elementary Schools: The State of Reform in Chicago.* Chicago: Consortium on Chicago School Research.

Bryk, Anthony, and Barbara Schneider. 2002. *Trust in Schools.* New York: Russell Sage Foundation.

Callahan, Raymond. 1962. *Education and the Cult of Efficiency.* Chicago: University of Chicago Press.

———. 1966. *The Superintendent of Schools: An Historical Analysis.* Final Report of Project s-212. St. Louis: Graduate Institute of Education, Washington University.

Campbell, Roald, and L. Jackson Newell. 1973. *A Study of Professors of Educational Administration.* Columbus, OH: University Council for Educational Administration.

Campbell, Roald, et al. 1990. 6th ed. *The Organization and Control of American Schools.* Columbus, OH: Charles E. Merrill.

Carlson, Richard O. 1962. *Executive Succession and Organizational Change.* Chicago: Midwest Administration Center, University of Chicago.

———. 1979. *Orderly Career Opportunities.* Eugene: Center for Educational Policy and Management, University of Oregon.

Casanova, Ursula. 1991. *Elementary School Secretaries: Women in the Principal's Office.* Newbury Park, CA: Corwin Press.

Chandler, Alfred D., Jr. 1962. *Strategy and Structure: Chapters in the History of the Industrial Enterprise.* Cambridge, MA: M.I.T. Press.

———. 1977. *The Visible Hand: The Managerial Revolution in American Business.* Cambridge, MA: Belknap Press, Harvard University Press.

Chinoy, E. 1955. *Automobile Workers and the American Dream.* New York. Doubleday.

Charles, Maria, and David B. Grusky. 2004. *Occupational Ghettoes: The World-wide Segregation of Women and Men.* Stanford: Stanford University Press.

Clark, B. R. 1960. "The 'Cooling Out' Function in Higher Education." *American Journal of Sociology* 65: 569–76.

Conley, David T. 2003. *Who Governs Our Schools? Changing Roles and Responsibilities.* New York: Teachers College Press.

Charon, Joel M. 1998. *Symbolic Interactionism.* Upper Saddle River, NJ: Prentice-Hall.

Cohen, M. D., J. G. March, and J. P. Olsen. 1972. "A Garbage Can Model of Organizational Choice." *Administrative Science Quarterly* 17, no. 1: 1–25.

Corwin, Ronald G., and Roy A. Edelfelt. 1977. *Perspectives on Organization: The School as a Social Organization.* Washington, DC: American Association of Colleges for Teacher Education.

Cremin, Lawrence A. 1970. *American Education: The Colonial Experience, 1607–1783.* New York: Harper and Row.

Cronin, Joseph M. 1973. *The Control of Urban Schools.* New York: Free Press.

Crow, Gary. 1985. "Career Mobility and Adaptation to Work: The Case Study of the Elementary Principalship." Ph.D. diss., University of Chicago.

———. 1987. "Career Mobility of Elementary School Principals and Conflict with the Central Office." *Urban Review* 19, no. 3: 139–50.

Crow, G. M., C. S. Hausman, and J. P. Scribner. 2002. "Reshaping the Role of the School Principal." In J. Murphy, ed., *The Educational Leadership*

Challenge. Yearbook of the National Society for the Study of Education 1, issue 1: 189–210. Chicago: University of Chicago Press.

Cuban, Larry. 1976. *Urban School Chiefs under Fire.* Chicago: University of Chicago Press.

————. 2001. *Oversold and Underused: Computers in the Classroom.* Cambridge, MA: Harvard University Press.

Dalton, M. 1959. *Men Who Manage.* New York: John Wiley and Sons.

Davies, Scott, and Linda Quirke. 2007. "The Impact of Sector on School Organizations: Institutional and Market Logics." *Sociology of Education* 80, no. 1: 66–89.

Deal, T. E. 1987. "The Culture of Schools." *Leadership: Examining the Elusive.* 1987 Yearbook of the Association for Supervision and Curriculum Development. Ed. Linda T. Sheive and Marian B. Schoenheit. No location cited.

Deal, Terrence E., and Kent Peterson. 1994. *The Leadership Paradox: Balancing Logic and Artistry in Schools.* San Francisco: Jossey-Bass.

————. 1999. *Shaping School Culture.* San Francisco: Jossey-Bass.

DiMaggio, Paul, and Walter W. Powell. 2007. "The Iron Cage Revisited: Institutional Isomorphism in Organizational Fields." In Amy S. Wharton, *The Sociology of Organizations.* Los Angeles: Roxbury Publishing Co.

Dornbusch, S., and Scott, Richard. 1975. *Evaluation and the Exercise of Authority.* San Francisco: Jossey-Bass.

Dubin, Andrew E. 2006. *Conversations with Principals.* Thousand Oaks, CA: Sage Publications.

Elmore, Richard F. 2007. "Education: A 'Profession' in Search of a Practice." *Teaching in Educational Administration.* Division A, American Educational Research Association, vol. 15, no 1: 1–4.

Elsbree, W. S. 1939. *The American Teacher.* New York: American Book Co.

Erickson, Donald A, ed. 1977. *Educational Organization and Administration.* Berkeley, CA: McCutchan Publishing.

Erickson, Donald, and Theodore Reller, eds. 1979. *The Principal in Metropolitan Schools.* Berkeley, CA: McCutchan Publishing.

Erickson, Kai, and Steven Peter Vallas, eds. 1990. *The Nature of Work: Sociological Perspectives.* New Haven: Yale University Press.

Feistritzer, C. Emily. 1988. *Profile of School Administrators in the U.S.* Washington, D.C.: National Center for Education Information.

French, John R. P., Jr., and Bertrand Raven. 1959. "The Bases of Social Power." In Dorwin Cartwright, ed., *Studies in Social Power.* Ann Arbor: Institute for Social Research, University of Michigan.

Gaddis, John Lewis. 2002. *The Landscape of History: How Historians Map the Past.* Oxford: Oxford University Press.

Getzels, J., J. Lipham, and Roald Campbell. 1968. *Educational Administration as a Social Process.* New York: Harper and Row.

Goldhammer, K. 1971. *Elementary School Principals and Their Schools*. Eugene: University of Oregon Press.

Goodlad, John. 1984. *A Place Called School*. New York: McGraw-Hill.

Gouldner, A. W. 1954. *Patterns of Industrial Bureaucracy*. New York: Free Press.

Gross, Neal, and R. N. Herriott. 1965. *Staff Leadership in Public Schools: A Sociological Inquiry*. New York: John Wiley and Sons.

Gross, Neal, W. S. Mason, and A. W. McEachern. 1958. *Explorations in Role Analysis: Studies of the School Superintendency Role*. New York: John Wiley and Sons.

Gross, Neal, and Anne E. Trask. 1976. *The Sex Factor and the Management of Schools*. New York: John Wiley and Sons.

Handel, Michael J., ed. 2003. *The Sociology of Organizations*. Thousand Oaks, CA: Sage Publications.

Hall, Douglas T. 1976. *Careers in Organizations*. Santa Monica, CA: Goodyear Publishing Co.

Hall, Oswald. 1949. "Types of Medical Careers." *American Journal of Sociology* 55, no. 3: 243–53.

Halpin, Andrew W., and Don B. Croft. 1963. *The Organizational Climate of Schools*. Chicago: Midwest Administration Center, University of Chicago.

Hanson, E. Mark 1981. "Organizational Control in Educational Systems: A Case Study of Governance in Schools." In Samuel B. Bacharach, ed., *Organizational Behavior in Schools and School Districts*. New York: Praeger Publishers.

Hauser, Robert M., and David L. Featherman. 1977. *The Process of Stratification: Trends and Analyses*. New York: Academic Press.

Hochschild, Arlie Russell. 1983. *The Managed Heart*. Berkeley: University of California Press.

Hodson, R., and T. Sullivan. 1995. *The Social Organization of Work*. 2nd ed. Belmont, CA; Wadsworth Publishing Co.

Homans, G. 1950. *The Human Group*. New York: Harcourt, Brace and Co.

———. 1961. *Social Behavior: Its Elementary Forms*. New York: Harcourt, Brace and World.

House, Ernest R. 1974. *The Politics of Educational Innovation*. Berkeley, CA: McCutchan Publishing.

———. 1998. *Schools for Sale*. New York: Teachers College Press.

Huberman, Michael. 1989. "The Professional Life Cycle of Teachers." *Teachers College Record* 91, no. 1 (Fall.): 31–57.

Hughes, E. C. 1958. *Men and Their Work*. Glencoe, IL: Free Press.

———. 1971. *The Sociological Eye: Selected Papers*. 2 vols. Chicago: Aldine-Atherton.

Illinois School Code. 2007. Source 89-572, eff. 7-30-96; 89-622, eff. 8-9-96; 90-14, eff. 7-1-97.

Jackson, P. 1968. *Life in Classrooms*. New York: Holt, Rinehart and Winston.

Jackson, Philip. 1977. "Lonely at the Top." *School Review* 85 (May 1977): 425–32.

Jackson, Philip, R. Boostrom, and David Hanson. 1993. *The Moral Life of Schools*. San Francisco: Jossey-Bass Publishers.

Jacobson, Stephen, and Kenneth Leithwood, eds. 2007. "The Leading Edge of Distributed Leadership Research." Special Issue of *Leadership and Policy in Schools* 6, no. 1.

Jenkins, Richard. 1992. *Pierre Bourdieu*. London and New York: Routledge.

Johnson, Susan Moore. 1984. *Teacher Unions in Schools*. Philadelphia: Temple University Press.

———. 1996. *Leading to Change: The Challenge of the New Superintendency*. San Francisco: Jossey-Bass Publishers.

Kanter, Rosabeth Moss. 1989. "Careers and the Wealth of Nations: A Macro Perspective on the Structure and Implications of Career Forms." In Michael B. Arthur, Douglas T. Hall, and Barbara S. Lawrence, eds., *Handbook of Career Theory*. Cambridge: Cambridge University Press.

Katz, M. B. 1968. *The Irony of Early School Reform*. Cambridge, MA: Harvard University Press.

Kaye, Elizabeth A., ed. 2006. *Requirements for Certification of Teachers, Counselors, Librarians, Administrators for Elementary and Secondary Schools*. 75th ed. Chicago: University of Chicago Press.

Kidder, Tracy. 1989. *Among Schoolchildren*. Boston: Houghton Mifflin.

Kleine-Kracht, Sister Paula A. 1990. "The Integrative Role of the Secondary Principal: Three Case Studies." Ph.D. diss., Department of Education, University of Chicago.

Kohn, Melvin L., and Carmi Schooler. 1983. *Work and Personality: An Inquiry into the Impact of Social Stratification*. Stamford, CT: Ablex Publishing.

Labaree, David F. 1997. "Public Goods, Private Goods: The American Struggle over Educational Goals." *American Educational Research Journal* 34, no. 1: 39–81.

Lane, John J., and Herbert J. Walberg. 1987. *Effective School Leadership: Policy and Process*. Berkeley, CA: McCutchan Publishing.

Lawrence, Paul, and Jay Lorsch. 1967. *Organization and Environment: Managing Differentiation and Integration*. Boston: Graduate School of Business Administration, Harvard University.

Levin, Henry M. 2006. Can Research Improve Educational Leadership? *Educational Researcher* 35, no. 8: 38–43. A review of William Firestone and Carolyn Riehl, eds., *Research in Educational Leadership;* Andy Hargreaves and Dean Fink, *Sustainable Leadership;* and James Spillane, *Distributed Leadership*.

Levine, D. U., and L. W. Lezotte. 1990. *Unusually Effective Schools*. Madison, Wisconsin: National Center for Effective Schools Research and Development.

Lipham, J. M., and J. A. Hoeh. 1974. *The Principalship: Foundations and Functions.* New York: Harper and Row.

Lipsky, Michael. 1980. *Street-level Bureaucracy: Dilemmas of the Individual in Public Services.* New York: Russell Sage Foundation.

Little, Judith. 1990. "The Persistence of Privacy." *Teacher's College Record* 91 (4): 509–36.

Little, Judith, and Tom Bird. 1987. "Instructional Leadership 'Close to the Classroom' in Secondary Schools." in W. Greenfield, ed., *Instructional Leadership: Concepts, Issues, Controversies.* Boston: Allyn and Bacon.

Little, Judith, Priscilla Galagaran, and Rudelle O'Neal. 1984. *Professional Development Roles and Relationships: Principles and Skills of "Advising."* San Francisco: Far West Laboratory for Educational Research and Development.

Lortie, Dan C. 1958. "The Striving Young Lawyer: A Study of Early Career Differentiation in the Chicago Bar." Ph.D. diss., Department of Sociology, University of Chicago.

———. 1975. *Schoolteacher: A Sociological Study.* Chicago: University of Chicago Press.

———. 1982. "The Complex Work Relationships of Elementary Principals." *The Effects of Collective Bargaining on School Administrative Leadership.* Proceedings of a conference. Kenneth Duckworth and Wynn De Bevoise, Eds. Eugene: Center for Educational Policy and Development, University of Oregon.

———. 1987. "Overlooked Aspects in the Study of School Policy: The Importance of District Organization." *Proceedings of the New York Education Policy Seminar.* Ed. Frances Kemmerer, with comments by David Istance, Gordon Purrington, and Alan P. Wagner. State University of New York at Albany and the Nelson A. Rockefeller Institute of Government.

McCarthy, Martha M. 1992. *Continuity and Change: The Educational Leadership Professoriate.* (Paperback) University Council for Educational Administration.

McCarthy, Martha M., and Nelda H. Cambron-McCabe. 1987. *Public School Law.* Boston: Allyn and Bacon.

McDowell, Harold D. 1954. "The Role of the Principal in a Metropolitan School System: Its Functions and Variations." Ph.D. diss., Department of Sociology, University of Chicago.

McGee, Glenn W. 1985. "The Role of the Principal in Implementing Technological Innovations in the Elementary School." Ph.D. diss., Department of Education, University of Chicago, Chicago.

McPherson, R. B., R. L. Crowson, and Nancy J. Pitner. 1986. *Managing Uncertainty: Administrative Theory and Practice in Education.* Columbus, OH: Charles E. Merrill.

McPherson, R. B., C. Salley, and M. F. Baehr. 1975. *A National Occupational Analysis of the School Principalship.* Chicago: Industrial Relations Center, University of Chicago.

March, James. 1978. "American Public School Administration: A Short Analysis." *School Review* 86, no. 2: 217–50.

March, James G., and J. P. Olsen. 1976. *Ambiguity and Choice in Organizations.* Bergen, Norway: Universitetsforlaget.

March, James G., and Herbert A. Simon. 1958. *Organizations.* New York: John Wiley and Sons.

Matthews, L. J., and G. M. Crow. 2003. *Being and Becoming a Principal: Role Conceptions for Contemporary Principals and Assistant Principals.* Boston: Allyn and Bacon.

Meskin, Joan D. 1979. "Women as Principals: Their Performance as Educational Administrators." In Donald A. Erickson and Theodore L. Reller, eds., *The Principal in Metropolitan Schools.* Berkeley, CA: McCutchan Publishing.

———. 1981. "Career Patterns and Choice Processes of Women Elementary Principals." Ph.D. diss., Department of Education, University of Chicago.

Meyer, J. W., and B. Rowan. 1977. "Institutionalized Organizations: Formal Structure as Myth and Ceremony." *American Journal of Sociology* 83, no. 2: 340–63.

Miller, Daniel R., and Guy E. Swanson. 1958. *The Changing American Parent.* New York: John Wiley and Sons.

Mintzberg, H. 1973. *The Nature of Managerial Work.* New York: Harper and Row.

———. 1975. "The Manager's Job: Folklore and Fact." *Harvard Business Review,* July–August, 100–110.

Miskel, Cecil. 1990. "Research and the Preparation of Educational Administrators." Special Issue on the Preparation of Educational Leaders, ed. A. Ross Thomas. *Journal of Educational Administration* 28, no. 3: 33–47.

Morris, V. C., et al. 1984. *Principals in Action: The Reality of Managing Schools.* Columbus, OH: Charles E. Merrill.

Murphy, J., and K. S. Louis, eds. 1999. *Handbook of Research on Educational Administration.* 2nd ed. San Francisco: Jossey-Bass.

Naegle, K. D. 1956. "Clergymen, Teachers and Psychiatrists." *Canadian Journal of Economic and Political Science* 22, no. 1: 46–62.

National Association of Elementary School Principals. 1978. *The Elementary School Principal in 1978: A Research Study.* By William L. Pharis and Sally Banks Zakariya. Arlington, VA.

National Association of Elementary School Principals. 1989. *The K–8 Principal in 1988: A Ten-year Study.* By James L. Doud. Alexandria, VA.

National Association of Elementary School Principals. 1998. *The K–8 Principal in 1998: A Ten-year Study.* By James L. Doud and Edward P. Keller. Alexandria, VA.

National Education Association. 1987. *Status of the American School Teachers, 1985–86*. Washington, DC: Research Division.

Nichols, Sharon L., and David C. Berliner. 2007. *Collateral Damage: How High Stakes Testing Corrupts America's Schools*. Cambridge, MA: Harvard Educational Press.

Ouchi, W. G. 1977. "The Relationship between Organizational Structure and Organizational Control." *Administrative Science Quarterly* 22, no. 1: 95–113.

Padavic, I., and B. Reskin. 2002. *Women and Men at Work*. 2nd ed. Thousand Oaks, CA: Pine Forge Press.

Parsons, T. 1967. "Suggestions for a Sociological Approach to the Theory of Organizations." In A. Halpin, ed., *Administrative Theory in Education*. New York: Macmillan.

Perlmann, Joel, and Robert A. Margo. 2001. *Women's Work? American School-teachers, 1650–1920*. Chicago: University of Chicago Press.

Peterson, Kent D. 1977. "The Principal's Tasks." *Administrator's Notebook* 26, no. 8: 1–4. Chicago: Midwest Administration Center, University of Chicago.

————. 1983. "Mechanisms of Administrative Control in Educational Organizations: An Exploratory Study." Ph.D. diss., Department of Education, University of Chicago.

————. 1984. "Mechanisms of Administrative Control over Managers in Educational Organizations." *Administrative Science Quarterly* 29, no. 4: 573–97.

Pfeffer, Jeffrey. 1981. *Power in Organizations*. Marshfield, MA: Pitman Publishing.

Pierce, Paul Revere. 1935. *The Origin and Development of the Public School Principalship*. Chicago: University of Chicago Press.

Pois, Joseph. 1964. *The School Board Crisis: A Chicago Case Study*. Chicago: Educational Methods, Inc.

Reller, Theodore Lee. 1935. *The Development of the Superintendency of Schools in the United States*. Philadelphia: published by the author.

Roethlisberger, F. J., and W. J. Dickson. 1966. *Counseling in an Organization: A Sequel to the Hawthorne Researches*. Cambridge, MA: Harvard University, Graduate School of Business Administration.

Rosenbaum, James E. 1989. "Organization Career Systems and Employee Misperceptions." In Michael Arthur, Douglas T. Hall, and Barbara Lawrence, *Handbook of Career Theory*. Cambridge: Cambridge University Press.

Rosenholtz, S. J. 1989. *Teachers' Workplace: The Social Organization of Schools*. White Plains, NY: Longman.

Sackney, Larry E. 1980. "Administrative Dilemmas of the Principal." *Canadian Administrator* 20, no. 3: 1–5. Department of Educational Administration, University of Alberta.

Sarason, S. B. 1971. *The Culture of the School and the Problem of Change.* Boston: Allyn and Bacon.

Schein, Edgar H. 1985. *Organizational Culture and Leadership.* San Francisco: Jossey-Bass.

Scott, W. Richard. 2002. *Organizations.* 5th ed. Englewood Cliffs, NJ: Prentice-Hall.

Selznick, Philip. 1949. *TVA and the Grass Roots.* Berkeley: University of California Press.

Simon, Herbert. 1947. *Administrative Behavior.* 4th ed. New York: Macmillan Co.

Shakeshaft, Charol. 1989. *Women in Educational Administration.* Updated edition. Newbury Park, CA: Sage Publications.

Smith, L. M., and W. Geoffrey. 1968. *The Complexities of an Urban Classroom: An Analysis Toward a General Theory of Teaching.* New York: Holt, Rinehart and Winston.

Smith, Tom W. 2007. "Job Satisfaction in the United States. NORC/University of Chicago." University of Chicago News Office press release, April 17.

Social Science Encyclopedia. 1996. Ed. Adam Kuper and Jessica Kuper. 2nd ed. London and New York: Routledge.

Spillane, J. P. 2006. *Distributed Leadership.* San Francisco: Jossey-Bass.

Stinchcombe, A. L. 1965. "Social Structure and Organizations." In J. G. March, ed., *Handbook of Organizations.* Chicago: Rand McNally.

Summerfield, H. L. 1971. *The Neighborhood-Based Politics of Education.* Columbus, OH: Charles E. Merrill.

Sumner, William Graham. 1906. *Folkways.* Boston: Ginn and Co.

Taylor, Barbara O. 1990. *Case Studies in Effective Schools Research.* Dubuque, IA: Kendall/Hunt Publishing Co.

Thompson, James D. 1967. *Organizations in Action: Social Science Bases of Administrative Theory.* New York: McGraw-Hill.

Tyack, David. 1974. *The One Best System: The History of American Urban Education.* Cambridge, MA: Harvard University Press.

Tyack, David, and Elisabeth Hansot. 1982. *Managers of Virtue: Public School Leadership in America, 1820–1980.* New York: Basic Books.

U.S. Census Bureau. 2001. *Statistical Abstract of the United States.* Table 238, Average Salary and Wages Paid in Public School Systems: 1980–2000. Washington, DC.

U.S. Census Bureau. 2007. *Statistical Abstract of the United States.* Table 241, Average Salary and Wages Pain in Public School Systems: 1985 to 2005. Washington, DC.

U.S. Office of Educational Research and Improvement Services. 1987. *Principal Selection Guide.* Washington, DC: U.S. Department of Education.

Van Mannen, J., and S. Barley. 1984. "Occupational Communities: Culture and Control in Organizations." In B. Staw and L. Cummings, eds.,

Research in Organizational Behavior, vol. 6, pp. 287–365. Greenwich, CT: JAI.

Waller, Willard. 1967. *The Sociology of Teaching.* New York: John Wiley and Sons.

Weber, Max. 1947. *Max Weber: The Theory of Social and Economic Organization.* Ed. Talcott Parsons. New York: Oxford University Press, 1947.

Weick, K. E. 1976. "Educational Organizations as Loosely Coupled Systems." *Administrative Science Quarterly* 21 (March): 1.

Weindling, Dick, and Peter Earley. 1987. *Secondary Headship: The First Years.* London, U.K.: NFER-NELSON.

Wesley, Edgar. 1957. *The National Education Association: The First Hundred Years—The Building of the Teaching Profession.* New York: Harper.

Wharton, Amy, ed. 2007. *The Sociology of Organizations.* Los Angeles: Roxbury Publishing Co.

Wirt, Frederick M., and Michael W. Kirst. 1982. *Schools in Conflict.* Berkeley, CA: McCutchan Publishing.

Wolcott, Harry F. 1973. *The Man in the Principal's Office.* New York: Holt, Rinehart and Winston.

Woodward, Joan. 1965. *Industrial Organization: Theory and Practice.* Oxford: Oxford University Press.

Wong, Kenneth. 1999. *Funding Public Schools: Politics and Policies.* Lawrence: University Press of Kansas.

{ Index }

237; promotions for, 239–40; sample
respondents to questionnaire for,
229; satisfaction for, 236–37; size
of school and, 235–36; suburban,
urban, and rural differences in interview answers for, 235–40; teacher
evaluations by, 238–39; teacher
supervision by, 238–39, 240
"Iowa School Principal, The" (Vittengl),
229
Iowa schools, 2, 190, 229, 235–40

Jackson, P., 78, 112
Jacobson, Stephen, 250n6
job evaluations. *See* evaluations, job
job security, 148

Katz, M. B., 12
Kaye, Elizabeth A., 25
Keller, Edward P., 200
Kidder, Tracy, 78
knowledge acquisition, 33t, 39–41

Lawrence, Paul, 249–50n3
leadership, 6, 177, 250n6
legislatures, 206–7, 249n5
Leithwood, Kenneth, 250n6
Levine, D. U., 3
Lezotte, L. W., 3
Lighthall, Fred, 249n5
Lipham, J., 50
Little, Judith, 245n1
localism, 25, 161, 183, 191
lock-step movement, 200
Lorsch, Jay, 249–50n3
Lortie, Dan C., 77, 81, 91, 156, 176
low "assignability" of staff members,
11, 120, 123

management and organization of
schools, 9, 187, 241n1; administrative teams and, 250n6; "administrivia" and, 32, 39–40, 49, 127,
180–81; authority of principal and,
92; baseline data for, 3; change and
stability in, 188–90; computer use,

and effects on, 197–200; consensus
work and, 12; cultural differences,
and effects on, 204, 249–50n3; data
and, 207; described, 1; differentiated program trends, and effects
on, 193–96, 250n4; distributed
leadership and, 250n6; division of
labor, and effects on, 204, 249–50n3;
evaluation of, 209, 251n7; external competition, and effects on,
200–201; gender composition shift
in, 190–93, 249nn1–2; high stakes
testing, and effects on, 204–11,
248–49n4; historical perspective for,
10; internal competition, and effects
on, 200, 201–3, 250n5; in Iowa, 2,
229; management rhetoric and, 5–6;
marketing and, 201; past decisions,
and change in, 6, 182; personnel
and, 11, 54, 55–56, 57, 120, 123,
244n4, 244n9; principals, and effects
of, 4–5; rate of change in structures
of, 2–3, 187; special factors in, 145,
161–65; trends, and lasting change
in, 187–88, 204, 211. *See also* authority system
managerial subculture, 170, 170;
authority of principal in, 33t,
175–77, 248nn2–3; career processes
in, 182–84; cause-effect relationships and, 115, 149n5, 179, 181–82;
caution versus risk taking in, 170,
182–84; coalitions and, 171; diffuse
goals, and uncertainty in, 178–79,
248–49n4; district policy and, 170;
emotionally charged setting in,
172–74, 186, 248n1; mediated solutions and, 171–72; parental trust
and, 173; parents, and relationships
in, 174, 248n1; parent/teacher relationship in, 177; past decisions, and
change in, 182–83, 182–84; private
and public differences in, 169; public
setting of principalship and, 46–48,
169–72, 189; shaky premises, and
uncertainty in, 179–82, 249n5;